SEMIOTEXT(E) NATIVE AGENTS SERIES

Published by Semiotext(e)
PO BOX 629, South Pasadena, CA 91031
www.semiotexte.com

Cover Art: Jack Pierson, *Grease Monkey*, 1990. Courtesy the artist and Cheim & Read, New York.

Back Cover Photograph: Peter E. Hanff
Design: Hedi El Kholti

ISBN: 978-1-63590-040-8

Distributed by The MIT Press, Cambridge, Mass. and London, England
Printed in the United States of America

10 9 8 7 6 5 4 3 2

FASCINATION

KEVIN KILLIAN

MEMOIRS:

Bedrooms Have Windows
Bachelors Get Lonely
Triangles in the Sand

Edited by Andrew Durbin

This book is for Dodie Bellamy
"I'm just a jeepster for your love"

CONTENTS

Introduction by Andrew Durbin   9

Bedrooms Have Windows   17
Bachelors Get Lonely   137
Triangles in the Sand   247

Sources and Acknowledgements   306

Introduction by Andrew Durbin

Every time I feel fascination
I just can't stand still
—David Bowie

Born on Christmas Eve, 1952, in a hamlet on Long Island, Kevin Killian began his first novel, *Shy*, in June 1974, after he graduated from Fordham Lincoln Center, a small liberal arts college in midtown Manhattan. It wasn't released for another fifteen years, when The Crossing Press—based in Freedom, California—published a small edition in 1989. That same year also saw the publication of his first memoir, *Bedrooms Have Windows*. "Freedom," George Michael crooned a few months later: "I think there's something you should know." What? Didn't everything happen in 1989? The year the world began, and the year it ended, too. Where had Killian been, in those intervening fifteen years? Both books place him near his hometown: "I lived in the upstairs flat of a summer bungalow on the North Shore of Long Island," *Shy* opens. It concludes with a place and a date, what might even be read as a declaration: *San Francisco, September 18, 1988*. "I grew up in Smithtown," he begins in *Bedrooms*, "a suburb of New York, a town so invidious that I still speak of it in Proustian terms—or Miltonic terms, a kind of paradise I feel evicted from."

By the beginning of 1991, Killian was living at the edge of the Mission District on Minna Street. He was a poet. He was married to the writer Dodie Bellamy. A friend and collaborator of many artists, writers, and actors in the city, he helped found the New Narrative movement—a loose-arrangement of poets and novelists centered around Robert Glück's writing workshops as Small Press Traffic. New Narrative, with its emphasis on critical theory and identity politics, offered a fiction and poetry that took itself apart in order to make its inner and outer workings— and worker—transparent: a writing about the writer who's doing the writing, a kind of authorial heroism, the splaying of the self. (Derrida was a touchstone.) In a conversation with Bruce Boone, the Language poet Charles Bernstein noted that Boone, like his counterparts, foregrounded the author through repeated interventions of a writerly interest in text *qua* text: "It would be as if Stephen King made [some of the] comments . . . that you're making to me, within the novel, and talked about its links with the high and the low European [literature], to French philosophy, and so on." If the author died in the late '60s, New Narrative attempted to account for the causes of his or her demise in order to resurrect the corpse in a poetry and prose of flesh and blood—stitched together, and electro-shocked back to life. The poet Cole Swensen once said that Killian's work is about the "palpability of being alive." One lives with it.

Fascination: Memoirs brings together Killian's two early memoirs, *Bedrooms Have Windows*, a choppy, autobiographical story about an aspiring writer named Kevin Killian who endeavors to find his place in a sexed-up, boozy world of Long Island and New York in the '70s and '80s, before and in the midst of the AIDS crisis, and its planned but ultimately unpublished sequel, *Bachelors Get Lonely*, sections of which Killian included in subsequent fiction collections (1996's *Little Men* and 2001's *I Cry Like a Baby*). It concludes with *Triangles in the Sand*, a new, previously unpublished memoir of Killian's brief affair in the 1970s with the composer Arthur Russell. Used or remaindered, Killian's early writing—including his little-known novella, *Desiree* (1986), and *Shy*—have long been difficult to find in the wild (the wild, not the web, being their rightful place, really), and have since accrued an almost cult status among readers of experimental and gay prose writing, like that of the early works of Killian's peers: Steve Abbott, Dennis Cooper, Dodie Bellamy, Robert Glück, Bruce Boone, and others. Cooper once described *Shy* as "mind-bending, trashy, and Dickensian." The novel "drove me wild." James Purdy, who Killian has long cited as an influence, called it "a book of sparklers." Boone wrote that *Bedrooms* would cement his place as one of "the brightest stars in the sex/experimental writing firmament[.]" Holding this two-part volume of such writing, a new reader, perhaps one more familiar with Killian's poetry (of which he has published four volumes, two in recent years), might wonder how exactly his non-fiction plots along the axis Boone describes.

In "Sex Writing and the New Narrative," a 1990 essay that alternates between a love scene with two men and an analysis of "language, narration, and representation," Killian writes that "all narrative is corrupt insofar as it attempts to ape the realities of our lives . . . Corruption of the body, of the text, of the story . . ." Killian argues that words are both insufficient in their effort to "formulate a representation of life" and irresistible, too. They are gamely partners in a cruise-or-be-cruised world, their corruption suggestive and tantalizing:

> "Sex writing" . . . differs from other forms of representation in that it has some kind of chemical effect on the reader. I get hard, I can't contain myself. A fugue results, between the closed system of language and the complex system of mole-cules that holds my body together a real communication

begins. Obedience . . . These include the disjunctions, strange-nesses and confusions of sexual gender we live with.

I read this as a distinctly queer, even specifically gay, update of Lyn Hejinian's well-known essay, "The Rejection of Closure" (1983), in which she establishes a handy binary of "closed" and "open" texts. In the latter, "all the elements of the work are maxi-mally excited; here it is because ideas and things exceed (without deserting) argument that they have taken into the dimension of the work." Killian is likewise interested in the excitability of language—so much so that it gets him hard. What about us, its readers?

Hejinian argues that the difference between the world and the word produces a gap, or let's say a hole, that most of us need to fill, prod, tongue. That's poetry, and that's sex writing. It prompts a feeling, a physical sensation. You put the book down, you walk around; you text a friend, you can hardly keep still. You grow pleasantly bored, filled with enough plot or verse for the day, and snoop for porn. Am I being too literal? Hejinian incorporates Umberto Eco's idea of "inferential walks"—those instances where "the reader has to 'walk,' so to speak, outside the text, in order to gather intertextual support," Eco writes—into her more general idea that language "is productive of activity." She notes that words appear to us as "attractive, magnetic to meaning." Flirtatious, Killian might add. We chase them, since they are the means to an immanent poetry or prose: that is, a forward-looking writing concerned with itself, with its own mechanics and the mechanic him- or herself. The open (or New Narrative) text develops as an evocative experience of reading rather than a mere recording of experience. In a later poem, "Helium," Killian puts it simply: "The balloon that once blown up assumes a shape and an ending. / Pop, then, deflates your sentence / into life." *Pop*.

Both *Bedrooms* and *Bachelors* concern Killian's "real life," though neither dwell on the provable connections between the living writer and his protagonist so much as they attempt, in their corrupt desire to ape and supplant reality with their own exigencies, to stand in place of private memory as a public document, as this book you hold in hand: the realer deal than whatever was once real. Scenes splurge, come-and-go, elaborate in non-sequential tellings and retellings of Killian's late teens to adulthood. Self-exiled from the gates of suburban Eden (anyone can be normal if he wants to be, right), Killian makes regular, restless visits to New York's profane streets, finding himself occasionally employed, frequently lost, "sealed in with the dismal frightened figures of subway America[.]" In *Bedrooms*, he meets Carey Denham while hitching in Smithtown, a man old enough to be his father, with whom he begins an affair:

"Take me to New York," I said.

"Show me where it is on the map," Carey said. His right hand touched my cock. The names of the roads on the map blurred before my eyes like a turning kaleidoscope. That's the night I fell in love for the first time.

Throughout both memoirs, Killian analyzes this poise of innocence as it becomes increasingly complicated by his growing awareness of it as a *poise*, as even a sexual politics—specifically through a friendship with George Grey, "the unclaimed son of Gypsy Rose Lee," who rouses Killian to a hunger for the broad belt of the wider world, for whatever the American mainland holds. (Funny to remember that Long Island, with its post-war fantasy of cookie-cutter America, is just that: an island.) Innocence, he realizes holds the key to personality—lie around long enough and eventually someone will tell you what to do.

I'm not sure if Kevin in *Bedrooms* or *Bachelors* could find New York on a map—not because he's unaware of his Northeastern geography, but that he's simply too distracted and too turned on to *really* get there. Men lead him along, and it is the appearance of new faces and bodies—new names, new words—that push him from A to B and back again:

> There has to be a person inside the story, I wonder why . . . But when a person came into my story I stood there and felt conscious of everything, like it was all new, like everything in my life was all new, and I wonder why; if our souls are so constituted, or if there's something sexual about it I don't comprehend.

Innocence is punctured by Killian's increasing alcoholism, by fear of AIDS, by depressive episodes of writerly self-deprecation ("At the end of my days, when I'm borne to my grave a hoary corpse, they will carve no hopeful verse upon my tombstone, for my dying hours were gloom"), and the progression from Smithtown to Minna Street is marked by the violence of sex and depravity of desire. Each crisis of timing or catastrophe of personality arrives as its own Sword of Damocles hanging in the air above him, ever ready to rend fragile happiness.

In *Bachelors*, Killian's need for booze becomes a dominant motivating force, both compounding and accounting for a desire increasingly complicated by the looming threat of AIDS in the years before protease inhibitors, when most anyone who developed the disease died from it. And everyone was dying from it. He scurries down the Long Island Expressway in summer, a scene-in-miniature of some of the fears that compel the narrative forward: "My little car vibrated under me, as though its engine were announcing exciting plans to fall apart, but I didn't pay much attention. Tears were drying on my face." The world is not whole; he is most grateful for the bottle between his legs. Life does fall apart: a boyfriend is impaled by a shard of mirror during a kinky shower session, blood darkens the running water. The guy manages to orgasm, but slumps over when he's finished. Killian can only imagine toasting their sex with Glenlivet:

> Was he sleeping? Unconscious? His blond hair matted red, brown, black; his smile gave no clue, his big lips slack, happy, purple and gray as the petals of a sterling silver rose. I nudged him with the Glenlivet. He didn't seem to want a drink, again I'm like—????? Then I dressed, found my keys, left the motel. I guess.

Throughout these three books, Killian is content with memory's ambivalences, its ambiguities, its moment of "I guess," when the distinction between fact and fiction dissolves. In situating themselves in memory's drift, its blur, Killian's memoirs remain as vibrant now as they did in the late 1980s, palpably alive with sex and politics, music and poetry. Killian's past is strange, drunken, a little lost, but it belongs to our present as a handy record for those of us who need a reminder that, sometimes, a direction can be found in the reckoning.

> Move along the velvet rope, run your shaky fingers past the lacquered zigzag Keith Haring graffito: "You did not live in our time! Be sorry!"

BEDROOMS HAVE WINDOWS

LOVELAND

I grew up in Smithtown, a suburb of New York, a town so invidious that still I speak of it in Proustian terms—or Miltonic terms, a kind of paradise I feel evicted from. Smithtown, Long Island, kind of an MGM Norman Rockwell hometown, a place so boring they gave it a boring name . . . When I was 14 I began to go to New York on a regular basis, sometimes on the train, sometimes hitchhiking there, looking for a jungly eroticism I supposed Smithtown, with its manicured lawns and its country club airs, couldn't afford me. I was right and wrong at the same time.

By day or night New York's a seedy Burroughs kind of place, and hurrying down the street I could hardly catch my breath, there were so many affecting things to watch and so much architecture. At Gristede's all the food's so expensive I felt I knew why everyone in Manhattan's so thin, but it seemed worth it, and thus I found myself buying things I never wanted before—simple things like: apple. Doughnut. Cup of coffee. I took a job clerking there for a month and famous people, like Jackie Kennedy, would come in off the street and buy these very same things. These would be my dinner; a fellow I knew in school had a cigarette, a cup of coffee and the *Daily News* when he woke up every morning, and he called it the chorus girls' breakfast. I knew another guy who always carried the same book in his back pocket, like Bruce Springsteen that red bandanna. A book of poetry: Bob Kaufman's *Solitudes Crowded with Loneliness.* I loved him for that: I used to touch the book in his pocket and feel direct connection to the ancient rain of San Francisco, now my home then only a mysterious flavor like guava, succulent, almost too rich. I used to tell him, "You are so cute with that book," and he would smile, unwillingly, as though he'd pledged never to reveal his connection to poetry.

The subway ride to his house seemed endless. Sealed in with the dismal frightened figures of subway America, I couldn't help but feel different and special, in that I was heading towards a love life that, I imagined, would have frightened them more, would have made them more dismal. "Loveland" I called it, as though it were an address like Rockefeller Center. It's when you look into someone's sunglasses and try to see his eyes, or the space you feel rolling over a cliff or a ramble. From these two fellows I took the sense that being a New Yorker involved high style, one was so camp with his "chorus girl's breakfast" and his operatic airs, the other so serious, a walking dictionary of soulful poetry like Kaufman. "Camp" and "Seriousness" themselves became characters I could cruise first, then nuzzle, then accept or decline.

Life's so much simpler here in San Francisco.

Then I was 20, still convinced New York's the most dangerous place in the world. I came out of the subway once, for example, and Francis Coppola was filming *The Godfather.* The cameras whirled as I made my entrance. I blinked and smiled, and lingered till I heard the word "Cut." One of the little people asked me to step aside so that Richard Conte, who was waiting inside the car, could get his face on screen. "If you want me to I will," I said. "You guys making a movie? Can I be in it more than I am already?" He explained that it was a period piece and that was why everyone was dressed in forties suits and hats. "I love those suits," I told him. "I love those hats men used to wear."

"Sorry," he said.

Out on the street it was four o'clock in the afternoon and girls were wearing summer dresses and acting soignee. My favorite time of the day. A large cloud, pumped full of black gases, loomed overhead. I felt goosebumps, perhaps because I was tripping. In my pocket a handful of red crystals, wrapped in pliofilm, gave me a kind of sexual energy I haven't felt since, and plus I made money this way, and plus I felt powerful, ambitious, and also I had lots of friends (and what they say about New York is true: eight million people, each with a different story to tell and a different drug habit); plus I was a homosexual primitive like a Frida Kahlo mural the Feds tear down.

In winter up on Carey's fire escape at East End Avenue and 86th Street I wrapped myself in a bearskin and sat there telling my diary the story of the novel I hoped one day to write. "This will make me famous," I thought. And what was fame, I felt, but an extension of my present being? I was seeing a man who had picked me up hitchhiking when I was in junior high, out on Long Island where I grew up. We'd known each other for six years—I'd grown a foot taller and my hair had changed color and I used to wonder, "If I grow any taller will I still be loved?" His name was Carter, but I called him Carey.

The night we met I noticed how warm his car was. A piece of toast. I'd sat shivering in it, in a black jacket and white buck-skin shoes. "Where are you headed?" he said.

"Take me to New York," I said.

"Show me where it is on the map," Carey said, producing a large roadmap from his glove compartment and unfolding it like an accordion across the width of the car. His right hand fell unerringly to my lap. The names of the roads on the map blurred before my eyes like sudden tears. "Show me where it is," he said once or twice, all the while playing with my prick. That's how I fell in love.

In many ways a cold fish, Carey was capable of surprising me with extravagant gestures I thought showed some emotion. He gave me a hundred dollars once. Another time he came out of a taxi filled with balloons to cheer me up after a depressing exam in Linguistics. Still I used to wonder, "Now that I'm blond no longer how much longer will we be tied together?" Even at 18, or should I say especially at 18, I knew balloons were corny and I squirmed and hoped to God none of my friends were watching. But as the taxi sped north up Third Avenue, the colors, the warm rubber suffocation, had the power to send fleets of taxicabs over the pier and into the blue and gray Hudson.

His wife I never cared for. She had a critical eye on me from the time I was 14. They lived in an apartment designed by *Architectural Digest*. Once I woke up there and only she was home. Anita gave me a steely look but fixed me a bologna sand-wich, though she kept rattling the knife around in the mustard jar like she was having a nervous breakdown or something. I sat at her kitchen table, nervous myself, twiddling my thumbs and rapping the underside sharply like a seance. "Quit fidgeting," Anita told me.

It was eight in the morning, and outside the sky was full of orange light, white clouds scuttling across the horizon towards Brooklyn Harbor. Under her cool black-eyed gaze, the white jockey shorts Carey insisted I wear seemed a little *de trop* at breakfast. I crossed my legs. Then spread them wide. "I'm reading a really good book," I said at a stab. "*One Hundred Years of Solitude.*" I thought this was a clever touch because Anita came from some Central American country or another, probably the same one Bianca Jagger did.

But she merely turned her head impassively and dropped the sandwich onto a plate, thrusting it my way. "Eat," she said. "Eat and don't talk." How much of my lovelife she knew about I'm not sure. It was as taboo as anything in Lévi-Strauss. Carey had a respectable life and liked it like that. He was capable of affection, although not in public, usually in a car.

Even when it was happening to me, I thought, "This will make a good story someday," but now that I think of it, its story's not that good at all. More important than its plot, it's the quality of feeling that strikes me now—something out of this world, "outlandish" in its literal sense. I had a pair of white shoes and a black jacket I used to regard in the same way, draping them atop chairs and talking to them in the stylish, sophisticated accents of David Niven or Peter Lawford. "I love those shoes," I would say to an imaginary visitor. "I love that jacket."

At my high school graduation I saw his face in the crowd. Afterwards I tried to find him, though I don't know what I would have done with him if I had. But anyhow I couldn't. Later he denied having been there, but with one of those roguish twinkles that can pass for truth or a joke. "I was not hallucinating," I said. "I saw you there."

"I think you've been smoking too many bananas." I never found his drug humor amusing, the way some people are turned off by bathroom humor.

"You were wearing your gray suit with a green tie."

"The luck of the Irish."

"You must have just gotten your hair cut."

"Oh sure," he said, "could you smell the talcum powder?"

"Bay rum I smelled," I said, "and you had a hard-on."

"Oh well then, that couldn't have been I," he said.

We drove somewhere in Westchester and entered an antique watermill preserved from Colonial times for its shock value. There, on its dusty wooden floor, he asked me what I wanted out of life. "Not to be like you," I said, first to annoy him, then also because it was true, plus he had a hard-on. I really liked being desired. And I liked money and kept hoping he would give me another hundred dollars. He kept peering around afraid that the caretaker would spot us. I liked the dangerous aspects of our affair, I liked even the fact that he did not. I thought that otherwise he would long since have tired of me and sought out someone else, someone younger, someone 12 or 13. He seemed old to me then, but working out our birth dates I realized sometime later that he must have been 35 when we met, and since that's my age now I get goosebumps. Here in San Francisco in October the sky is a pale and delicate blue, like a robin's egg in a child's picture book.

It's four o'clock in the afternoon as I write this: my favorite time of the day. A car is moving slowly down the street, pushed from behind by two sweating workmen in grayish overalls. I want it to roll down the hill. I want its trunk to leave their hands. I want them to stumble a bit in surprise, then begin chasing the car, as it picks up speed and strips its gears, then they fall back out of breath and grow fatalistic. Then the car plunges off the cliff and you see the faces of the lovers rising from the back seat, steamed in a kiss, the kiss they can't feel, and you see the car hit a rocky mesa way down below. From vertiginous heights I watch and smoke a cigarette, humming a little tune and acting very debonair. I am reminded of a misspent youth—someone's misspent youth, not necessarily mine.

Once Anita was knitting me a sweater and waxing sarcastic: how kind Carey was, taking a disadvantaged child out of the suburbs, bring him to Manhattan! "Fresh Air Fund except in reverse," she snorted.

"Well I need to get streetwise," I said, "brush some of the country cobwebs off me."

"Carey's not the man to teach street smarts. We were mugged by three Guatemalan borrachos on Lexington and Carey told them to take the Lady Seiko that they didn't even know I had."

"He helps me with my school work," I said.

She said nothing, kept rocking and knitting. Presently she spoke again. "*Espera*," she said, her voice and face deadpan. "*Espera* Kevin."

"Esperanto you mean," I cried. "Talk English to me, you know I don't understand that loco lingo of yours."

"When you grow up I will talk to you, not now. If you want a sandwich you know how to make one, so go."

"I don't want a sandwich," I said. "I'm so awfully hungry."

"How are your parents and your brothers and sisters and boys' school?"

"I guess everything's fine," I said, suddenly frightened. "Tell Carey I'll wait for him in the car, okay? I'll skip the sandwich all right?"

She shrugged. "If I see him I'll tell him." The needles began to flash in the light. "In English," she added. "In the language you and he have."

When it came time for me to go to college I picked one in New York, actually three, but that's a different story. In my cheap room, all grays and whites and pinks, he and I met one night so I could tell him it was over. Carey washed his face in the bathroom and came out with water cupped in his hands. He threw the water on my face, meaning to wake me up. "My classes are all very interesting this semester," I said, ignoring him. "Sometimes I feel like an ashtray—like you're a cigarette and you put yourself out in me. Ever wish you had passed me by on that highway? I bet you do, cause I've caused you grief." I didn't really believe this. "But I got to like you, Carey, your candy breath, your mouth stuffed with cotton, your pleasant gray eyes. O baby don't come."

He wasn't about to come; coming was far from his mind. He stood up and pulled off his pants. What is the trick of description, that writers must use? How do I make him more clear, vivid, real—or even imaginary? You know the film actress Rosanna Arquette? He had the sulky pouting look of a Rosanna Arquette. But what happens if you don't know her? I could say: Pia Zadora; Brigitte Bardot; but at each remove the similarity fades a bit more, so you don't get my picture. Shall I stick to Rosanna? But then I'll seem obscure, oblique. He had the sulky pouting look of a male Rosanna Arquette, while I, who knew I could never pull that off, thought it politic to ape the vacuous, slightly zombie drug store of the '50s singer Johnnie Ray.

Carey told me so many stories about growing up in Wilkes-Barre, Pennsylvania, that I came to feel I knew as much about that city as he did. One of the stories was of a little boy who worked a paper route, all summer long, to earn enough money to buy a new suit for the first day of school. The paper he sold published his picture on their front page. So Carey and some other boys pushed this boy in a ditch and laughed at him and pissed all over his neck and throat and chest. Sometimes I felt like that paper boy, that all my love did for him was to give him a big laugh.

"You want ice cream, Kevin?" he said. He put his pants back on and zipped up the fly. "I'll go down to the store."

"Sometimes I feel like a piece of paper," I said. "That you wrote your name on then pissed on."

"What flavor?" said Carey. "I know your favorite."

"I don't want any ice cream." I said. "Why don't you take off your pants and listen to me?" I loved him so much I couldn't let him out of the room. He had had everything and I had only been able to give him just a little. "Remember that old woman who lived at the end of the block and you were never allowed to step on her lawn?"

"I remember," he said gravely, his pants round his knees.

"She'd come running out of her house to chase you away if you stepped in her yard, a lawn so shabby and unkempt you never understood why she got into such a dither about it. After you broke her mailbox with your fists, she came calling on your mother in moth-eaten black widow's weeds with a calling card and a reticule. I feel like that old eccentric widow woman—that you're the meanest boy on the block. Under my windows I crouch and wait till you've stopped vandalizing my house. Then I straighten up and breathe again. She smelled like mothballs and sour cheese and her house was unpainted and one day she was dead. She had turned up the gas to light the stove and she fell forward, asleep, while her face burned away. It burnt completely away like strips of bacon leaving only grease and fat behind. Sometimes I feel I'd like to burn in Hell with no face if it meant you wouldn't be looking into my eyes with your devil's look. Your mother worried about your bad temper. At night while you slept she'd watch over you and cry, thinking of you. She wanted your happiness and could see none for you in the future. She couldn't even talk it over with your father because it seemed to her that he'd lost all interest in his family. He, your mother knew, was dicking that little girl in Philadelphia—the one he'd told her he'd given up. When she touched him it was like he or she wasn't there but never both at the same time. Sometimes I feel like your mother, that when I turn to you, you're not there, that you're somewhere else and never were in my bed. Sometimes I feel like your father and I feel you touching me and I wish I wasn't in bed with you and I dream or daydream of someone else. She needed your love so much then but you were embarrassed by her affection: weren't you, Carey?"

"She tried too hard," Carey answered.

"John Lennon said, 'Mother, you needed me but I didn't need you.' Or, 'I needed you but you didn't need me.'"

"The latter I think," Carey said, a towel made of an expensive material knotted around his waist.

I wish I had that towel right now. Whatever happened to it? Anita probably has it along with everything else.

"And I say, 'Kevin, you're going out of your mind!'"

"If you love me why do you have to go out tricking with those tricks not to mention your wife . . . O baby don't come. Prove to me, Carey, I haven't wasted my time."

"What do you want me to do?" He was exasperated with me and my constant demands and I knew it; yet I couldn't stop going on and ruining it all. I didn't ruin what counted but I ruined whatever I could. He got up and went out in the rain to get me my ice cream but I didn't like ice cream.

"I don't want you to do anything," I said. He was walking in the rain and probably picking someone up in the bargain as well as the ice cream neither of us wanted. "My name is Kevin Killian," I said. "I come from Smithtown, Long Island. I'm going to send away for a gun I saw in a magazine."

I never did send away for that gun, probably because I didn't have enough money for it. Instead I wrote more of my novel. In grad school, years later, I decided to write my dissertation on child pornography but I had yet to connect my decision with my own experience.

That night Carey got into his big warm car and drove out fifty miles to Smithtown, the town where we'd met. I'd said something to him he couldn't forget. He took his razor and opened a little vein in his cock, trying to expiate for the awful way he'd treated me. The car was warm as a piece of toast. Yet once, I'd sat shivering in it, in a black jacket and white buckskin shoes. "Take me to New York," I said.

"Show me where it is on the map," Carey said. His right hand touched my cock. The names of the roads on the map blurred before my eyes like a turning kaleidoscope. That's the night I fell in love for the very first time.

Now he was somewhere in Manhattan's oily dark streets getting drenched to the skin for the sake of my love. A boy passed him on the street. He had no conscience. That's what was so remarkable about him. Two boys passed him on the street. He was like nothing in the world I had been brought up in. A double life was exactly suited to my consciousness, so I went along with him and got excited. His voice was so much deeper than those of my teenaged friends that when he called my house asking for me I told my parents he was one of my teachers. Then I told them he was a writer in New York. They said, "But I thought he was one of your teachers."

"I never said that," I told them, full of scorn and counting the days till I could get away from them. "No, he's a writer in New York." Later on I made him a piano salesman I had fooled into thinking I had enough money to buy a piano. Who knows what Mom and Dad made out of my lies. They probably thought it was a drug dealer. After writing hundreds of pages of it, I gave up on my dissertation not too long ago. I remember thinking that to lie and deceive, to lead a secret sexual life, was to me the greatest of all pleasures and by far the most natural. Maybe I should have been a spy for a foreign power, or a better Catholic.

In Loveland, only a few colors stain the crystal radiance of the skies, gray, pink, white, black; someone holds you for a few minutes, then lets you fall to the rocks, and nothing hurts, and you're never betrayed. All your allegiances are to the holy. All the phones are tapped. If there's someone younger than you in the nightclub he or she's an enemy agent to whom you must show the marked roadmap and speak the secret words. Once you've made your way there, you never, never grow old. First he frightened me, then he made me come, then he amused me, then he left me, then he made me recall him.

I went to the window, shivering in jockey shorts, holes in the seams in required places, and drew back the cheesecloth curtain. I looked out onto windows and chimneys. I saw shabby storefronts and New York rain of the pearly white and gray. I looked over my shoulder to quick-trip on our unmade bed, a sprawl of similarly pearl and gray mattress and stained sheets. Then to the glass again. Once I kissed his face in a mirror. Another time I kissed a glass ashtray. Out on the street a car was lurking, its motor running. The car seemed sinister and it hummed danger.

The noise was incredible.

The walls were thin there. Glossy magazine covers hung from the walls to increase their thickness. Once he said he wished we had no windows, since glass is too thin and lets in and out too much heat and noise. I remember arguing with him. I asked him how else if not for windows would we be able to see out onto the city streets. I reminded him that they, the streets, were what provided him with almost all his excitement and inspiration. "But I don't need any windows now," he said, "since I fell for you." You can imagine how that made me feel. I looked out into the rain and I was glad to be indoors. I began to spit on myself because, if he was getting wet out there, I wanted to feel wet too. The night is long. I didn't have much self-protection. I opened my pants and maneuvered my cock and pissed all over my chest and throat and face.

Years later I read a poem, by Eileen Myles, that exactly answered my need to express what I felt about that time in my life, during which I grew from a little boy into a young man, so that I felt then that I'd never have to write about it myself, only relax and wait and then someday be wrapped in swaddling clothes.

THE HONEY BEAR

Billie Holiday was on the radio
I was standing in the kitchen
smoking my cigarette of this
pack I plan to finish tonight
last night of smoking youth.
I made a cup of this funny
kind of tea I've had hanging
around. A little too sweet
and odd mix. My only impulse
was to make it sweeter.
Ivy Anderson was singing
pretty late tonight
in my very bright kitchen.
I'm standing by the tub
feeling a little older
nearly thirty in my very
bright kitchen tonight.
I'm not a bad looking woman
I suppose   O it's very quiet
in my kitchen tonight   I'm squeezing
this plastic honey bear   a noodle
of honey dripping into the odd sweet
tea. It's pretty late
Honey bear's cover was loose
and somehow honey   dripping down
the bear's face   catching
in the crevices beneath
the bear's eyes   O very sad and sweet
I'm standing in my kitchen   Oh honey
I'm staring at the honey bear's face.

THE THINGS OF A CHILD

At the same time that I was seeing Carey Denham, I was trying to maintain the normal life of a Long Island teenager. This wasn't always easy, but it gave me a unique distinction—or so I then felt. The boys I knew in Smithtown were like suns, each radiant and clear, and I was the sun with the spots on it. I had a best friend, though. His name was George Grey.

George wasn't an adopted child, but this distinction he falsely claimed, like a merit badge of some kind. He was never able, so far as I know, to shake off from his life the romance he associated with adoption. Even into adulthood that romance still irradiated within, deciding for him what to do, how to behave. Many adoptees form grand theories about the identities of their natural parents (the more far-fetched, the more fitting) and George followed suit: he believed himself the natural son of the famous dancer and entertainer Gypsy Rose Lee.

Until he was thirteen he kept his own counsel about his "true parentage." Then he let me in, and showed me his evidence. Exhibit "A" was a faded clipping from the *Messenger*, Smithtown's weekly newspaper, dated one week after his birth. The article, illustrated with grainy photos, said that Gypsy Rose Lee had visited relatives in our town the previous week, in seclusion, practically incognito. George flapped this clipping at me and said: "This is the proof I've been after for thirteen long years! She must have left me on the Greys' doorstep, pinned with a note, 'Please call this baby GEORGE.' She had the motive, the means, the morals, the method and now—I find out—the opportunity." This was why he always said, of Mr. Grey and his wife, "They're not my real parents." I could understand that, but why'd he say it so *witheringly*?

I only flipped through some baseball cards and chuckled, like a cat. "You goon," I said, too used by then to George's high-flown talk to pay much attention to this, the deepest and more far-ranging of his fantastic neuroses. George was in any case the master of hyperbolic bullshit. A little of it rubbed off on me, I guess, everyone says so, and maybe they're right. Most of the time our gang only laughed at George's bullshit because it was so outrageous. On the other hand we rarely knew how much of it was true. Yet on the third hand we knew enough not to give this mysterious-birth story any more credence than we could help giving it. I guess we were pretty small-minded, but kids are like that, aren't they? In any case I could comfort myself, sometimes, and think, "Wow, Kevin, you may be a queer but George Grey is really *really* fucked."

Now I know how small it was of me to snicker when George expounded his theory of Gypsy Rose Lee's Smithtown confinement. But what would you have done or said? Here was this 13-year old kid, brandishing fucking "proof" that his rightful mother was a Playboy Playmate stripper—or whatever she was—back in the twenties or sometime. I didn't then realize how much George, like W.B. Yeats, desired a connection, however tiny, improbable or precious, between the dancer, and the dance.

"Here look," George continued. "I hold here in my hands old copies of such respected family tabloids as the *Midnight Tattler* from 1952 through '53. Read them and weep! Gossip items ranging in size from blind tidbits to full-length feature articles which scurrilously imply that my mother was secretly pregnant during this period." He handed me layers of old dust which fell apart between our hands. "Damn it—those old mags fetch twenty bucks a pop."

"If your mother was Gypsy Rose Lee who was your father, Clark Grable?"

I tickled myself pink with this question: boy, oh boy! I wasn't even abashed when George corrected me. Gable, Grable, whoever. What did it matter? They were all stars: therefore, they were all insignificant nothings. George's face was blank.

He hadn't really thought about his father, he admitted. "I don't suppose I could have been another Immaculate Conception."

"I don't think so," I said, straight-faced.

"I don't think so either," George said. We went on to talk about getting drunk, getting laid, getting high. George had a million opinions on every topic. Women fascinated him, even old ladies like my grandmother, who lived with us sometimes, and whom I once had loved but now frightened me.

George met her for the first time when he was thirteen. "Hello there, sir," she croaked. "And what's your name?"

"This is George Grey," I hollered. "He's in my class at school. GEORGE," I repeated, a little desperately, because after all I didn't want George to think I had a relative who was not only old and not only crazy but one who was deaf too into the bargain. "GEORGE GREY. Oh, what the fuck, George, she—can't hear me," I confessed.

"Is he now! Well, well. Well, well, well. And what grade are you in now, Kevin?" Her small gray face was covered with hair and wrinkled bags—God, she was gross. She was my grandma, and I loved her and everything—or did once—and because she was senile I pitied her; but I hated her face and her very smell.

George, however, was taken by surprise at an erection like a redwood tree—or so he claimed as we left my house.

"For her!" I said.

"O yeah man. I mean older women have this—I guess it's a scent, it's something to do with hormones, it kind of hypnotizes me."

This possibility repelled me, enough to deny it; then George showed me the erection, put my hand on it like Jesus putting the hand of doubting Thomas on the wound in His side.

"I guess maybe you're right," I said, impressed. "But I think she's *too* old, besides which she's my grandmother." His cock was hot and pulsed in my hand like a trapped skinned animal, and we grinned at it, and at ourselves, then we hopped on our bikes and began gliding down the hill towards the footbridge over the pond. I was thirteen, too, but in comparison to George I was still a little boy, or felt myself to be a little boy—a late bloomer. In my bike spokes, but no longer in George's, baseball cards still flapped like frenetic tap-dancers. The cards snapped faster and faster as I gained momentum downhill. When we sailed and skidded to the pond's edge, we boys were both too exhilarated to breathe or think. Then we walked our bikes back up the hill and George swore at the unforgiving asphalt as though it were his worst enemy.

If ever George changed my life, though I don't believe the whims of others have much effect on one's life, it was surely at this juncture. His arousal made me long for a paradigm, a construction around which I could wrap my life. That night, I threw myself to work. I tore the baseball cards from out of the clothespins that held them to the spokes of my bike, and burnt them, one by one, in my parents' backyard.

The blackening, shrinking faces on the burning cards were those of my idols—Mickey Mantle, Sandy Koufax—but as I watched the blaze I could only think, "I put away the things of a child." I wanted to grow up and be a man.

USED TO

In high school, George and I used to drive around in incredibly new and shiny cars, and meet girls. George would tell them his name was Mike Hunt. "Now say it real fast ten times." These game girls, full of pluck, kind of taken, would leap into the fray: "Mike Hunt, Mike Hunt, Mike Hunt Mike-Hunt Mike-Hunt my cunt my cunt—" Then they would stop or drive away. This was considered a "liberating" line. Maybe the girl would come to her senses and realize that she was basically an animal walking on two legs. That was, at any rate, the theory. Twice this actually happened—a day or so apart, and my friend, jaded by his success began, in a heavy, Teutonic accent, to introduce me as "Mike Hoch." When I think of all the writing I've done since those days in 1970, sometimes I have to jump back and consider that "Mike Hunt" and "Mike Hoch" aren't, after all, dead themselves. We are still young and still weak and this weakness, like all weaknesses, is so strong.

George and I went to a boys' high school, Catholic school; we wore beautiful sweaters and coats there, black and gold our school colors. You don't see those colors much in San Francisco, which is pretty much a pastel city, but sometimes I go to China-town sin parlors, open all night, have a drink, have a few laughs. You know. In one of these bourgeois bars not too long ago I spotted this guy drinking this cocktail that looked black and gold under the pink-shaded lights. "Make me one of those whatchamacallits that man's having," I told the barman. "It'll stir up some nostalgia in me. It's black and gold, like a hit parade of high school memories. And do me a favor, por favor, round me up some teenage boys, cheez nips, salty bar nuts or other canapes to wash down my drink?"

He nodded and complied. Soon my left hand cradled the drink, an anise liquid, black as a squid, corseleted with goldfish like a chain of gold on which the hidden ring is hung Juliet can't wear on her finger. This drink, sweet as the devil, dramatic when stirred, is everything a teenager wants. A teenage boy sat on my right hand.

When I put it to his lips a hair fell off his face.

He smiled and told me two lies about sex. He was fifteen or sixteen. One of those boys. "You're very much like I was at your age," I told him. My ears were ringing and my face was red: how often I had promised myself never to use that expression: *when I was your age.*

In school the glass walls of our homeroom would fog from so much hot breath and steamed cotton and wet snowy water spreading in circles on the wood floor, like the rings old cocktails leave behind when your hand moves them. The odor of damp wool, made piquant with sweat and that old-timey purplish mimeo smell, rose towards the musty wood ceiling in waves and waves of heady, cloying perfume. Our desks were outdated and clunky, furniture made by the Nibelungen dwarves. Outside, the Long Island woods, moving with snow, heavy, but evanescent at the same time, shivered under the shortness of the day and the thickening wind. Snow covered the outbuildings of the campus; snow clung menting flake by flake, to the nape of George Grey's neck as he sat in front of me, hunched over, writing a lengthy letter to his girlfriend, as the teacher droned on oblivious. *Dear*

Jane, Mr. and Mrs. Grey are off to Bermuda come Friday. We're running the taps and letting the floor of their rec room freeze over, winter carnival Jane, please come and bring skates. "God," said our teacher, a Franciscan friar in a black robe and sandals, chilblained toes poking out in a Dickensian way, "God has a bone to pick with you." This homeroom was a warm box of wet dark in the brittle cold sunny world, it kept itself to itself. Years later when I heard the California expression "heat on" ("he's got heat on" = "he's drunk"), my mind would jump to that room instead, and to the Long Island woods outside, moving with snow, that made me write in my yearbook "Remember me!"

I open the old yearbook and always turn to page 11; it flies open by itself like the Sorcerer's Apprentice, to George Grey's picture. I took the photo myself, he's tied to a tree behind one of the school outbuildings, tied by the ankles and strung up like a beautiful hung mermaid.

Boys' school: One of our teachers died and we were left alone with his body for a moment. George rolled a joint of marijuana on the dead man's shirt-front and we passed it to each other across his fading whitening face. Later we sang "Give Peace a Chance" at this dead teacher's funeral, because it was in the spirit of the times. Later still, we took to calling his widow the "Merry Widow"— the Merry Widow has a waltz of her own. Their son Billy went to our school and he was kind of a friend of ours. I suppose I guessed even then there's not much ado about anything much.

Boys' school: This other time we were stoned in the dark, at a dance, crepe paper tied to his waist to make him into a girl. I sometimes imagine life in high school to be the most hieratic time of one's life, with a court of breeze nipping, like the players of an air guitar, at every new pore of new skin that grows and flows across one's body on wave after wave of chill and chastisement and heat.

George could play the piano faster than anyone I have ever known; though I suppose this is more of a knack than a talent, I thought I could make money off of him by exploiting his fatal facility. When he and I saw Antonioni's *Zabriskie Point*, a taste or love for the devastated and the colorful began to develop within me like a tooth in a fetus. Sitting next to him in the theater, watching hundreds of young people make love all over Death Valley, I forgot to eat my popcorn. When the lights came up I looked at my lap and I didn't know what I was seeing. But it turned out to be popcorn. The whole point of the picture is that noise, stratified into degrees of toleration, is the way Americans measure distance (time, space, Bergson, etc.)—it made me want to become a famous Californian. This meant taking a lot of drugs.

George's mother once reproached me for being what she called a "bad influence" on her son. This left me speechless, or almost so, since as far as I could make out of the lives of Verlaine and Rimbaud, they were almost equally to "blame," and even if they weren't good company was there really room for reproach in our lives, Mrs. Grey? "Leave me alone," I told her, stumbling out of her kitchen and down the split-level stairs of her patio.

On the inside of one kitchen cabinet, Mrs. Grey had taped a yellowed fading Xerox of a composition of gray and black shadows. It looked like an example of Action Painting till you stood a certain distance from it, whereupon the shadows reassembled themselves into the image of Christ. Under the face of the title was printed: "Famous Invisible Picture of Christ." But like I say, you had to stand a certain distance away from it—like say if you put your hand in the cookie jar, that was far enough: you saw Him then.

School Building: We had this one teacher, a very smart man, a Franciscan brother no less, and I had a kind of crush on him. I wrote a novel, *Atlantis*, to give my teacher and impress him. It was to serve as my kiss of love (he was very religious but religion, I thought, is only sex without color) (like lamb with mint jelly).

I was so preoccupied with this crush and with writing this "novel" that I didn't see Carey for three or four months in a row, which seemed like a long time back then. When I finally made a date, he stared at my hair. Last time I'd seen him, I'd been a winsome blond. Now my hair had turned its present color, a studious maple.

"You're growing up," Carey said.

"Oh, no," I said. I felt guilty about it, guilty on two counts. My teacher was receiving all the adoration I had to offer—the adoration Carey demanded of me. And also I felt guilty about time, that time would pass by and no one would want me, no one at all.

"It's okay," he said gently. "Gentlemen prefer blonds," he said, "but it's okay, honestly."

As it turned out, Brother Felix never commented on my "novel"—I thought he was shy like so many older men are or were. Now I realize how impossible I must have been. One day, *purely by accident*, the house all the brothers lived in burnt to the ground like a curtain, while we boys stood outside cheering on a green hill. In the cloud of smoke and falling debris, I saw what I believed to be the pages of my book fluttering and weeping in the nauseous air, trying to die, under a sun as gold as beer and as warm and as flat.

This picture stayed with me, a MS. blown by hot air and fire, and afterwards whenever I considered a dramatic suicide, this image restrained me. If these pages refused to die, dying couldn't be that easy. I stood on the hill, thinking, so when you try to die you can't, you jump over a wall, you decide *I will not be a nun, what I will do is fuck up for twenty-five years then see what exactly is what and what's not even that much.* That was the beginning of summer, the last day of school. I walked back to our deserted classroom and stared down at the eccentric rings in the hard-wood and said to myself, "Boys' school."

How do I explain further? We boys lived in time, in a seething jungle the vines and contours of which, while never as gruesome as, say Vietnam, have now vanished with progress and OPEC and MTV and AIDS. When something happened we could place it real quick, just the way it happened for us. Now there's no time, and here in San Francisco no seasons, and sex, I now think, is religion with no color—like a bag of liquid on a dead man's chest.

I think going to a school makes one think more often of going outside, just to get away from the teachers and to try to find out what process inside bare trees leaves them so alluring to lightning, so easy to carve, so kind to the wind in the open vatic mouth of a nature I haven't believed since I was fifteen or sixteen—one of those boys.

I was one of those boys who walks around your kitchen like a dog trying to get to sleep.

Then he lies down in your arms and you blow a sensual music through him like Keats. In the morning he gets you to eat all the wild plums in the icebox and to drive him to school or to, at any rate, a big parking lot stunned with Porsches and fallen leaves. A little bell rings in the side of your head like the ear of Van Gogh. He'll mount the steps and he'll sidle into homeroom. *His* wonderful teacher descends into the room and begins to talk about living in history and how this time we live in will never have its duplicate, it's special, it's a typological snowflake like something out of Dante. He forgets about you and thinks about—the Mall.

Once George stood in the middle of a field of snow, himself layered in snow, his hair was the color of patchouli, but whitened by the natural weather he had brought down on Long Island by his own essence. His powers were not to be sneered at. I loved the snow and connected it to my best friend. The other day I read in the paper that scientists now don't believe each snowflake is different after all. There are apparently something like six thousand types, and that rings true, doesn't it, but how disappointing!

Every time one melts, anyhow, it's an act of perfect taste.

Melodrama and reversal have always come easily to me. In private a Fassbinder-Sirk festival runs in my head from day to night, whenever my eyes shut, but once upon a time I was more sedate about it, a nicer boy with some gorgeous friends, and wore black and gold and stole a ladder to bring it to school at night, stoned on a new drug. In the wondering starlight flecked with seeds of marijuana, George and I mounted the Stonehenge handball concrete wall, spray paint like roses in our teeth, adventure and art at heart and I wrote Wordsworth. THIS IS THE HOUR OF FEELING. And he wrote the vacuous lovely words of Brian Wilson: BE TRUE TO YOUR SCHOOL. JUST LIKE YOU WOULD TO YOUR GIRL OR GUY NOW.

George had five brothers, one of whom was a professional tennis instructor and for this reason rather the "black sheep" of the Grey family. This brother and George sometimes went out with two sisters, the Mulhall girls, and I thought this was an appealing project. The eldest sister, Lizzie, was the reincarnation of Lizzie Siddal, D.G. Rossetti's model and later his wife.

At least I thought so. I'm alive still. "Time has too much credit," says Bridget, in I. Compton-Burnett's novel *Darkness and Day*. "I never agree with the compliments paid to it. It is not a great healer. It is an indifferent and perfunctory one. Sometimes it does not heal at all. And sometimes when it seems to, no healing has been necessary."

STILL

I haven't thought about the two Bernhardt brothers in some time, but I was staring at the floor, the radio playing Barbra Streisand's new record, and I was thinking of how long she's been around and why is it I still don't know if I like her or not, as a person. The floor started to whirl round and around, like her record or as if to denote extreme dizziness and nausea . . .

One spring afternoon I left school on my bike and rode downhill about fifty yards to a tiny, mushroom-like delicatessen that sold delicious Fudgsicles. School was so dull, and the spring air so vital, I wanted to see something made out of my life, not just books and papers and unappreciative teachers who didn't understand me. Me, Kevin! I wanted a Fudgsicle. Wonder if they still make them: I loved Fudgsicles then, loved buying them, unwrapping them, looking at them. Loved pausing before plunging them into my mouth. Then I'd start to chew, swallow, eat.

As I entered the deli, an Italian woman came from behind the counter, about five feet tall, making a pizza with her hands, rubbing it and catching it playfully as though it were a cat. Over a purple housedress she wore a white apron, basted in the reds and scarlets of secret sauces. To help me she pointed where the Fudgsicles were kept and said how popular they were. The door was propped open and little bells rang in the breeze, and she moved closer to the sun, her eyes opening and shutting like a camera's lenses. Leaning back against the cool white box, filled with bagged ice, I peeled off the Fudgsicle gratefully. "Cool meat," I said. From where I stood I could see my bike, and a hundred green hickory trees, lying low into the street, cool shadows turning the rippled, bumpy asphalt into a black and gray and blue river. We were near an actual river, too, quite near. Sometimes fishermen walked past the store armed with boxes of tackle and rods and red coats, stubby hats. The Italian woman clapped her hands, she was so full of glee, and also, I suppose, to improve the taste of the pizza.

This woman was used to the boys from my school coming into her store at all hours, in twos and threes, to buy ice cream and cigarettes, candy and wine. She liked to play operas on an old phonograph from the fifties and to sing. A colorful character like someone who lives in San Francisco.

Then Billy Bernhardt came into the store.

There has to be a person inside the story, I wonder why; surely the pattern alone of this changing, breathing nature should satisfy, but I couldn't tell why clearly or make it seem. I could feel the breath inside my chest, and I didn't smoke then, and then I ran a lot, trying to keep up, but then in stillness it blew through me and kept me alive. I didn't think much of it, just as I ignored the marsh birds and the violet, dusky reeds along the roadside. But when a person came into my story I stood there and felt conscious of everything, like it was all new, like everything in my life was all new, and I wonder why; if our souls are so constituted, or if there's something sexual about it I don't comprehend.

He looked so familiar, though I knew I hadn't seen him before, that I asked him his name, while the Italian woman nodded in precision and whistled one of her airs from Puccini. I thought of her as a kindly, stupid person. "I'm Bill Bernhardt," he said.

"Hey, you related to Chris Bernhardt?"

"He's my little brother."

"You look kind of like him."

Billy considered. His face grew gloomy, his white lashes bristled.

Then he told me about his life and why he looked so much like his brother, and why it was a troubling matter to all who were concerned. I didn't really care. "I'm on vacation from my job and I'm spending a few days in America with Chris."

"Why, where do you live?"

"Kumquat," he said. Some Arabian state. "I haven't seen Chrissie in five years." I got on my bike and followed his VW to the apartment of Chris, who I knew from school but had never really cared for. I'll say this right now: Billy was by far the more attractive of the two Bernhardt brothers.

Chris Bernhardt was the kind of guy you take one look at and say *But for the Grace of God, baby, there go I.* He was so vacant you wondered why he was still in school, why he hadn't been expelled long ago. I shared one class with him and he always stared straight ahead at the blackboard, never saying a word, never writing a word, and not replying when the teacher spoke to him. He had a personality problem; it was as though he felt too stupid to be alive. One finds this kind of problem intriguing at first, but after a few days you tend to forget it, the way I remember the first time I went into New York, a child, and saw hoboes sleeping in the street, I was so upset I wanted my parents to call the police and have them all arrested. But now I pass by these people all the time and I could care less.

Chris stood about six feet tall, with a shock of light brown hair and slow, frozen eyes like a dead cow's. His skin was pale, milky, and the more so for the giant strawberry mark that ran up the right side of his face to disappear into his ear like a slug caught in the light. He liked to shave and once caused quite a commotion in the locker room by getting carried away and shaving the hair off his legs. All in all, a mixed bag. Many there were who said he was retarded, but I never thought so, just boring. Despite all this Chris was kind of popular because, alone out of all the boys in school, he had his own apartment. And no one knew why.

We were so used to living with our parents and having to cope with their rules and guidance that Chris Bernhardt seemed at once very lucky and the awful example of what would happen without their restrictions. In a way he was the wild child, the blank page, into which we could read whatever scenario we saw or felt or could ever imagine, in relation to our parents, in relation to love, to relation itself. He and they were so stupid they all became the true and ideal. He was a legend in his own time.

"Your assignment," George told me, "is to go over to Chris' apartment and find out everything you can about him. You and I are going to write a book exposing his life and we'll call it *96 Tears*."

"I'll go, and I'll find out what I can," I said. "But I don't know about writing any book. You're the writer," I told George. "I'll tell you everything I find out and you can write the book."

I don't think George ever did write his book *96 Tears*. I'm having to write this book all by myself, and as you know, I've chosen a far different title.

"I was struck by lightning," Chris Bernhardt told me. We sat on the floor of his apartment amid a litter of hubcaps, beer cans, TV dinner trays, moldy clothes, broken sticks, pebbles, dirt and water. We might as well have been outdoors, in a junkyard, or in the "Waste Land" our English teacher was trying to drum into our heads. "When I was a little boy I was struck by lightning on a golf course and that's how I got my strawberry mark."

"Oh Chris that's not how you get those marks, they're birthmarks."

"No, until I was four years old my face was unmarked. It's something that happened while I was alive."

"Well, tell me what happened."

"I told you."

"You told me a little," I said, "but there must be more to it." Or less to it, I thought.

"I told you all I can remember."

"It's not good enough, Chris."

"Asshole."

"Shut up," I said. When I looked at him I saw he was almost asleep. He was more relaxed than most of the teenagers I knew, few of whom ever seemed to sleep at all they were so horny, worried or amphetamized. His hands curled around a steering wheel, and his knees pulled up to his chin. "Shut up, Chrissie," I said to him. The sun went down. I didn't hear anybody calling me for dinner. The windows were smeared with filth and the rich warm smell of gasoline stung the twilight. I had to go home and do something, jerk off, watch TV, do something.

The sun went down and spilled into dark. His leg thrust out like a hard-on, pulling together the seams of the split leg, like a curtain closing. The turtle retreats into his shell, the ostrich to sand, the narrative spills inward and begins to examine itself like a Buddha . . . a love bizarre.

I followed Billy up the stairs and into Chris's apartment. *Hiya Chris. Fuck you.* Billy spent twenty minutes scrubbing a square into the linoleum, ten feet by eight, then unrolled his new sleeping bag into it. All around him garbage piled up to the height of eighteen inches, but he kept his space clean.

"Mr. Prim and Proper," Chris said, kicking off his sneaker into the square towards Billy's face. Billy threw it back in another direction.

"I'm trying to read," he said. I wonder why he wasn't in Vietnam.

"You two are like cats and dogs," I said. "Can't there be any peace between you?" Maybe he worked for the CIA.

The father lived in Arabia, worked for a US oil company. The mother was dead, I think. Maybe she'd killed herself and the family hushed it up. Or maybe Chris had killed her and that's why he'd been abandoned by everyone else in the family and left to live by his own devices on Long Island. Maybe, but you'd think someone would have done something.

And no one did anything, any more than the rook, that from the silver birch shoots across the sky to stop again at another nowhere place. It was enough, perhaps, to grow, like the shock of purple iris from the trampled riverside patch of weeds.

The child says, "I don't want to go to Arabia!"

"Then don't come, who cares . . ." And one day you come home from school to find that indeed, the child's dreams have at last come true. The whole family has packed and split, leaving money in an envelope in the middle of an otherwise empty room, and food in the unplugged refrigerator, enough for a long weekend. That never, ever ends.

Chris had a guitar and liked to play the songs, popular at the time, of Paul McCartney and George Harrison, *Rocky Raccoon*, *Badge*, *Martha my Dear*, *While my Guitar Gently Weeps*. When he picked it up with Billy there, his hands fell away after a few broken chords and he threw it down. After a while he left the house. The open door showed a shot of him hitchhiking, grim and determined in the salt-laden air, behind him the colorful beach grass and wild onions and roses. "He's got spring fever," said Billy. "He's like this every Spring."

As though a story was uncoiling out of the ring of rope on board the ship to Arabia. A coral snake or red snake unscrewing itself out of a hank of hemp, lifting towards the watery horizon, towards the sun, exultant, a snake out of control, its tongue in an arc and the sky, rose red, half as old as time, its only limit. The story of the two brothers, continues, as though the basket has only half opened.

Billy was so good-looking Arab women raised their veils to compete for his attention. At least that's what he told us. But he went out with an American girl from the American Embassy. "Don't want to pick up kumquatitis," he said. "Better the devil you know," said Billy, "than the devil you don't."

He didn't want to pick up fleas from Chris' floor because Arab Airport Customs would send him packing back to America. This was the first I ever heard about Arabia being a clean country. "I guess it figures with all that sand," I thought. Chris and I sucked out of one can of beer, hearing the brother, a million stories, a million Arabic characters, all for nothing.

Close-up—say this was a movie: The mouth of the beer can, Chris's eyes sullen above it. Then Chris storming out, down the rickety gray stairs, and hopping on a motorbike so hard you'd think his balls would ache. Then:

VROOM!

"You two guys know each other pretty good?" Billy asked me.

"Well, we've never slept together," I said. "Still we have this same teacher who's kind of a prick so we have something in common."

"I know what that's like," Billy said. On the muddy floor a can of beer, or piss, sat open and he put a cigarette out in it. "Man do I know what that's like."

"I guess you're glad your brother's so popular."

"Am I?" Shrugging, he pulled his shirt over his head. "I guess I am but I don't really give a shit. He has his own thing. Always has."

But what was it? What could Billy possibly think Chris had? I searched him closely, from the sheen of his glossy, gardenia hair to the intricate, pale leather web of his sandals, to find his reasons; anxious, but not yet aware of the pressure of compulsion. I felt for my neck and massaged it. Billy opened a beer and sank down into the open sleeping bag. He stared thoughtfully at the sagging plaster ceiling, where part of a neighborhood pizza still shone, dreamy and vague as a sleeper's kiss. "I'm only in town for a few days, I thought he'd be different. I'm twenty-five now. I'm so fucking old. He's just a kid." The walls were battered, the consistency of fried chicken. What a dump. "Still. Still just a kid."

A classic case of the *right hand* not yet knowing what the *left hand* is doing or how or travelling, why or just pumping, up and down, absently, as though two trains pass by each other in opposite directions but slowly enough for Passenger A to spot Passenger B in Train B strangling Passenger C . . .

When I saw Billy's cock it reminded me of mine, this I really flashed on, wider than it was deep, like an egg roll—no—like a Fudgsicle, and wider at its base than its head, very unlike your classic egg roll or *lumpia*, more like the logo of some World's Fair, but hot and heavy and the colors beige and pink and scarlet prominent, present in the room, but absent from the discourse between us, or between Billy and Chris, a clean study . . . a sudden insight—and so on and on about Chris's thing and how he'd always had it, always been a loner, with his own form of dealing with the world and how that was cool. "Cool meat," I said, leaning against a battered wall, my legs thrust out and smelling like flowers and money.

The absent father is the central figure in this case. I couldn't make him out. Still can't. He certainly neglected one of his sons. This makes Chris the Scapegoat, anagogically speaking. Why, he's like Christ in that sense.

Because he lived alone Chris found himself the center of things, but being so dull his classmates sinned and made him feel ignored in his own home. Sometimes you'd go over there and find the place a whirlwind of TV, tequila, *Racing Form*, *Playboy*, flash bulbs and noise, but Chris sitting slumped in a corner, fingering the strings of his guitar and being stepped on. "Who's that goony guy?" this girl said. She was frying an egg in a smoking skillet, smoking herself, and looking covertly around like Madeleine Carroll in a Hitchcock Nazi spy picture.

"Who's him? That's Chris Bernhardt."

"He keeps *staring* at me," she sighed, flicking long blonde hair over her shoulder. "Like he's never seen a girl before."

"You like the attention."

"Yeah but I'm screwing up this omelet, what is he, hostile?"

"He's just a guy in school."

"I bet they don't even know this is my apartment," said Chris. "They just don't know, do they?"

"Ah, Chris, I don't know."

Twang. Broken string. "You ever see what a cunt looks like, Kevin? You ever really take a look and see?" The girl at the stove swore as a lick of flame and grease spattered her arm. "When you walk right up and look at a cunt your eyes die."

"That guy is sick," she said out loud. She licked her arm, slowly and thoroughly. Her own eyes were dark, rubbed in with a smutty finger. She was rather a legend of sorts herself, because she'd been put in the trunk of a car as a little girl and held for fifteen days by a gang of airport bandits. Her name was Kathy McLaine and she never took off her makeup. Just put more on, morning after morning, so nobody really knew what she looked like from the neck up. I used to wonder if being kidnapped had made her what she was today. Perhaps she had become a changeling. George Grey said he was writing a book about her called "*Up from the Gutter—and Back Down Again.*"

"The cunt's eating my food."

"Oh, the hell with it," said Kathy, sliding the fried eggs onto the floor, where they crackled and sizzled for a minute, then lay still. Abruptly Chris rose and left the house, the screen door slamming behind him. I heard my bike skidding away across a bed of grass and gravel. He was headed for the harbor. "So I'm eating his food."

"He doesn't have very much," I said.

"You stick up for him like he's your pet," she said. "Besides he has plenty of food."

"I didn't mean food," I said, kind of lamely, because lots of makeup always makes me feel lame. "He was struck by lightning on a golf course when he was little."

"Oh, poor thing," she said. "Too, too bad. If he wants to swap sob stories, he's come to the right place. I was kidnapped—held for ransom when I was only six!"

"Like Elizabeth Barrett's dog, Flush," I said.

"What?"

"*Flush,*" I said, "by Virginia Woolf."

"A wolf or a dog?" she said.

"And you know W.S. Gilbert, of Gilbert and Sullivan," I sped on, hardly waiting to hear her deny it or watch her fumble with her compact. "*He* was kidnapped and released and when an adult he wrote *A Policeman's Lot is Not a Happy one.*"

"Well, I was released too," she announced. "I guess that's why I'm not glum and neurotic like your friend Chris Bernhardt."

"He's not my friend," I said. A car slowed down and Chris got in.

"Where are you headed?" said the driver. Or maybe Chris said this.

I picture these two brothers as the characters in *East of Eden*, walking up a long road to a dim little town with about twenty cents between them.

Another picture: Chris is sick and nobody comes to visit him or give him aspirin or Tab or anything.

A third picture is Billy water-skiing in the Persian Gulf in a blue Speedo bathing suit the color of hydrangeas, and so is the sea. Chris turns the picture over, and reads *Having a Wonderful Time, Wish you were Here* in a hand he doesn't recognize, but I do. First he crumples the picture and dunks it in the toilet; but later he fishes it out and lies it to dry in the sun on the windowsill where a pot of marigolds lies dying.

And the final picture is Psyche, and her ugly older sister, Orual, Psyche about to light the fatal lamp on the malicious advice of the sister, who's shown bending into her delicate ear and whispering words of bad faith and ill-omen. The temple is vast, the temple of Aphrodite's love. Mystic smoke billows from the gray stone floor, like in Prince's videos for *Kiss* and *A Love Bizarre*.

Saturdays Chris helped the Italian woman in her store, hauling trash, sweeping dust, stocking the freezers with ice cream treats. She didn't pay him but seemed happy. She would clap her hands from joy and she told him, "You are the best helper I have ever had."

Sweat fell into his eyes from a fringe of brown hair. She sang and hummed the songs of another century, filled with simple emotions, grandly expressed. There was a broomstick right up his ass.

The open door of the store rang with bells. He felt sorry for her so he kept working for her. He felt strong in her love, his muscles opening and closing like the factories Bruce Springsteen is always moaning about.

Three guys from school called up from a pay phone down the street. They wanted to come over and smoke some reefer in "a safe house." Billy picked up the call and told them don't come over and to get fucked.

He asked me if Chris did a lot of drugs. *Not one* I lied. How come he acted so stoned all the time? C'mon, it's all right, I don't have to lie for my friend even though it shows I'm a good scout. *Why don't you ask him yourself then?* Well we have one of those relationships where we don't talk and that's cool. *Yeah well that's cool then* I said. "Billy Bernhardt," he said again into the phone when again it rang. I waited. "Yeah and I still have the same message. Get fucked, scumbags." I've waited and waited for fiteen years, still the stars through the open door don't say why or how or what they want. Silent still. When I reach for God I fall back on one impression, that I don't do it well. People come into my office with tracts and pamphlets and I say *No Peddling*. Seems to be cool with them, real cool. They just leave. I give them the same message Billy did: *get fucked scumbags*. The hands of the clock race forward, and I consider the alternatives: backwards? Like a trick in a home movie. Or stay still?

So it would always be some time or other, all the time, some time that I don't like and want to change and get away from.

Chris got into a car, then a fight. He came home moping. His brother was on the phone making plans for the weekend. "I'm just gonna be in town for a few days, I thought, why not have some fun?" He lay in his magic square in his underwear, pulling at his cock from outside, absent, yet too present for Chris' taste. Chris looked in the mirror and dabbed at the blood on his face.

A tooth had gotten knocked out. He could hear Billy try to talk the old girlfriend, now married to a doctor in Northport, into a kiss for old times' sake. "No I've been in Arabia for five years, yeah, the whole family, except Mom of course."

"And except Chris," Chris said to the mirror. He could hear the squeak and the slither of his brother's discourse. "Cool meat," he said. "Hey, dickhead, get off the phone," he yelled. "I have important calls to make to my pals."

In an instant Billy had bounded into the bathroom. "Don't ever you fuck with me while I'm on the phone," he said. His eyes were fierce and his breath sweet and torrid. He opened a cut in Chris' face. "And who the fuck are you trying to kid about *pals*."

"Okay, okay, okay, cool off, fuckface," Chris said. "Look I got the big man upset. Look, his cock's hanging out he's so upset. Like a Fudgsicle," Chris said. "Cool meat."

"Who did it, Chris?" said Billy, pointing to the new scar on Chris' drawn face.

"What the hell do you care!"

"Ah, Chris, who did it?"

Chris turned again to the screen door, away from his brother. After a while he spoke again, not answering—only speaking:

"You rent that car, Billy?"

"Borrowed it—from your 'girlfriend,' Kathy McLaine."

"Billy, that girl . . . she was standing in the airport with her Mom and Dad, and she wandered away a little ways, and somehow she got into the back room of the baggage area and she saw these guys from another country, and I guess they thought she knew too much."

"She does know one fuck of a lot."

"Billy, she was only seven years old."

"I know," Billy said soothingly. "I know."

"Did you fuck her?"

"Did *you?*" Billy replied.

"They grabbed her up, Billy, and put her in the trunk of a car."

"Did they fuck her?"

"Come on Billy! She was only seven!"

"Well, I like her car. That's why I borrowed it."

"When are you going?"

"I might decide to stick around a while," Billy said. Behind his aviator glasses his eyes were blue, blue as the river of Old Dock Road. Chris would sit on his steps, strumming his guitar and looking as though he were looking at it, and we'd come bustling up the steps and ask who was over. He'd shrug and moved his ass to let us pass. No one liked to tousle his sweaty hair when they went by, but usually someone would as we mounted the steps to reach the apartment, out of charity, noblesse oblige.

"Good guy," I said. "I want to come here and be alone and write my story." Behind me the strings of the guitar ring out a little plangent and affected, like the Beatles. Up so high Chris looks out over the Nissequogue River. A heron rises up out of a ring of beach grass and red reeds, pokes his beak to the sky; then before Chrissie knows what's happening the bird has flown. The key is difficult. Still I'm a million miles away and I don't really care. The pages I wrote in that house fly by, round and around like a record of the Beatles or of Barbra. As a person I don't really like her, but her voice is beautiful, a million times better than that crazy Chris Bernhardt. "Move it, Chris," Billy said.

Blood ran down his chin like a shaving cut, or the impossible piss of the bum on the sidewalk. He moved closer to the mirror, a magic square cut into the bathroom wall. "I might decide to live here for a while," Billy said. "Then again I might not."

Better the Devil you know Chris thought, *than the Devil you don't*. He left the house, mad. For the first time the driver spoke. "Where you headed, Chris?"

"He didn't even say goodbye," Billy said. The shower was a cool white box, filled with ice, standing upright and stained with the reds and scarlets of his brother's blood. From the base of his cock a cool blue vein twisted languidly towards the sky.

The temple of Aphrodite where Psyche sleeps. She has to win Aphrodite's love and respect. They tell her to descend into Hell where Persephone reigns and take back the box of beauty. Along the way, they warn her, she'll be besieged by the figures of those who deserve her pity and might wring her heart. But they'll only be phantoms, don't let yourself be taken in. Wonder can I get it across. I'm on a search for God that never ends and won't be satisfied: the long weekend—the money in the envelope on the floor of a vacated room.

Chris walked out of the house, pissed off as all Hell, and got in his car. He realized he had left his car keys in the house. He got out of the car and started to hitchhike. Chris looked out at the night and at the road with mixed feelings. He was a regular emotional cocktail. Somebody, somewhere, would have his difficult keys. "I'll go down River Road; I'll go to Little Africa."

A car pulled up and Chrissie got in. The Beatles: *You're gonna lose that girl. You're gonna lose that girl.* The driver was dangerous but Chris was very drunk. The slightest curve of the road broke through the plastic seal of blindness into the slit-eye-ball-land of plenty.

He would go there, to that house. He couldn't go "home." Vietnam was only just around the corner. In the middle of the road a squirrel or muskrat froze as if in a dream or an icecube tray, its mellow eyes turned to pinpricks by the car's open headlights. There, in that house, he could reach a resolution. He inserted as many fingers as he could into his mouth. Spring nights! The radio. "Trying to make yourself puke?" He took out his fingers and sat on his hands. Chris felt strong, his teeth filled with spinach and his biceps covered with pictures of pile-drivers and TNT. The driver of the car looked at you separately from your background. Behind every tree lurked a tiny civilian. His foot thud-thudded on the fireboard/firewall.

5 STEPS TO MURDER

In January 1971, I had just turned 18, and I felt over the hill, older than God, I decided to spend a few days with my best friend George Grey who boarded at a now-defunct college in upstate New York called Eisenhower.

"Won't I get to see you Saturday?" Carey asked.'

Saturday was "our day."

"You can put me on the bus," I told him. "Spend the weekend with your kids, that'll give 'em a shot in the arm."

By a previous marriage Carey had several sons, all of them old enough to occupy himself with. He loved those sons and I couldn't be sure I wasn't really one of them. "I leave Port Authority at midnight."

I wonder now if this confusion about paternity isn't what led to my present-day addiction to TV soaps.

When my bus left New York there wasn't a snowflake to be seen, but the sky was threatening and cold.

When I got off the bus, the sky was white, very Brooks Brothers. George didn't meet me at the station, but that was only to be expected. My satchel hit my right calf over and over as I slogged towards the campus through the morning storm. The sky stayed white for days, white, thick and choppy, like cioppino, and due to the blizzard I was trapped in that dormitory for five weeks. After a while, no more food got through, only acid. A tunnel was engineered between the dormitory and the cafeteria and we would go in and get trays and silverware and eat acid three times a day, ceremoniously, like disciples of Mishima. Then we would go back to the bedroom and think of things to do. I hadn't expected to stay as long as I wound up staying, but I'm glad I did, because that month in the country "turned me out"— I became a writer and this is how.

George's two best friends were Flip, a real short dwarf, and Skip, kind of a tall rangy Joel McCrea. These nicknames sounded acrobatic to me, and certainly in their appearance there was something rather Circus World about these two boys. I asked George about their names—if they were jokes. He said, "No, that kind of nickname is an implication of breeding." I suppose nowadays I'd recognize preppy, but at that time I thought of breeding as something that made you look beautiful, like Grace Kelly, and there was little conventionally beautiful about either Flip or Skip, just goofy, especially when they got dressed. Once we played hide and seek and Slip hid Flip in a dresser drawer. This was no wide chiffonier either but a high narrow dresser the kind you associate with Emily Dickinson.

We turned out the light, to be careful of it, to conserve our looks and to squander the dark.

It took one glass of beer to get me drunk. To stay passive like a smile, to derange me like a snake, and to shed my skin, I took the light out and threw it in a snowbank.

Skip was sleeping with a woman named Maureen, later his wife, but the spirit of the times saw no reason why George shouldn't sleep with them too, especially since he had all the comforters.

"It's so easy to write a novel and this is how," he said. "Just pretend you're writing a letter to me." Using an entirely different method George had himself already written over twenty novels.

He would re-tell the plots of the Warhol movies he had seen as though they had happened to him. I still remember his opening to *I, a Man.* "I am sitting on the beach at Fire Island in a tight white sharkskin bathing suit and then men are watching me. A dark shadowy bulge between my legs attracts their attention because I am so gorgeous." Nowadays for every movie that's released a so-called "novelization" pops up in drugstore racks to accompany it so I think George was ahead of his time. Avant-garde. His novels were decorated with stills of the films involved, or with photos of himself or of me. *I, a Man* was cleverly "bound" in tight white sharkskin as though ripped from the shadowy bulge of its hero to wrap up his story. I did not think I could learn from his methods so he said impatiently well then, think of your favorite songs on the radio. Like what I said sulkily, like a baby. His eyes grew wide. "Do you like IT'S MY PARTY AND I'LL CRY IF I WANT TO?"

"Well not really but I see what you mean."

"It has possibilities doesn't it?"

My first story was called *After the Cheese.* The heroine, Lesley, gives herself a gala birthday party and kindly, somewhat conde-scendingly, invites her country cousin Judy. Everyone's prepared for a quiet shy girl to show up (and to act like a wall-flower) but when the party's in full swing Judy proves to be even more seductive and wanton than the city girls who are Lesley's regular friends (I must have had Judy Garland's image in mind I realize now). When Judy is spotted dancing with Johnny, Lesley's steady, Lesley bursts into tears. The party seems ruined. In full swing—and yet ruined. "Judy and Johnny just walked in the room, like a queen with her king. Oh what a birthday surprise—Judy's wearing his ring." Things look bleak—curtains imminent—for Lesley. But she's saved from complete misery by the attentions of the same band of helpful mice and birds who aided Cinderella in the Disney picture of the same name. The birds effectively put Judy out of action by wrapping crepe paper around her body over and over again and stuffing her into a closet. Today I find this an eerie forecast of my favorite sex kink: mummification. Back then I was just a prophet without honor in my own country, I guess. Meanwhile the mice somehow manage to get Johnny so drunk that they are able to play the old "bed-trick" on him beloved by Shakespeare in his "problem comedies." At midnight he wakes up to realize that although he thought he'd lain down with Judy, he's woken up with Lesley. So now he'll *have to marry* her. And thus the party ends happily for all concerned, except for Judy of course. Now it's Judy's turn to cry. George's writing teacher gave him an "A" for this story and thus began our collaboration which was to continue for many years.

Next we wrote a romance novel called *Laughs in the Cake*, the story of the French Revolution. Its dramatis personae were the keys on the typewriter vs. the cards in a playing deck. The haughty lovely Queen of Diamonds, beheaded by fiery peasants Y, #, T and @ (Circa)—their leader, the mysterious Citizen X.

Without reading Agatha Christie's novel *Towards Zero*, George read the back cover blurb and decided he could write a better novel than hers based on the same incidents. This became *Life in the Mud*, or *5 Steps to Murder*.

Then we embarked on a musical comedy based on *Madame Bovary*, but there weren't enough lovable characters in *Madame Bovary*, so we added Felicity the maid, and her parrot, from Flaubert's *Un Coeur Simple* as a subplot—it became kind of French *Upstairs Downstairs*—or a French *Doctor Dolittle*. The parrot had all the best songs and the best sex too. She had to decide between simple pastoral domestic tranquility with Tweety Bird or a walk on the wild side with the sinister, sexy Maltese Falcon. Then George said, "Why don't we write a novel about my parents? They're a subject even Tolstoy couldn't exhaust. He wrote that all unhappy families are unhappy in different ways. I wish he had known my family, he would have changed that to 'All unhappy families are happy in different ways.'"

"What should we call it?"

"*Desiree*," George said. Nowadays I'd be more artful and call *Desiree* a "piece" instead of a novel, but he and I sat down and wrote it anyhow, without thinking. Besides its take on Victorian porn, large swatches of which we copied from an invaluable compendium called *The Pearl*, we prized it for the autobiographical sidelights it threw onto our own sexual identities. Today I can't make up my mind how I feel. George's hands were never still. They kept reaching for whatever was brightest in the room, in the snow, in the car, in my life, in his bed, on his body. I thought everyone was bisexual when I was eighteen.

I further thought that the fields of snow and the close, moist, warm air weighing down our bed was a factor in it. Even vision—what I saw from the window, wavery, vibrant and distinct—and taste—the sugary feel in my mouth from mescaline—I folded in, like a swirl of vanilla in a chocolate cake. One night we decorated a piano from a pillowcase half-filled with pubic hair, George had been cutting up a book of Duchamp's; to the black keys we glued swatches of darker hair like mine, and covered the white with the reddish blond hairs that spring from breeding. Dozens of participants tiptoed around afterwards through the snow, shaved and chafing, yet dazzled to realize Art through genital pain.

These are the five steps to murder as outlined by Agatha Christie, as taken up by us: 1.) A model child, Miggs, turns in ugly fury on her innocent playmate. 2.) Inspector Smythe uses his knowledge of tennis to solve a puzzling crime. 3.) Roadie, a beautiful if troubled woman, tries but cannot hide her feelings. 4.) A man with no memory comes back to the scene of his attempted self-destruction. 5.) A blood-stained handkerchief, found on a "slippery" window ledge, spells trouble for a muscular traveller from the Far East.

On the bus back to Manhattan I read and re-read all our manuscripts repeatedly, clutching to my chest, clumsy as a lover. I'd fallen in love with a world of art that knows no consequences or reversals. Ever since then I've been the same person, no growth, no development, just an aging body falling faster and faster towards death. When I began to write this book, that you're slogging through now, I tried to recreate the snowstorm that led me to his painted dorm room. The Greyhound windows were wet with cold rain and fog. The ticky-tacky houses of the Adirondacks whizzed by, the stately homes of Scarsdale, the inveterate rest stops and billboards, the Bronx, burnt out, the towers of Manhattan, while I sat unnoticing in the bus's back seat. My mind was spinning with plans. I saw no reason why I couldn't write a novel in a month, why not, I had so much to tell! When I stepped off the bus I was surprised to see Anita there, come to shepherd me to the house she shared with Carey. "Hi," I said, prepared to be friendly.

"*Venga aqui*," she told me. *This way.*

"You shouldn't have bothered," I said.

"I don't do it for you," she said, her shoulders bobbing this way and that, as I followed her hastily through the Terminal labyrinth. "Carey asked me to. So I came. *Venga aqui, ablamucho.*"

Ablamucho: big mouth. I forgot to mention that George had decorated his room at his parents' house with gigantic colorful oil murals. It would take him weeks to finish a wall. Each mural illustrated a scene from the novels of Harold Robbins. My favorite was the one from *The Inheritors*—it's the scene where the naive hero arrives at the 18th birthday party of Marianne Darling, and what the hero doesn't know is that Marianne's no ordinary debutante but instead, to use her own words, "crazed and blazed, flashed and trashed." George's painting represented Marianne in costume, dressed only in whipped cream and maraschino cherries, being licked all over by a dozen men dressed as Satan. Beneath her feet were inscribed the appropriate words of dialogue from the novel, as though this wall were an aquarelle from a Victorian romance. Another panel represented the meeting of Jennie Farrell and Rina Marlowe, the two heroines of *The Carpetbaggers*, as they rendezvous in a quiet Hollywood restaurant to divide up Jonas Cord's future. By the time George got through with the picture, that quiet restaurant had turned into the Hall of the Rhine Maidens. Mrs. Grey, George's mother, said nothing about these pictures until it came time for George's younger brother Jeff to move into that bedroom. "Those women are too sexual for Jeff," Mrs. Grey said. We just stared at her. Hadn't she ever met Jeff?

"Nothing," we said, "—not even a train going into a tunnel— is too sexual for Jeff." I felt sorry for Mrs. Grey. Her husband, a junior high school principal, was keeping a mistress named Babs, a waitress he'd met at the Hot Dog Diner. To spite him, Mrs. Grey had embarked on a series of belly dancing lessons and was also becoming an Episcopalian. Eventually, Babs gave birth to Mrs. Grey's seventh son. I slept with four of them at one time or another but since, in folk-fairy-tale material, the "seventh son" is supposed to embody miraculous luck, I regret that I'm so old and he's so young because it would have been nice to have lain down in darkness and gotten up in light.

CHERRY

So there—I had learned to write, but unless I kept up a rapid pace of living I'd have nothing—or so I felt—to write about.

A year went by, I kept changing college courses and colleges, going to parties, and living in a half-world. Soon I would turn nineteen. I started taking creative writing courses. "One day I'll be *giving* courses," I swore, "in creative living." I met Robbe-Grillet, Marshall McLuhan, Margaret Mead, Nicholas Ray, Marguerite Young, Paul Blackburn, all of whom were living and teaching in New York at the time. And over all of them I felt a half-acknowledged and contemptuous superiority, for who among them but me, I wondered, was having a secret affair with a married man a son exactly my own age? You can't teach an old fool new tricks, George Grey used to say, and these living masters were, in my considered opinion, hardly of the '70s at all—they belonged to culture, whereas culture belonged to me, by dint of vanity and my increasing self-absorption.

The progress of a life, its growth and development. When we'd met he'd said, "My name's Carey, I want fun with a boy." He smiled sheepishly, as if in on a joke, but it wasn't a big smile. Soon it became clear, soon as he dived in, that he did want fun with a boy, I only wondered if I was that boy. I was fourteen. In his car he took off his coat with the portentousness of Jack the

Ripper, and had sex with me, but all the time he kept yapping the most outlandish lines I've ever heard, offscreen or on:

Words of love. Words of adventure. But mostly these *stories* about the ordinary days and nights of his oldest son—Nicky. "I'm me," I thought. "Stop talking about him and pay some attention."

In shadow his face was a moving muscle of fat. I couldn't believe a thing he said; his hands pulled at his cock like they wanted to throw it out of a window. Finally from out of it came this enormous spurt of come, dappled in streetlight—green, yellow, lacy, just when he was telling me about Nicky's hobbies. This I found off-putting, but in another corner of my mind I recognized a fellow traveller, another who knew the moves but lacked conviction or intensity. The car door creaked open like a mausoleum, our two bodies slithering to the ground. He swung me around in his huge arms, and threw me onto a patch of weeds. He said, "And so I told him, get a haircut, but sure enough next day rolled round, no haircut, I dragged his ass over to the Singer machine and chopped his damn hair into the needle." He went down on me, gently, and with my cock in his mouth kept talking, barely decipherable words and I think, yes, probably, this was the first time language had been used on me quite so intimately. The sensations varied. Fricatives tended to scrape the straight underside vein; sibilants were sucky, babyish, *lisp blowjob*; it were his long vowels and his aspirants that thrilled me. So I got to dislike "Nicky" right away, and if his son's name had been "Hugo" who knows? maybe we'd still be together . . .

"Had another little escapable on Tuesday."

"Say the day," I gasped.

"Tuesday." Oh it felt so good. "Took Nicky to a Vet's picnic."

Please, no "Nicky," no "picnic," these little bursts of sounds that thudded my balls in rabbit punches. I wrapped my legs over his neck and drove him down into the dirt, but he kept sucking, cupping my ass, talking, and I came and then fell back and let the trees and the wind cool me off and still, after all that, for five long years, Carey kept talking and talking.

Soon I would turn nineteen, so it would be Nick's birthday soon, too, and his father took me shopping to get the young person's point of view. "I don't know the styles," he said, reasonably, in his car, "and you're just Nick's age, same size, build, coloring."

"I don't think I should," I said. "I'd feel funny." We were parked outside a hip store with the unprepossessing name of "Loose Threads," at a deserted shopping mall on Long Island. Carey wouldn't take me anywhere crowded; in too big a crowd there'd be too big a chance of running into someone he knew. One of his wives perhaps. In consequence we spent a lot of time riding aimlessly in his Cadillac, a lot of time in mirrored motels, and a lot of time in different Howard Johnson's, where I learned to go for fried clams in a big way. "I don't want to."

"But you're exactly his size."

"Yeah. Same—same . . . same everything I guess."

Now he was hurt. "What's the problem?" Puzzled too. "Tell Carey. You don't want to do Carey a favor, that it? One little favor and you don't want to help out?"

I pouted for him.

"Well, what's the problem here, I really don't understand." He held open my door and grudgingly I got out, followed him. Four or five drowsy salespeople leaped into life. Here Carey was in his element, beaming broadly, pushing open his fat wallet so they could see all his credit cards. "My son here," he said, "my son here's having a birthday soon. I want to dress him up, the way the kids are dressing nowadays. Carte blanche."

Panic hit me, I don't know why. Yes I do: I was stoned. Each face in the shop seemed to wear a spectral grin of greed and sick pleasure. (You know how these things go.) A young man reached out to touch my shoulder, and I recoiled as if a snake was biting me. "Don't," I said out loud, just like that, Carey waved his hands around like a Texas oilman in a movie, pointing to this and that, craving attention. Now that I think on it, he would have been a perfect shoplifting partner. He liked to distract. When I became involved with him it was for something to do, but as I got to know him I felt all fly and he loomed like a spider. I closed my eyes when he kissed me, when he murmured that he loved my skin and my dick. I always thought that he wanted to make love to his son, Nick, whom I'd never met, and that if I opened my eyes I'd know this for sure, and I kept waiting for the day he'd call out Nick's name instead of mine.

A saleswoman bowed to Carey in a geisha way. "Anything you say, sir."

The young guy's smile was a fixed thing on his skinny face. My eyes begged him: understand me man, this overbearing man I'm with is not my father. At the same time I knew that so very many real sons' faces must plead the same thing in connection with their real dads that my look must convey little or nothing to him. This man is not my father. I'm not his son.

"We don't get many clients like you, sir, if I may say so," the young woman said. *Oh boy!* I thought: *she don't know the half of it.* "What with inflation and all."

"What the hell. 'You can't take it with you,' right?" Carey quoted with a sigh.

She nodded sympathetically, as though there was something sad about all this.

"Look at it this way," Carey said, "My oldest son. His birthday. What he wants more than anything else: new clothes. Put them altogether they spell V I S A C A R D, right? Nowadays Dad has to do what Sonnyboy wants or where are you? I'll tell you where: smack in the old generation gap? Am I right, Miss?"

"Absolutely," she replied, still melancholy.

The young man and his gang herded me away to a thin dressing room at the rear of the shop, and threw clothes in at me, clothes so new they smelled of the factory. From floor to ceiling a mirror hung, and velvet nailed over plywood covered the walls. It was just a dressing room, but like a madhouse cell in so many ways. "He's doing all this for Nicky, that goddamn son of his," I said to the mirror. "I'm being used. Or maybe he's going through this whole charade to convince me there really *is* a Nicky, in either case I'm still being used."

From a slit in the velvet the young man poked in his head. "Excuse me," he said. Again he winked at me. "I thought you'd be undressed by now." An unusual thing to say, maybe, but it had its effect. I perked up and said:

"I know you. From somewhere but where?" Because I never went shopping . . .

"You're a friend of George Grey's."

"Oh yeah." This dispirited me all over again.

"I've seen you with him half a dozen times," said the young man, introducing himself. "Acting lovey dovey." He slipped bodily into my room and began to unbutton my shirt for me. I was sad. And this young man—"Roger"—was very much the dextrous pro. "Though I didn't know your name is Nicky, that's cute."

I was about to say it wasn't Nicky. I was about to say, *My name is Kevin. Kevin Killian.* But, embarrassed, I kept mum, thinking of all the dopey things I'd ever done and said and felt in my life. Eyes narrowed, brain sizzling I used, for example, to brag, "I could have that husband in thirty seconds." Just like Joan Crawford in Cukor's film *The Women.* Now some think Crawford's acting is awfully exaggerated. Not me. She's a mistress of understatement compared to my own machinations. A kiss on the hand may be quite continental, but I wanted diamonds, diamonds and cherry, like some Dali valentine. And look where it got me! You tell me, is or is not Crawford a perfect model of representational cool?

"Don't worry, I won't blow your cover," teased Roger. "And no I won't tell your dad the naughty things you do in your spare time; the way you dance or the men you dance with."

"No, don't," I said. Roger stood behind me pulling my shirt off my arms. "Spare him, please."

"He might get upset then."

"He might cut off my hair," I said. Then I laughed. The close dressing room, Roger, the fusty velvet breathed dust and the metallic shiny scent of new pins. "Or my balls," I told him, warming suddenly to the part. "He might cut off my balls with a Singer sewing machine." I flashed: what a part to play! I looked in the mirror and my image wore a funny look on its lips, a look that said, "In for a penny, Carey . . ."

Roger read it a little differently though. "Now try these on, why don't you? Yves St. Laurent. The old man's paying right? Yeah, right. Oh yes, I've seen you in the bars, in the bars with George Grey, right? Now there's your Stud Glorious. He's wasted on the dance floor; he should be lying on his back in bed; my bed; legs pedaling. I tell you what, Nicky: introduce him to me, a real close intro, next time we all meet again. Hear me?"

I was noncommittal.

"He's not yours, is he?" asked Roger in pretended alarm. "What a fool I am!"

"Oh, I'll introduce you," I capitulated beginning to see the line of complications. I pushed Roger's hands from my waist. "But make me a promise—two promises: don't tell my father anything about me and George; and don't tell George about my dad bringing me in here . . . Promise?"

"Can I call you?"

"Oh, you can call me," I cried, dizzily. My new pants—the pants destined for the son of Carey—rode halfway up my thigh, the tip of my prick chilled in the open metallic air. "You can call me Ray, or you can call me . . ." I wrote down my number. "Call me—any time." I kissed his mouth and his tongue moved beneath mine like Dial-A-Kiss. It seemed logical at the moment. His hands were warm like suds and smooth like velvet, or Black Label. I don't know why I kissed that awful oozing clone, as hard as I did, as much as I cared to. My erection broke me up, broke me in two. Couldn't keep my mind on one man at a time. "You had falafel for lunch," I said. I wrote down my phone number. I gave it to him. I gave it away . . .

About fifteen minutes later Carey and I got ready to leave "Loose Threads," laden with wrapped packages like beasts of burden. "Thank you, Dad," I said for the salespeople's benefit. "You're the ginchiest."

"Sign here, please sir," the young lady murmured, with a breathy, light, floating smile. She should have been a cruise director with that smile. Instead her job consisted of thanking people for spending their money. "Thank you and—have a nice day!"

"Who was that boy," Carey growled in my ear.

"He's the best Dad in the world," I said to the saleslady.

"This better be good," Carey said.

"You're a lucky fella," she told me. "To have a Dad so generous." It brought tears to her eyes, too deepset for tears.

Later I sat among the snappily wrapped gifts that filled the back seat of Carey's car. "Take me home," I said haughtily, regarding him as little more than my chauffeur. "To Shakespeare Mansions." This was the name I called my house, because it was decorated with Victorian lithotypes of scenes from Shakespeare's plays. The car pulled up before it. I didn't want to go in and face my roommates. Shakespeare Mansions, lit from within by candles, now, and glowing in the night like a cathedral or jack-o-lantern. I whispered to Carey wait a second, wait, wait . . . He held up his hand in the dark as a signal, don't open the car door, a light will come on. The Cadillac purred, its motor finely tuned, a great grave smiling cat in the night. Must have been a blackout with all those candles inside. And no electricity anywhere.

"Kiss me," he said.

"Your hands are cold."

"Your ass is red hot," he said. "I want your cherry." (He'd had that, of course, a hundred times or more, and he'd told me I had his. This was Fantasy Life, adult country, where the real and the sore don't matter. Still almost every time we had sex that's what he wanted, I got tired of hearing about it.) "Give it to me!" (The first time it had hardly hurt—it was like giving candy to a baby.) "Give me your ring of fire."

"Thanks for dinner, Carey." Fried clams and hot dogs, wow. "And give my love to your ex-wife and to Nicky and Anita and all the other little people. In your life." In the dark I walked away on rubber soles and found refuge behind a large range of scented bushes. I licked my lips and spat. The huge black car rolled down the hill silently, filled with motive power.

I closed my eyes but the night was so stark I might have left them open. Sometimes when your eyes are shut you see pinwheels of color and light, and stars; that night I saw all these and something more, a band of ribboned colors arcing around my eyelids like a rainbow tipped on its side. Against my back I felt the splintery ridge of a telephone pole; I leaned into it, cracking against it. Somewhere down the pike falling wires had caused this blackout. Above me more wires. If they too fell I'd be electrocuted or would I? Were they dead now too? I was surrounded by a rainbow, inside my skull: Cinerama. Above the dead wires, above them a hundred kinds of constellations, patterns, motives, reasons.

"There's a reason why we're in each other's arms . . . it's because we need each other."

"Some reason," I cried.

"You said you needed a father figure."

"You need a son, Carey? You have two or three of them. Nicky for example."

"Oh fuck that."

"But I am your son in a way, don't get me wrong, don't get mad, I was just wondering."

"Wondering? Wondering what? You can tell me anything, ask me anything, I've shown you everything, I've done everything. All for you, Kevin."

"I don't feel like this is really happening," I said, dazed.

"I've even shown you my house where I used to live with my previous wife!"

I didn't care much for any of his wives, not even the ones I hadn't met.

"I was wondering if you ever did it with Nicky," I said casually. And Carey had turned away, hurt, vicious, his teeth came flying out to bite or chew my cock . . . Maybe then I'd come too close to the truth; who knows! When you're dealing with variables it's hard to say what makes a person's blood boil and what makes the same person say he will love you forever if he can only have your cherry. "Get the fuck away from me with that overbite . . ."

"My boy's no fag."

"I didn't say he was."

Then I remembered to get on my high horse.

"Isn't a crime, you know," I said acidly. "So what if he is. I am. You are. At least you say you are. I don't know what Anita thinks, all she does is rock in the rocking chair and spout Spanish at me."

"I am! I'm a fag in a heterosexual's body!"

"You treat Nicky like shit."

"I treat him swell, he's got everything, he's got a big allowance."

"But he's always got you on his ass."

"Cause I'm his father and I want to see him grow up right, that's all."

I used to slam the car door and run in the night up the flagstone steps, and open my door and tell my roommates, "I'm home, I had a lovely night with the worst shit in the world," angry with him because he'd turned me into some kind of freak. My roommates would blink and say why not drop him, but I considered that what he and I had was little more than a continuous, slow-moving drop, like a glacier melting over all Minnesota and Michigan and making great lakes. But he was ever charming, and bought me plenty of fried clams, grilled frankforts, other treats . . .

Yet despite all his charm if he was conducting a full-blown sex affair with his own son I felt, foolishly, I had the right to know. Once when he and I were at his ex-wife's house and in Nicky's room, making love on Nicky's bed, while the rest of the family was summering in the Poconos, I vomited onto the floor. For no reason. I pictured Carey and Nicky entwined on the bed, creating each other, snaking like a conga line. Only Nicky was smaller than Carey. Not as big. Thin. His child.

"Just don't say you've given me everything, Carey, that you possibly could! I don't want to hear those words any more, cause what you give to Nicky you take away from me, yours truly Kevin!"

I was thinking, these words will be my text, when I grow up, get out of this love, and write my memoirs someday. Carey pulled away from me and stood up, undecided. He got some towels from a linen closet and ran water through them in the bathroom. After a while he came back to the bed and cleaned up the vomit in silence.

I was silent too. I heard nothing but our labored breathing and the moist susurration of the towel swamping the floor. On the wall above the headboard hung a framed photo of Nick winning some trophy or another from a bald portly man dressed in bright warm-up clothes.

"I should more be like Nicky," I finally said. "Turn myself inside out trying to please you. I should grow up and develop a healthy interest in the opposite sex. Go out for organized sport. Learn cunnilingus."

"Maybe you should," Carey said. "Nick's a very good boy. One of these days maybe you'll realize that."

"Maybe one of these days I'll meet him and fuck him," I said. Tit for tat. Of course what happened to me when I finally did meet Nick was something far different. We have a strange way, don't we, of prophesying our futures? Always wrongly, it seems; you'd think after awhile we'd get the hang of it and go by opposites, the way dreams are supposed to?

"One of these days he'll be my boy, as well as yours."

POW

A GIGANTIC MISTAKE

So I developed an interest in the opposite sex—not a healthy one, maybe, but an interest nonetheless. I went so far as to get married. I was twenty-two, and so was my bride and this is our story, *A Gigantic Mistake.*

The two of us hadn't let ours be a very "legal" marriage, not in the sense of marriage license, Wassermann tests, the other bourgeois City Hall hoopla. No, we held our own private intimate ceremony in the apartment, near New Rochelle, in which we'd lived for the previous six months. Never too steady, I was now thinking of becoming a diamond salesman (a friend's dad was the right-hand man to Roussel Reilly, the "Diamond King"), but made pocket money by performing magic shows at children's birthday parties, badly. She was a real oddball who belonged to a local witches' coven, or so she claimed at first. We told our parents we'd been married in a Black Mass, hoping to shock them. We succeeded. Of course it hadn't been an actual Black Mass, what we'd done is simply to introduce some of Michelle's occult paraphernalia into the apartment and let it work its spells in an unspecifiable way. The bride wore black. Even her bouquet was black, a mass of geraniums, induced into blackness by an overnight plunge into a vase of a water heavy with lead pencils. Streaky and wet, they waved and whistled in her long beautiful arms. "I'm glad I *didn't* wear white," Michelle teased. "If I'd worn white it'd a gone black anyhow. I'd look like a witch."

"You are a witch."

"I know but besides that," she said lightly. Michelle was very into her witchcraft, challenged as she was by the idea of Elizabeth Montgomery's perky nose and Aleister Crowley's coked-up beak becoming, in the person of one modern and sophisticated teenage girl—in her own being—the Nose that Made News. And it seemed to work. Perhaps that's why I fell in love with her in the first place. She made my milk turn sour and I never, ever cared for milk.

Also, she thought she was pregnant. When I looked at her I felt the blood run cold in my veins: I had to have her. She belonged to a sorority house at Mount St. Vincent's, and sailed through the New Rochelle night like a golden dark dove, her eyes on fire, half feral. We'd met when I stood on a line to pay for a deck of marked cards at Woolworth's. She arrived behind the register late, apologizing profusely to the girl she'd delayed. She wore a long black coat with a red silk lining, and when she took it off, I leaped to the front of the line and asked her her name. We started talking; she started ringing up; the next thing I knew she was explaining witchcraft to me. "I guess I'm into magic too," I ventured. "I do tricks like at kids' parties." The look of scorn I received made me wince as if from a blow, but it continued to knock in my mind. All of a sudden I was seeing colors I'd never seen before. I didn't care for her *particular* explanations but I had to admit that my own magic wasn't magic at all, only a ragbag of tawdry tricks. Hers was the real thing.

I told my friends I'd met this new salesgirl who was into witchcraft. Their eyes lit up with the same kind of enthusiastic fire. "Maybe I could pay her to put a hex on my mother," George speculated. "There must be some kind of voodoo jinx that would cure Mom of belly-dancing." This was around the same time

George and I were reading *Helter-Skelter*, the Manson book. Some of the ambience of the far-off Spahn Ranch turned Michelle's third-floor apartment into an excited movie set. Each piece of furniture was charged with holistic rhythm. The charcoal brazier beneath the bay window smoked the glass panes from inside, forming indecipherable messages from another planet. Did my friends know there are all kinds of complicated dietary rituals to Satanism? No? Innumerable affairs of the mysterious menses which must be observed in a strict routine? No? Some they might think of as arcane, maybe disgusting? No? One of my friends dropped me—even George, who claimed he had no time to visit New Rochelle, he was burning the candles at both ends, writing a thesis on the actress Hope Lange, and taking up water-skiing.

"Hope Lange's a horrible actress," I said angrily.

"That's what they used to say about Garbo," George replied coolly.

"And that water-skiing's the stunt of a fool!"

"So is marriage," sighed George, "though I have to say Hope's tried it three or four times and each divorce seems to sharpen her acting skills."

All I had left was Michelle. Her turns and twists began to seem everyday, a part of life, yet never palled. My friends, my ex-friends now, didn't know what they were missing. They didn't know the half of it. I moved in with her. We married. We married ourselves.

So it was that when she said to me, "Kevin, what do you think we should do tonight?" on such and such a night, I said to her:

"Why don't we just go out and maybe go down by the river."

"Why the river?"

"I don't know, maybe we can trap a couple of hoagies."

We walked down to the turgid numinous Hudson and Michelle tried to concentrate on willing the hoagies to come into our hands. I thought of the bags full of diamonds I might by now have held in my hands, had I not "married" Michelle, and when she turned a flashlight on my face, she saw it contorted into a mask of living crawling grief. We dropped the flashlight into a net, and sunk it underwater. One or two fish, attracted to its beam, swam toward the trapped flashlight but avoided the net. Their quicksilver shapes replicated in the murky water. Michelle told me she wasn't pregnant after all. We forgot about fishing and started to quarrel.

I wanted to end the marriage. My mom and dad horned in on the act and demanded a showdown with Michelle, whom they conceived with my connivance, as an impossibly wilful and wanton whore. She said to my father, over the phone, "Fuck you Mr. K." I got on the phone and apologized immediately, but my dad couldn't listen, he'd had a bad shock.

Over and over again my folks told me, "She's no good, she's no good." When they changed to "She's evil," my feelings began to tilt again, and I realized once more how drawn I was to my fantasy of my wife. Were I to love her at all I needed to think of her as Satan's bride—perhaps of myself as Satan. The crisis came at a time when no one was listening to anyone. Michelle said her stars had told her that ours was rapidly becoming diseased sex. She pointed to my disjointed knobby cock, about which I was so sensitive and so madly proud, and accused it of having given her a venereal disease. She had me go to a doctor of her choosing and take a humiliating examination. The doctor wore Coke-bottle glasses and squinted close between my spread thighs. Behind the thick lenses his pupils looked like long needles. The viscous sweat of my fear left my silhouette behind on the doctor's leather-covered table. I pulled up my pants so hard I walked home bowlegged. Even after I'd been certified as clean Michelle refused to accept the medical facts. She insisted that in some mystical way I profaned her body each time I lunged into it genitally. She stood on the bed and spat down on my refulgent defenseless form, and threw a can of Tab at me. I jumped up and hit her across her lying face. She began to shriek in a foreign tongue.

Within a few days she had left me and had begun to tell anyone who'd listen that I'd given her reason to suppose me a homosexual. Alone, in a set of sulks, distraught, I had checked into a motel room for a week; then I'd gone out determined to make the name my game. I wasn't able to do so, although I did spend a lot of money.

"Room service," I called.

"We don't have Room Service," they said.

My motel room was small. The TV was only black and white. Once, I called Michelle, but she was too busy arguing with my parents to be able to speak to me for more than forty-five seconds. Why didn't she want kids? My parents, I knew, would love a couple of grandtykes. I'd make an ideal father. What the hell was wrong with her? She hung up on me and I kicked over the TV. After that I only saw her every now and then. Without any of them consulting my feelings one way or the other, she and my folks annulled the marriage behind my back. They said that someday I'd thank them. They said that right now, they knew, I was upset, but in years to come I'd look back and realize it had all been a gigantic mistake.

Michelle shortly after kicked over all traces of magic and went to work for SAS as a baggage handler, later an air hostess. After taking a degree from a New York City college, I moved out to Kings Park into a summerhouse, almost unattached. I took a job as a waiter slopping down food in front of hungry hogs, and applied to grad schools. Across the quiet street stood an asylum for morons and maniacs. I lived with a little boy too old to be my son. What was my problem? Was I afraid to remarry? Maybe I didn't really want kids after all. Sometimes while talking to the teenage dishwashers at the restaurant, or to my boyfriend, listening to some tragedy of bad complexion or dateless Saturday, I fell into a daydream and saw the flashlight, caught in netting, disappear plunged into darkness under the dark river waters. This image of a piercing light, plunged into darkness to trap an unwary prey, seemed to me symbolic of the drift of my life in a way I couldn't put a finger on. I spread the fingers of my hands and watched them crawl of themselves towards whatever was brightest on the desk; in my bed; in the car; in my life.

Then one day, I must have been 23, I called up my old friend George Grey and asked him to come over, *The Best of Everything* was playing on TV.

He paused before answering. "I'm kind of off Hope Lange, tell you the truth."

"Are you?" I said. I twisted the phone cord up and down my calf. "I thought you were the steadfast type."

"Oh, Kevin," George said. "You have no idea what type I am."

"Still water-skiing?"

"It's bad for your posture," he said. "If I'm going to be led by a rope I'd rather not have a powerboat on the other end." He paused, as if searching for his imagination. "Some big lug like Wallace Beery, I might go for."

"Is that your type, George? I'm bored," I whined. The circulation in my calf felt feeble, I looked down and saw red welts rising from it in '50s kitsch Slinky patterns. I pulled tighter at the phone in my hand. "Come over," I insisted. I felt constricted, wrapped in a plastic cord, a modern-day Andromeda. "Come on and rescue me."

FACE VALUE

The street is called Upper Dock Road, the town—Kings Park, Long Island—a charming colonial backwater. While in this area don't forget to visit the historic yellowish cottage where, a plaque of bronze informs you, Kevin Killian and George Grey once lived. Though tarnished by sea air, and littered with the violets and vervain of visitors moved to floral display, the plaque maintains a stern composure in the face of erratic North Shore weather. Inside the carefully preserved landmark—actually little more than a bungalow—the fruity tang of Sangria, the grim earthen miasma of beer, still may drug the sensitive pilgrim. An imposing bank of gym lockers stands in the center of one room, hung with fetishes and surrounded by oversized replicae of household objects (razor blades, cigarette boxes) filched from five and dime stores—when you could still find a five and dime, when filching was still a thrill. Why the gym locker? Why has this house windows, complete with shutters, in every bedroom wall? Move along the velvet rope, run your shaky fingers past the lacquered zigzag Keith Haring graffito: "You did not live in our time! Be sorry!"

On the face of it, the arrangement he and I came to was perfectly sound. We were both at beam ends, and we loved each other, so why not share rooms? Egocentric myself, I imagined George—imagine everyone—subject to my own fits of sex obsession, "crush," alternating with periods of cold hauteur so total you feel nothing counts but style. The fugue state. My tendency to welcome the depraved and the vivid into my life quarrelled with a taste for the closed, contained; with a taste for elegance; and long after George had left my world for another would continue to do so.

But was I supposed to know that? I ask you! I wanted croquet, watercress sandwiches, assignations, gossip: I thought life with George would be one long party, like the Cliveden set's between the wars. More than any other of his Warhol-derived novels, I liked *The Chelsea Girls* because he and the other characters went to so many parties. "I am Eric Emerson," it begins. "Welcome to my body." Meanwhile like any other divided nature mine was hard to take, even in small doses, and cohabitation's such a heaping one that men far more full-throated than George Grey have choked on it. Once I opened a letter he'd written but left unmailed, perhaps on purpose. "You may think I'm happy here," I read. "Hardly. Living with Kevin is far from a picnic. He's such a slut. He lets people walk all over him if it'll get him someplace. He is a Capricorn like you—you 2 are the men who put the 'prick' into 'Capricorn.'" The letter piqued me no end, but its taboo nature prevented me from complaining overtly. Instead I emptied a chilled pan of linguini, clam sauce, and meatballs into the foot of his bedclothes and labelled it *embryo*. Toy body for a toy death.

Body of pain, body of implications, references, statements.

He slept in a screened-in porch, thus to get in or out the front door you slid by his bed. Sometimes he'd glance up from his work, see you pass by, and pull you down into a sprawl of chenille. If he wasn't acting broody, Heathcliff, haunted, then he'd light a cigarette in your mouth and sell you new schemes talking faster than Joan Rivers and nearly as sincerely. "Let's go to Las Vegas, let's write Ayn Rand, let's become astronauts." George smoked continually, blowing the smoke out the very farthest corner of his mouth, so as not to obscure his almost candid blue eyes. "Let's buy a tobacco farm like Gary Cooper and Lauren Bacall in *Bright Leaf*." Learning that Lost-and-Found ads in *Newsday* may be placed for free, he decided to retell Proust in the long gray columns of Long Island's largest newspaper. "Found: suede jacket with 'Odette' designer label." Well, announcing the loss or discovery of red shoes, madeleine recipes, "altered" photos of Vinteuil, caused little or no comment. (One crafty woman did call claiming to have lost the red shoes. That was no Duchesse, George growled, slamming down the phone. Unreal shoes, ergo: criminous woman—how deftly Life imitates Art!) But when "Grandma" alerted readers she'd found—in a public toilet no less—a packet of letters from on Charlus to Morel, George was exposed. But not deflated. "I only regret we didn't get up to *La prisonnière*," he said. "I want everything to be real. I don't want to wind up like my brothers."

From George's bed life took on the frivolity I'd wanted so long as I could remember. He wore thin blue pajamas with a tiny whip sewn onto the breast pocket. Beach pajamas. "Let's rent Peter Frampton and dip his body in latex." His favorite record, "Love Will Keep Us Together" by the Captain and Tennille, blared and squeaked from tinny stereo speakers. "Let's hold a seance and contact Bobby Kennedy." Rows of bayberry hedges hid our little house from goggling passers-by. We began work on our memoirs, to be called *The Bungalow Mystery*. This drama's ostensible subject was the tale of Kiki Garfield, a strong-willed clerk discovered in the process of reinventing womanhood. By day she sorts files in a metropolitan police department, but at night she goes home and locks her door and becomes an underworld Queen. She's the head of the Key Ring (hence her

Christian name), and is aided by two henchmen: Bones—a Skeleton key, and Roxie—a Roller Skate key. I think we'd been watching the Late Show: Judith Anderson in *Lady Scarface*. Face of dead pain, face of implication, ellipses, patience. We felt outside society. It was so delicious. But he is lost to me now.

"When you come to write about me—and I know you will," he said, trying to pin me down with a smile, "remember: I am your Steerforth." So I was David Copperfield? I don't know if he meant this as a compliment, but I took it as an insult. In Dickens' great novel, Steerforth is David's schoolfriend, hero, lover; he's amply the most dashing and alluring of all the beautiful young men in Nineteenth-Century fiction. But he's bad, too, where David is good; and in later life spots of evil and decay fester across his portrait's face. His death nevertheless has all Nature crying out: the sea, the sky, sands . . . the stars . . .

I don't know why George married Karoll. Never have I been able to fathom it. And then to up and move to Hawaii! Everyone was flabbergasted. Karoll was a nurse's aide at the Veterans' Hospital. She was tall, fair, rangy; initially thus she seemed akin to George, a sister, a confidante. After six brothers, I thought, surely he'd like a sister, no? But I never should have introduced them. In high school an adviser had told her she could become a model, and the rest of Karoll's life proceeded serenely from this deluded assumption. Her brother Buzzy was a real lowlife with a furnished flat on the railroad's edge. (As in Vincente Minnelli's film *The Cobweb*, our whole village revolves around a mental hospital. I knew a guy whose mother worked there, and she was in the drug cellar one night just tidying up—and a crazy man put a knife to her throat and stuck it all the way in!)

Buzzy was a mess. His head looked like semen had dried all over it. Long and listless as his empty gunnysack, his body irradiated the kind of drugs kids try, drugs with pop names the handbooks don't list. His tiny red eyes seemed round and misplaced, pimples you could love on an ass but behind lenses look stupid. Karoll treated Buzzy like dirt in general but family ties linked them, and thus from hospital records she supplied him with addresses he could break and burgle. Picture her patients in the ward, her cool hand on their foreheads, healing them; and meanwhile her brother climbing in turn into each of their homes with gunnysacks to fill! Once we were sitting around in the heat listing our hobbies. Karoll: hair drying (her own). Mine: parlor tricks, falling asleep, reading *Women's Wear Daily*. George: writing. Buzzy said he'd once collected stamps but had given it up, too much trouble. Someone should have put a stamp on him and mailed him to Cambodia.

These two now became our constant companions. At first I liked them, then I felt faint and dizzy near them, then I rejected them. This couple who lived next door to us were Christian astrologers. They had named their children Asphodel and Cancer. I never liked that system of naming. "Hi Cancer,"—I couldn't bring myself to say it. And a dog named Spider. "Why?" I couldn't follow their system yet managed, in the perverse way of the disenfranchised, to believe my own superior. Anyway one night I babysat for them, and the little girl said her prayers and she said, "Surely good Mrs. Murphy will follow me all the days of my life." She was so cute. When I went home I told George and Karoll about it but Karoll said, "What kind of sick prayer is that!"

Yet George grew ever closer to Karoll until one night they made love, and this had the odd effect—odd at least in my book—of bringing them even closer still. I was in despair, but I kept thinking, ah he has too much taste, this must be some kind of nouvelle sex experiment—grist for *The Bungalow Mystery* perhaps. They couldn't be in love. George had done a lot of silly things (once he'd tried to kill himself by swallowing a packet of pipe cleaners) but this took some beating. Hadn't he the awful example of my own marriage to reflect on? And I had married a wonderful woman, not a model like Karoll! Maybe, I thought wildly, it's really Buzzy he's after. Neither alternative seemed the least bit likely but there they were, in bed all day and all night, the three of them, and others too: wharf rats dredged up by them out of the ass-end of human society. But love? Surely not.

Nevertheless the day came when George put his arms around me and said, "Kevin I've been au courant, and homosexual, and now I'm twenty-two. I'm getting married and becoming a priestess."

George and I had gone to high school with a guy named Bruce and everyone thought he was gay—I think because of his name—and also because of his parents. The father was a banker but had once been a pugilist—his nose was broken so many times he looked like a mean bulldog. Then there was Gertrude, his mother, a home economist who collected cookbooks. Between the two of them you'd have gotten a terribly distorted version of sex distribution. But Bruce had the last laugh. He was no more gay than—than—a box of soda crackers; for some reason he liked to play at it. People called us the Three Musketeers. Our six or seven parents were in despair—especially Gertrude. Once Bruce had a cocktail party on the roof of his parents' house and invited these anxious parents to meet for the first time. (They sat inside, in the Colonial living room.) It was heaven above, disaster below. ("Like Wales.") No one got along. Cats and dogs. My dad told me he'd never met an uglier man in his life than Bruce's father. "Ugly?" I said, suggestively. "What's so ugly? I think he's sort of distinguished." I rolled my tongue inside my right cheek to denote an attraction I couldn't act on or feel. Ignoring me my father bit his pipe. "And that finger food was for the birds."

"I think Gertrude's a fabulous chef. Why don't you write a cookbook, then criticize!" Grrrrrr.

When he made me the scapegoat for a sex crime he'd committed, anger at George roiled and churned within like vomit. But then I reconsidered and grew calm. Everything I know about life, after all, I'd learned from him: how to write, and why; how to make friends, how to draw, how to make drinks, to drive, to trick. Couldn't I forgive an unforgivable transgression? What else are steamy jungle bungalows for, but to mend irreparable rips of the heart! No matter how anonymous one's sex partners are one always finds out something about them one hates. So how could I continue my snit, this right real thing, this verminous cross I dragged behind me like I was Jesus or someone? I would turn the other cheek and tell George I didn't mind.

What happened was this. For some time Jeff, George's younger brother, had been driving him mad with his overtures, his underpants, with the darkish blond hairs running like rodents up the inside of his thighs. At night they'd share a bed and feel each other up until they were half-drunk. Maybe that room, decorated with the Harold Robbins frescoes, *was* too sexual for Jeff, just as Mrs. Grey had claimed in the first place. Could be! She was a wise sibyl in her way and at parties performed a famous takeoff on Marlene Dietrich, top hat, weltanschauung, husky rasp. She used whipped cream on her face the way some people use mud, as a beautifier.

Anyhow after a few years Jeff had begun exhibiting some of the wilder symptoms of Sex Disturbance—nightmares, heroin abuse, indiscriminate tattooing—and George knew it wouldn't be long before their Incest Secret became common knowledge. Jeff was in the tenth grade and seeing a very nice girl named Anne Violet Hunt. (Anne Violet never got along very well with Karoll; after they became sisters-in-law a big contretemps erupted over who gave who what Christening gifts and why: like the way Sleeping Beauty begins.) So he and Jeff got together and decided to say it was me. I. Kevin! No one who knew me well could fail to believe this story—another victory for naturalism. But did you ever hear anything so malicious? And George was supposedly my best friend too; and yet here he was turning on his own kind.

I kept my mouth shut, took the rap. Mrs. Grey was scathing. "Kevin you're full of book learning but it's poisoned you." I guess I'm lucky she didn't call the police. But maybe she realized how far to press the issue . . . I was discovering a streak of masochism to lay aside, spoon-fashion, my already colonized sadistic strip. Discovery's its own reward. Keats and Cortez. A new world was swimming into my ken, like hoagies into a flashlit net. Bedrooms have windows to spy into, to comport oneself before, the way you or I might first read a book, then write one.

Life in the mud is not for everyone, George wrote. *If you are squeamish or easily shocked proceed no further. Burn this book.* Remember the Alice Crimmins case? Crimmins was a local cocktail waitress convicted, many thought unjustly, of murdering her two kids during the '64–'65 New York World's Fair. Often during these years, her case came up for appeal; at each appeal George and I sent her cheery letters and Hallmark cards of empathy. We brought matters to a head one day by setting up a card table in front of the Mall George worked at. Behind the table we sat before several large placards reading FREE ALICE CRIMMINS and a cleverly worded petition addressed to then-Governor Nelson Rockefeller. *Surely you, as a man who's also lost a son under mysterious circumstances, will be the last to throw stones at, and the first to show mercy to, a woman like Alice.* Headlines of ten years before had depicted young Michael Rockefeller, an aspiring anthropologist, as the victim of cannibal headhunters in New Guinea. His body was never found. Most people will sign petitions without bothering too much about the whys and wherefores. I know this now.

Our neighbors the patients, after taking the thorazine given them, were then made to walk ten times around our block. They used this opportunity to walk into houses and examine real, human furniture. Once I came home and there was a man in my bed masturbating with my nicest pair of dress shoes. And I did not even know him. He just came in off the street and lay down. I told him, "I'll give you ten cents if you put down my shoes and leave this house." He didn't seem to hear me or see me. He looked thin and glazed, like a stick of Wrigley's gum. I do not think they feed them right over at that mental hospital. Pale face; copper red hair. When at last he wandered away he left a pair of gray institutional pants behind like a ring in a bathtub. Later George said, "Maybe *that* was Michael Rockefeller!"

He is lost to me now, like the word the stroke victim can't remember. Surely goodness and mercy will follow me all the days of my life. Here on Guerrero Street in the night of San Francisco, I stand and press my face to my bedroom window; it feels cool, but I come away with dirt on my cheek and no vision.

A lime green Lotus pulled up silently to the front steps down from George's bed. Through the net window we watched the driver alight dressed by Sonia Rykiel, sunglasses pushed upside her hairline, and I recognized Michelle. So did George. Though we'd been unhappy together, auld lang syne feels lucky when you keep it up, so whenever a new Clint Eastwood picture opened, Michelle and I managed to meet to see it in a first-run $5.00 theatre. But she'd never come out to Kings Park, I couldn't figure out what was up. I thought: *bull in a china shop, no,* I thought: *whatever is the reverse of bull in a china shop* . . . She looked around her aghast—dusty drive, tangle of green leaves and hickory, greige furry weeds waist-high, ironwork across the road behind which spread the neat manicured lawns of the asylum, ten patients in white nightsheets walking in circles. Above everything a blue white sky washed with clouds.

"You were married?" Karoll began to giggle. George massaged his throat and nipples with a melon liqueur, and stared. The muscles along the inside of my arm began to twitch, like fingers in a fist inside a deep, humming, lubricant. There was a lot of violence in my relationship with Karoll. Isn't this a good illustration of it? The sun, slanting in through thousands of wire squares in the screen windows, cast light on a bed I didn't feel could bear much exposure. Michelle and I stumbled down the porch steps down to the beach, she nagging, I fagged out. Her shoes were "sensible" maybe for the city of Blade Runner not for the seashore Michelle . . . "I know *tons* of gay guys, Kevin, who'd be much better for you than George and his crowd, cute guys, mobile, assertive, Giorgio Armani suits, private keys, great jobs, one of them's the dentist who fixed Ann-Margret's face when she fell off that stage, Kevin!" She kicked a pebble into a silvergreen surf. Her voice rising till it met the wind and the caw of the gulls. "Don't throw yourself away, I'll take you dancing at the Ice Palace or I'll give a big brunch for you."

"He needs me," I told her, all reason. "Like meat needs salt."

She framed my face in her hands as if a deep searching look could find something deeper in it. Was I being ironic? Or had I fooled myself so well I needed a clown to match my wits? "A brunch," she repeated. Her totem. "Brunch or the Ice Palace, which?"

Much of my early life remains clouded in mystery. Like the— inside of a balloon. "The time came in its season," writes David of Steerforth, "and that was very soon, when I almost wondered that nothing troubled his repose, as I looked at him. But he slept—let me think of him so again—as I had often seen him sleep at school; and thus, in this silent hour, I left him.

"Never more, oh, God forgive you, Steerforth! to touch that passive hand in love and friendship. Never, never more!" One night in our back room, a long low hall covered in pastel mortarboard, studded with college lamps that looked like megaphones. A party over. A cherry sat sodden at the base of a bottle of tequila. Hangover chill weighted the air, the heat, the cold. George lay slumped on his stomach in a morass of white clean linen in a darkened space. My dear dear friend. His eyes were green and empty and blue, his hair the surf in a picture postcard. Australia. In silence we smelled our ornate wintry bodies and got hard, but nothing new came into my room. What should have been a hesitant magic should have settled, airy as Firbank, redolent as L'Interdit. Audrey Hepburn's favorite perfume. Instead I tugged his pants down and made first love to him, awkwardly, a force of nature I haven't believed since I was fifteen, or sixteen.

The most contained, the bruise is the most aesthetic form of bleeding.

He turned his weary profile and said *don't you know that it's true*, he whispered hoarsely, quickly, an auctioneer *that for me and for you, the world is a suburb?*

I took his words at face value, for beneath the sleeping gold and cream and capillary blush of his gaze lurked a being so alien I didn't care to take it in, preferring to watch the planes work up and down or rest in repose like a Redon deathmask. When Mme. Tussaud et fils fled the Terror they knew the value of these precious masks, smuggled in trunks, under furs; too high to declare, it would float the rest of their lives into history. And deeper into his mouth I penetrated with my tongue as though to stifle a never, like a dentist's drill employed to bring surcease to a killing pain. His pain or mine, his nerve or mine? Not apparent whose, on its misty apparitional face. "Don't you need me?" I said. "How does this feel," I said, moving the very head of my cock further into his luminous haunches. I was curious. "Oh George look at the stars: they're only the diamonds in Tiffany's window. Oh George look at the stars and the starlight!"

The face is the most valuable of icons, how else shall I remember people? I blank out their weights and heights, and colors of hair; in my memory, as well as in intercourse, genitals run into a blur. Tone-deaf voices, insensitive to the touch direct, I see money, *l'argent*, in the human face, as if in a mirror; had I a photo of George I would kiss its mouth and act very Salome all over it. The face of Garbo, Barthes says somewhere, is an Idea, that of Audrey Hepburn an Event, but Barthes died without a glimpse of George Grey's face: the face as model of Economic Indeterminacy. "Do you think I'm good looking?" He lived inside a mirror. "Do you think I should grow a mustache?" Mirrors tell tales, the face lives on inside the mirror as time goes and grows. "I am butch." He lay out in the grass on a bed of tinfoil—splendid, unreproachable, like a hoarfrost killing the green grass with the weight of his body, the sun in his eyes. "Rich man, buy my body." Hard pressed to say what I loved in it, I bit into his face like a diamond ring etching a window and tried to write my name: Remember me! Tonight I looked at the stars and out onto this Spanish California street. George, if I wanted you to live in the modern world, I'd kill your children first off. But the kids are so cute, and in any case I think—you'd be scared to live, where the muggers dance on top of the pizza. Surely all the days of your life you'll be followed by goodness, and mercy.

BEDROOMS HAVE WINDOWS

Squashed onto the car ceiling, my feet keep pounding. I think his name's Gil. His cock feels the approximate size and shape of a dart, and he keeps sticking it in, humping his hips like a jackhammer or jackrabbit; and I'm his dartboard, made out of cork. Except cork doesn't ache, or does it, and this little steel dart in and out of my ass is killing me. I try to let out a scream. My mouth is stuffed with a red bandanna. Midnight in a parked car with a Puerto Rican bully. "Well," I think to myself to console myself, "he's such a jackrabbit maybe he'll come soon. I would in his shoes." Then I think maybe he'll burst a blood vessel, my vessel, with that hypodermic needle or dart he calls his *bate para jugar baseball* and I wonder what I've gotten myself into.

Maybe you know him. He was dating the daughter of a neighbor and played on the soccer team. Annoyingly he began to intrude on my life—for everyone bar none would come up to me and ask if my little brother was now going to the same school. "Except he's taller than you, he looks just like you."

Well he didn't look *just like*, and wasn't backward about snarling so. I know I was sulky, but I didn't know why. But really it was because he had a kind of beauty about him I didn't feel I would ever attain, and he was fourteen, and I was seventeen, and he was straight, and I was gay. One day he surprised me by commenting on the resemblance, but I made him feel pushy. One evening the rain was rushing down out of the sky soaking the fur trim of these ridiculous parkas that were fashionable in that climate, at that time, and we huddled together under a tin roof for shelter, he and I, to smoke a joint. There the breath blew up over his face as though warmth and friction itself lived in those planes, and I made him feel pushy again, whereas in actual fact I resented him for looking so much like me—but the real thing, where I was not. I was amazingly affected then, though I can't regret it. I was looking for a personality to inhabit and thought "willful" would be a grand one.

Carey, who managed several HoJo franchises for Morgan, could have done TV commercials for them—"They're the neatest, cleanest places anywhere in America," he used to say. In Western Pennsylvania, I looked around for a suitable Howard Johnson's motel to check into. At midnight, though, all the vacancies in Bucks County were filled. I pulled up into the spotlit parking lot of one and tried to sleep sitting up behind the steering wheel, the orange and blue lights filtering my face with the motley pattern of the harlequin. A low wind out of the north kept things tolerably cool.

A lazy mosquito circled against my window, over and over in a dulling hypnotic pattern—like opening and shutting a drawer. Its body no bigger than a seed, I thought I could see its eyes and read an expression there the look of megalomania. As though it thought it were King of the Universe. Eventually it lost interest in me and disappeared.

The calm cool night was soft and still and in the orange-and-blue pajamas the light arrayed on my bare skin it should have been a night of restful slumber.

But I couldn't get comfortable enough to sleep. After a while I got out of the car to stretch my legs and to use the bathroom inside the restaurant. While I was there I checked to see if their menu was the same as the HoJo menu I was used to on the land. It seemed identical, which made me happy, and then I noticed this place served "scrapple," which sounded really hideous.

I thought to myself, "You've come a long way from home, Kevin." A man sitting at the counter started talking to me about the rich people who summered in Bucks County, he said he was one of them, he bought me a big plate of scrapple when he heard I'd never had any. When he found out I was driving to California he insisted on taking me back to his house to show me pictures of its wildlife. I followed his car down a series of dark hills, and a couple of times my new pal had to slow down completely, to stop the car at a strange crossroad and to come out and kiss me, so I'd get the idea. See it's simple.

But that scrapple was definitely for the birds.

One night I left my room to fetch a glass of water from the cellar pump. Descending the rickety wooden steps, pushing holes through the webs of the ornate spider family, I dropped my flashlight. Down the steps it bashed, bang, bang, bang, like the gunshots that killed Marvin Gaye. Finally it came to rest with its lighted end wavering across the dusty basement floor, pointing like a weathervane to what wasn't a man or boy, but rather a whole climate of erotic opinion. I was caught—captured—by a pair of blue eyes so vivid and so sleepy they seemed those of Loretta Lynn . . . but they belonged to a sleeping boy—a boy who sleeps with his eyes open, and his mouth open, and his clothes open, and only his sense of identity seemed closed to me in that intolerably close room. The cave walls were slimy and covered with graffiti, big pictures of big cocks and big words, I began to see the connection. The attraction, the allure, of a language.

Once I watched dispassionately as the boy of the hour, Harry Van, sat opposite in a chair across the room, his pants down among his ankles, wrapping a long limp rose around his—around his—"Look out for the thorns," I said.

"Pretty?"

"Who taught you," I said, "flower arranging?"

"Taught me all by myself," Harry said, grinning. He tied the rose then lifted his hands above his head and clasped them like a champion fighter. "Look, no hands!" The flower bobbed between his legs, his sparse white pubic hair rustled, entreated with the greenish-brown of the rose's stem. "Crown of thorns," Harry said with a wink, beginning to whistle a hymn popular on the radio: *Everything is Beautiful, in its Own Way*. "Feel it, Kevin. Tower of ivory."

I wouldn't.

"Your loss. Now watch." He lowered his hands and pressed them into the encircled rose. "Tighter."

"No, don't, no don't."

"Tighter."

One drop of blood, and a flood of tears, then he fell on the floor, pretending a deep wound, but laughing and ejaculating at the same time. I went to the window and called out, "He's gone loco this time. He's singing *Everything is Beautiful* and he knows I hate that song." And presently we did more tricks with flowers and weeds and lay on the rug like Adam and Eve in the first bower of bliss. Occasionally one or the other of us would peel the thick skin off an orange and feed the other its sweet pulp. In the sultry summer heat of Long Island, a jinky haze sat upon us. On one wall was pinned a large poster of Raquel Welch in a swimsuit in a blue shower. She smiled at the camera and her silver body sweated hot water. We loved Raquel, who doesn't?

One evening several years ago I was lying in bed, after some unsatisfactory fumbles towards "safe sex" with a writer I used to admire, Dennis A. He turned his head—exactly as he'd turned mine, an hour earlier—and get this, he said, "why didn't you think to take home that Tom B. too and we could have had a threesome?"

"Why didn't *I* think," I replied, an echo of disbelief. "Dennis, I did think; I thought and thought. If I thought any more, I wouldn't be having this safe sex. Madness won't be safe from me." I felt attracted to him when he spelled his name in plastic magnetized letters on Aaron's refrigerator. Then he spelled mine with the same colorful letters. Language fused. It was like William Carlos Williams. "There were plums in that icebox," I said to him. "Forgive me. Forgive me. I couldn't help it; they were so ripe and so purple and so cold."

In St. Louis the vast cement arches reminded me I hadn't stopped at a single McDonald's in days.

The guy in the back seat was sleeping still. An unruly lock of red hair dangled over the scar on his forehead. "Like Cain," I thought. One hand nestled his crotch, but the hand was so light it couldn't have weighed more than a pound, and any time I wanted to I could have taken that hand and pinned it to the floor, like Nabokov pinning a butterfly in a mounted case of glass. Motel life wasn't disagreeable to me, no more than it was for Humbert Humbert and Lolita. So long as I stuck to Howard Johnson's I could take comfort from the indistinguishable sameness of American life—only the face changed, and sometimes the accents, like this one, in the blue leather back seat—the mouth that opened doorways on several impoverished southern countries and backwater *towns you-all*. A few miles later I saw a McDonald's—red and gold as the Queen's embroidery. I wasn't impressed by the Mississippi, smudgy, roiling, impossibly dim and wide—unless fright counts as a kind of impressure. Crossing bridges always threw me into a panic, and this was one long motherfucking bridge for sure! Good thing I was full from my hearty burger lunch.

I was in New York having an awful kind of sex on the night of the Stonewall riots in 1969. I was sixteen, that part was OK it was only that I was made to feel so uncomfortable. All night long these muddy fucked-up white fogs rolled up to the window pressing in, looking in, as if to signal that from now on everything was to be first examined, then analyzed. I didn't hear any police sirens or drag queens protesting, only the familiar Manhattan rumble of ironwork and street noise. The face on the pillow didn't belong to me, it squirmed and averted its eyes no matter how steady my stare, how intimate or abusive my words. I take this face as the model of the love that resists, yet endures, everything that can be put to it: all trials, sorrows, all caresses. In the morning it rises and in the summer sunlight gets splashed with lukewarm water over a kitchen sink, in front of a mirror. It floats out of the apartment to be confronted by the headlines, black as the dark glasses through which it scans the news. We took a Lexington bus from East End Avenue and 83rd, then hiked over to what he still called "Greenwich" Village. I was really into Italian ice then, I remember: the man I was with for example, Carey. He and I stared at the controversial site amid a big crowd, that grew bigger by the minute. Where had all these faces come from? Out of little bedrooms, down from uptown, off of these perfectly white pillows and into the open air. And all these sunglasses! Like a crowd on the beach—witnesses of some jaws-type accident or attack. Everyone moved as if in shock or underwater or both, and began to swell.

So if I'd conceived a baby that night it would now be the age I was then, but born and bred under a different condition and I do not know if we'd get along. We would need someone to mediate between generations. If the old only could! If the young only knew! I shut my eyes to try to call up that face, substituting the blackness of memory for the shades we wore, to call it up as though it were a number, I don't get much of a response. To him

I said, "You're old enough to be my father," and that seemed to please, like a token of a love too long denied and a tongue too twisted. "I'm pretty happy," Carey said, admitting to something very like a crime. "Then treat me right," I said. "Let's go back to your apartment. I have to go to summer school tomorrow."

"Not after this," he said, sweeping his hand. "Never, never, never."

But oh yes, I sure did.

THE BOYS FROM BRAZIL

After George and Karoll left for Hawaii, I remained where I was, and lived on, please write for details. I took a series of roommates, one by one, two by two. One of them I'll call "Aleck Varney," as he might have grown up to become a prominent attorney, though it's not very likely. I don't recall either where or when Aleck Varney picked up Marion Martin to come live with us, but the night he brought home two boys from Rio de Janeiro I've long remembered. Up in town Aleck, who was my age—25, managed the hardware store of his aging father, and these two guys came in—couldn't speak much English— asking could he fix their Porsche for them? "I don't know how they knew I'm good at motors," Aleck marveled.

"You are, you're a whiz," I said. "It *is* funny they'd come into a hardware store for auto maintenance but maybe that's a Brazilian custom." I was thinking of those places in the dessert that sell not only gas but ice cream, souvenirs, liquor, snake-skins, tongue depressors,—hardware even . . . In the American desert . . . "But why are they here, Al?"

Aleck looked embarrassed, began to fiddle with his boot. Eventually I pieced it together. Aleck Varney could speak marijuana in any language and when the two boys produced ounces of it in gratitude he closed down the shop and sat miming with them all over the cash register counter, for about two hours, after "accidentally" slipping the phone off the receiver so his dad couldn't bug him. Then he decided to show how Long Islanders know how to party. He took them to 2001, a space disco. One thing led to another and he couldn't tell them not to set up camp in the front room of the house we shared. Just couldn't. Not because he was a bashful guy, though often he was; it developed onto a level of language so deep he had no resources to bridge it, outside a kick up their asses. Which, he reckoned, would be un-American. Unfriendly. So here they were all twelve foot ten of them, two boys from Brazil with a Porsche and ten beautiful matched luggage pieces and one hundred white pearly teeth and no English. Lots of money, no English. I weighed these pros and cons on a scale of my own invention, I thought, well maybe they'll be all right. "They sure are loud motherfuckers though ain't they!" Aleck said.

"This used to be a quiet home," I called to him, "and now it's a Samba-rama I can't sleep in or take to." They'd unpacked some records and were even now rolling some joints to the beat of *The Girl from Ipanema*. Apparently they were college students, checking out New York party life on an extended vacation, and as someday they'd go back to Brazil I at least could feel they weren't squatters.

"Marion likes them," Aleck told me defiantly, with the air of one who won't mince his words.

"They're kind of cute," I said, up on the bandwagon: as usual, but with a few reservations. I didn't like drugs especially. I'd become a homosexual. I was afraid of myself and what would happen to me next in life. But in a way I was telling the truth.

I took to the looks of the two boys right away, it was their personalities I came to hear. Their names were both "Pedro." And so were their looks. Pedro looked much like Pedro, at least in my untutored eyes: two young Cary Grants, a bit more exotic, lounge lizard, but very very Cary Grant. They wore expensive clothes with Cary Grant's ease, I thought they should have been GQ models. On the night they arrived I had sex with one of them but never could remember which one so it was hard to schedule a return engagement. Everything about them said money, *dinero*. On the bench down our street they swam in jockstraps, which they removed to sun themselves—I thought this daring, cosmopolitan, almost medical. So did the lifeguard who called the police. "Is it me or don't they look like twins?"

"They do look roughly similar," Aleck said. "But I don't think they're related. It's like these two cats my dad has."

"They are two cats," I said, struck by the simile. "Two big lean sinuous jungle sex animals."

Meanwhile the two boys were playing a game with string in "their" room, lying on their stomachs face to face propped up on their elbows and kicking their legs to accommodate their moves. The wrinkled white linen suits they wore fell down their calves, exposing reams of tanned pinky brown leg with no hair, L.L. Bean type socks clocked with bluebirds. I wondered if they shaved their legs, then I recalled some of the smooth Indian chests I'd seen in Cochise movies. But why? I thought: Indian blood, yes, there's something very cowboys and Indians going on in this house and I intend to exorcise all my racism out of my body somehow. String fascinated these two Brazilian playboys, string and American blondes like Aleck's girlfriend Marion. What South American game were they playing with that string? Not cat's-cradle, something more complicated; but it couldn't have been folk art could it? Marion claimed to be able to distinguish between the two, but I came to believe this only another airy bluff—I noticed she called each of them "Pedro" as uninflectedly as she called all non-Brazilians "babe." When she worked as Calvin Klein's babysitter (before the kidnapping—she was exonerated) she called *him* babe. One day at breakfast I overheard her talking on the phone. "Well babe," she was saying, "what goes around comes around. One guy breaks your heart, you break the next guy's legs." When she hung up she took my toast and said, "That was Linda—Linda Blair."

"What! The star of *The Exorcist!*"

"Linda and I go back a long way, B.C., babe." She said casually between bites. "Back Centuries."

"That's not what B.C. stands for," I thought but I didn't say it, I was so interested in finding out what Linda Blair is really like!!!

Marion boasted that once she and Linda had eaten cat food for three weeks before hitting it big. "All kinds of cat food, Frisky Vittles, Happy Cat, mostly seafood styles, it's good for your teeth, ever see a cat with stained teeth?"

Pedro and Pedro seemed never to eat at all, although sometimes their largesse was so grand we would open the freezer compartment and find a turkey or goose dead there, frozen and flesh-colored like a transplant. Eating seemed to disgust the two boys in a Swiftian way, like his land where people fuck and excrete in public yet lock themselves in tiny rooms to eat guiltily. These two boys wouldn't even take a potato chip at a party! Their exquisite waists and flat stomachs were, I felt certain, less the product of expenditure than of disdain.

"Was Linda Blair ever really that poor? When *The Exorcist* came out, they made such a big deal of her horsey Connecticut background."

"We were *coldwater*," Marion said firmly. "I remember Linda when she was so poor she took the bottles of Thunderbird from bums, sleeping in the gutter, if she saw a little inch left—inch or less."

"Oh my."

"And pennies from penny loafers! Sometimes a chiclet from the subway machine would be the only solid food she and me would have for a week." Marion spoke of these hard times of hers complacently, almost with regret. Evidently the picture—two games, pretty girls up against it in a cold cruel city—she'd imagined meant a great deal to her and she had no intention of tampering with it now or ever. Maybe too from this same imaginary past stemmed her affection for the TV sitcom *Laverne and Shirley,* but I'm just guessing. I do know that almost everything Laverne and Shirley did had a seedier counterpart in Marion's life with Linda Blair. In one episode Laverne and Shirley find themselves entered, without their knowledge, in a Milwaukee twist contest which naturally they win despite their utter ignorance of twisting. ("Pretend," Shirley hisses to her chum, "there's an invisible hulahoop around your waist!") Likewise Linda and Marion had once unwittingly been drawn into judging a "Human Ashtray" contest in a Manhattan waterfront sex club. "They called us 'Cigarette Girls,' kinda cute ha babe?" After a while I found Marion's parallels so far-fetched as to seem desperate; and finally I came to think of Manhattan almost as black-and-white as Woody Allen's version of it, while Milwaukee screamed and blared pastel dayglo color like a trip to the Mall on acid. What Linda and Marion had, that Laverne and Shirley must purposely have discarded, was a preference for grit, soot, ugliness of a Diane Arbus sort, that couldn't be accidental; ugliness sought and cultivated with vigor. Her lies, her frame of reference, were so thorough I wanted a pattern made out of them to darken my belief: a doubting Thomas in reverse.

But because I thought of Linda as an almost entirely fictional person, Marion's lineaments became less and less real to me, even though she was one of my roommates. I knew she was game, I felt she was pretty; but I doubted whether she was a "girl" as much as a—fabulous *phoenix*. She was doing the same thing I was—constructing a life from the ashes of an old—but with what different materials! "Do you think she really knows Linda Blair?" I asked Aleck once.

He shrugged and grinned, a little painfully. "Sure," he said, after lacing his boots for a minute or so. He straightened up, red in the face from exertion and hunger. "And I'm Arnold Schwarzenegger."

"Well you are in a way," I said, absently flirting as usual and not thinking: as usual. All I could think of was the construct. Oh he was so attractive! But the bird that immolates itself then rises out of its own flame is—more curious still . . . I'd sit there, reading the *Midnight Tattler* with Marion, and she'd say,—I almost slept with that one, or—I slept with this one, kind of a deadhead, or—her, she's a coke freak and the world knows it. Often, if they were small enough to fit in her heavy green leatherette wallet, she cut out the stars' pictures. She put up her thick blond hair in different ways to suit her plans for the evening, which shows she was going to watch, which men were going to watch them with her. From childhood she'd kept a scrapbook of current events, Man on the Moon, cancellation of *Petticoat Junction*, death of Alan Ladd, Brian Jones, the grain boycott, bombing of Haiphong Harbor ("I had a P.O.W. boyfriend, never got none of the Entenmann's I sent him"), Three Stooges reunions. She balanced this book of her head and walked from room to room in a bikini, arms akimbo and precarious, biting her tongue, her grayblue eyes focussed intently on a travelling spot in the ceiling. "Calvin used to say—Grace is the word for Marion Martin."

Restaurants are constantly looking for talent, too, just like Hollywood; there are talent scouts out there always trying to grab up a good-looking or efficient waiter, and in my time I considered several offers. One was from, I remember, a healthy middle-aged couple who made me quite a few exciting overtures. Finally, on their invitation and with their card, I went to eat at their restaurant and I noticed something creepy about it I couldn't put my finger on. They joined me after dessert and I realized what it was from their effusion and their smiles. They wanted me, they said, but only if I could become a born-again Christian like all the other waiters in the place. That's it! I said to myself. Then you got the hard core hard-ons like this one guy who comes into my story right now. He got me into talking and said he and some partners were opening up a swanky joint in the South Shore and he liked my style and could we meet after I closed up, have a drink, kick the future around a little? I thought this pretty obvious but I agreed, playing *faux-naif* for him, swishing my ass around. I knew he was a conman but I felt like going to bed with him. We met for a drink at the bar next door then "went home" to my house. The two Rio boys were in the front room talking their language and flipping through Aleck's vast collection of *International Penthouse*, and my collection of *Harper's Bazaar*— which then as now featured plenty of naked, thin women. "Stan" and I fell into my yellow room, but it was too small to contain our passion. So it was that when Aleck and Marion came giggling home in the wee hours the kitchen door flew open on my ass while "Stan" and I were poking at some awfully vicious 69. Which I think is so stupid, but that's what he seemed to want. Aleck said, "Whoops!" like a comedy and made as if to vamoose again, but Marion lingered.

"Look at them," she said, in a dead voice.

"I don't want to look at them," Aleck Varney whined, in the darkened doorway, jiggling his hips like a schoolboy who has to piss but isn't allowed to. Maybe he had to: they were even drunker than I. I took the cock of "Stan" out of my mouth and laid it on the linoleum, to say "Hi," to apologize. "Stan" wanted to—I didn't want him to—come in my mouth.

You see even then I knew what I like and what I don't like. "No, look babe," said Marion.

THE PULL

Dear George,

You told me that whenever I can't think of what to write, pretend I'm writing you a letter. Remember that George? You stood in a field of snow, clouds full of snow high above your palms, and brought a snowstorm down upon us. Yours were great powers, greater than you knew. Inside your dorm room a typewriter hummed and I drew myself closer to it, ever closer. *Oh what a birthday surprise, Judy's wearing his ring*. Those were the first words I wrote, everything else grew round them, accreted, a snowball racing down a hill massed round a single stone or snowflake.

I picture you and Karoll in Pearl Harbor, opening this letter. Hawaii like the gilded shell Botticelli's Venus steps out from. Its delicate pinks and silvers frame the blonde tans of you and your wife. A letter pokes through your mailslot, drops to the lanai floor, amid the faded orchids and leis of all yesterday's parties. Remember my boyfriend, Harry Van? He called me up the other day.

All it takes is a telephone call. "I used your name in conversation, Kevin. Today this piece of pork he wakes me up he goes when can I see him again. I don't want to see him. He say's what's your name and what's your number. So I said *Kevin Killian*, gave him your number, hope you don't mind, maybe he's your type, I guess a little. You know. Okay? It's just I felt the pull, that's why I did what I did, you know."

I met him in a candy store, I looked around from side to side, no one was watching so I leaned over and pulled him into my pocket. "Can I help you?"

"No thanks, just browsing."

On my way home I petted him repeatedly to keep him soothed. He took to me like a house on fire.

For the whole of one year I kept him, then I lost him to another.

"With no mother no father or sister or brother I wind up stiffed all over the map. That's the way it is. You gotta have someone to protect you. You name the place I was screwed there. I say that's life. No one to take care of you, you get screwed but good. I laugh it off. Feel it pulling all the time. You get a lot of laughs that way."

Harry was always laughing. Before he met me he'd never seen any of the famous *I Love Lucy* episodes. Lucy gets carried away with her poverty, years to break free of Ricky's coattails; doesn't every man feel this way when he's in love? Lucy and Ethel on the assembly line wrapping chocolates: it's a time line as well as a conveyor belt. Soon enough you're falling off the belt, but Harry was only fifteen.

"When it got heavy I just said well them's the breaks. I came up all through Hard Knocks School. When it got super heavy I knew it was Jesus calling me like a voice from out of the pit. What did I know about Jesus, right? I didn't know Jesus from the backside of the barn. The rain was pouring down a motherfucker, man, I just about to keel over collapse, I pulled into Gunther's house, I'd been put on earth to be his servant. He got to me. We were into a real heavy S and M trip. He got to my religious convictions that you don't say No to. I didn't even know what they were. I knew Jesus was out there but that's Jesus, not a real person. I used to do a lot of angel dust hell years before it was vogue like disco. Disco sucks. I was ahead of my time always have been and always will. Don't mess with me cause you're messing with the kid. Religion and shit Gunther didn't want to know from, so I had to hide my feelings from him, even my feelings about human affection even the animals believe in, when you pet them, they purr back, cuddle up. But he just laughed. I said to him, I'm fifteen or sixteen now but some day like everyone else I plan on dying and going to heaven like the rest of the jokers. Except for you, Gunther, who's going to hell. He just laughed. Between the two of us, me and him, we had a lot of laughs, good and bad, but in the end the whole scene got too heavy and he did something terrible to me. Besides which he wasn't Jesus. Jesus can't be a real man. But that's something you don't know when you got no mother or father. And like when you don't have a mother, stands to reason, you don't have a father either."

Like he always wanted to find this absurd father figure, this search of his reminded me of nothing I'd ever felt or experienced in my life. I guess because my own father's so good and so wise, I didn't need to find another. So sometimes Harry's fumbling around, under the streetlight, dusted with coke or brown powder, got my goat instead of tickled my funnybone, I mean you can't find your father or find Jesus hanging out . . . you know.

"And you can't find your father or find Jesus just by hanging out on a street corner and letting any old piece of pork take you back and you know. One night I woke up all tied up in electric cord. I loved it. I mean. You feel the pull, you follow the drill. I ate the crusts Gunther threw off his sandwiches. Then he switched to submarine sandwiches that don't got the crusts. I sat up like a dog, I begged and rolled over, I fucked like a dog. That's kid stuff, but you know.

"I say to him, I'm fifteen or sixteen now but I won't be fifteen or sixteen forever, some day soon I'll be born again. One of these days you will see what I mean."

"I don't want to hurt your feelings or play Hearts and Flowers with you. If I use your name in vain tell me Kevin and I will be sorry, I will be glad, to make it up to you."

"You don't have to," I interposed. But he swept on.

"I picked some winners all right. But now I don't know. That's the pull. You feel it right under your balls but it's not sex, it's just a thing, you don't stop to say no, you don't say slow down, will this do damage to my chromosomes, what do you say, you say Yes. You get pulled all over the map. You go from New York New York to the West Coast. You see a girl, that's the pull. You see this guy all covered with sauce and spaghetti, you say Yes. You wake up and maybe you're in bed with maybe an asshole. Rub your eyes all you want it's still real. That's the whole thing and what is it? The power of Jesus moving within one another! You get dragged up from being a naughty squawking kid, it's for real. All without you knowing it or wanting to, you got a big cock, what do you say, No? No way man, you just go out and do it."

I had the feeling his continual use of the second person was only a mannerism he'd perhaps picked up from—whom? Stand-up comedians? When he said "you" he rarely meant "you," he meant "I," only a more lapidary, concise "I" than the one he'd been saddled with. A perfect "I" is what he meant, the "I" of the Lord.

"Maybe you're tired of everyone laughing at you," Harry continued, "so you run to be locked up, people giving you the treatment, well say, who gives one shit in hell. Ever bite on the pillow, bite on the edge of the mattress where the tag comes from, 'Do Not Remove,' inside your eyes you see the stars man, and the big halo? That's Jesus. Means you've grown up and you don't have to take no for an answer or put up with any shit. Except if you want to, and no one's stopping you. That's the breaks then. Maybe you like it after all, maybe you like the pull.

That's growing up. I had this one date Kieran otherwise known as Queeran who said 'Growing up means learning to like salad,' but that's not what it means, it means getting the message. That's what it's all about.

"I was a kid I got bounced. Now I'm eighteen or nineteen and all of those people—where are they? Living their own lives because they have to, but that's not my style. I'm the kid is why. That's that. That's it. When you're free you're free I say. Don't matter you're tied up or maybe locked in or there's a pretty girl spread her bush in your face or there's a big gonzo dick up your ass. Someone smacking you with a ping pong. So, it may be the doctor slapping you make sure you're alive. It's the pull. You're like a lizard, you move inside your skin. I'm no baby I said. I said to him don't be afraid of me man cause you're afraid, so what? I'm fifteen or sixteen, I'm the kid, but I'm no baby. You do your own thing and don't worry about me squawking or squealing. That's what irks me when people think you're a squeal. I'm no baby and I don't squeal. I'm not a minion and I don't go around squealing and I don't go turning on my own kind."

"That's good, Harry," I said, soothing again, Kevin's cough drops, patent pending. Oh, George, you and I were 18 or 19 once. Did we need so much consolation? Like Harry? I remember when I first thought of writing, I was afraid to pit my strength against the proven prowess of our favorite writers, Proust, Dickens, Ian Fleming, Dorothy Sayers, Faulkner, Cowper Powys, Carolyn Keene, Colette. I'll never be as good as they, why even try!

"They're terrible writers," you told me, yawning, your hand flippant with dismissal. Our bookcases snarled with bulldogs. "They're nothing but a pack of old fools," you said. "In ten minutes you could write a best seller, thirty times better than theirs." All I wanted from you was permission, I didn't even want you to like me.

And all Harry wanted was permission. "I don't turn on my own kind," he repeated. What utter bullshit.

"Which I never have done, never will." Of course he had, dozens of times, and of course he would in the future, if he ever got off of the phone. He breathed into the phone dreamily, like an obscene caller, he'd forgotten who he'd dialed. I pictured him on the other end of the line, lying on his back on the rug, his feet kicked in the air, the phone upside down like a scene from *The Patty Duke Show* or *Bye Bye Birdie*. His green and white eyes were closed, darkness reigned within, a peaceful darkness like the forest glades of Hardy. His hair's tousled and wet, the color of peaches. A twisted towel lies draped across his waist imitating a belt, and his skin's soft as velour. He's one of those boys who walks around your kitchen like a dog trying to get to sleep.

I don't mean "your" kitchen, George.

"That's real good, Harry," I told him. "Now hang up and go to sleep like a good dog."

"Okay," he said happily, amazed. Who was speaking to him? CLICK

POETRY

The Cruisemobile practically drove itself, and in under an hour I swam up through the Lincoln Tunnel like a rat drenched in sweat. At noon lower Manhattan, teeming with inferior life specimens, sweltered under a huge beating sun yellow and orange as a Douanier Rousseau. My lip curled in complete and utter disdain at the fleabag hotels and the street people who littered the winestained alleys. At a stop sign one bum staggered up to her car and spat on my windshield, he wanted a quarter or something more hefty, what he got was the bum's rush. In California, I thought, I won't get all this riffraff. At the same time I found myself thinking, Kevin, you're a liberal—why are you going into this snob infusion mode?

Nevertheless I drove my fist into the horn and blasted that bum way the hell into the Bowery.

Uptown I found a good parking spot opposite the Gotham Book Mart. Ted Berrigan was inside reading from and signing copies of his latest book. Do you remember the late poet Ted Berrigan? As I recall him from that long-ago afternoon, he was an abundant colossus of a man, with a red face and beefy linebacker's hands. I take him now as the *exemplum* of the artist, supremely talented but self-destructive in a way that seems foreign to our chaste nineties. Casually, enthusiastically, I cracked open a copy of his book and at a random page, read a few lines to myself, then backed up and started over. "Wait a darn minute here," I thought. I couldn't follow what he was trying to say in the poetry! I felt stupid as Archie in the comics: you could have drawn me with a balloon above my head saying "Huh?"

A tall vase filled with carnations stood beside me: tight folded sprays of white, purple, and pink. I stared at the book, shook my head in defeat. I guess my pride was wounded; I, after all, considered myself an artist too, and I'd always believed that we artists live in a fraternity of our own, each one helping the next one, no man divisive, each man commodious. But with the book in my hand, and beyond the confusing words printed there, the moving mouth and swaying stomach of the author, all I knew was that, no matter what his poetry "meant" or "said," Mr. Ted Berrigan hadn't missed very many meals in his day, or in the day of about 20 other people who were probably starving. Watch out or he'd eat those carnation petals too. Not me: smelling carnations always takes me to a funeral home, I couldn't imagine eating one, though they do resemble some Japanese appetizers I've seen people eat here in San Francisco.

For every reaction, I've come to learn, a compensatory action results. What would mine be? Taking a panoramic look at the interior of the Gotham Book Mart, and spying, in a far corner, under a photo of Edith and Sacheverell Sitwell, a table laden with white pale pastries and hors d'oeuvres, I made my move. "Excuse me," I said loudly, stepping between two people who looked more important than they really were. "Are those snacks reserved for the reader or can anyone have some?"

"Help yourself," they told me acidly. I was famished. Ted Berrigan stood there by the cash register reciting this long, long sonnet sequence almost by heart—as though he had really lived the lines. When I slid one of his precious egg rolls into my mouth, he gave me the Evil Eye, but I was too hungry to care. Let him think what he wanted, the hell with him. Maybe I was a little disruptive at this event, but that's the condition his poetry called out in me. I felt like I was drunk—actually I hadn't had a drink in almost 24 hours. So it was definitely time for a drink.

Behind a rack of books, an old woman with white hair, Frances Steloff, was quietly pouring red wine into a group of water glasses. Oh, Christ, was I ever glad to see her! She must have been around ninety years old but pouring that wine she resembled the ageless Goddess of Vesta! Noiselessly I slipped behind and reached round her waist to grab one of the filled glasses, and when she slapped my wrist I whispered in her ear, "It's for Ted," whereupon she let me go. My ruse had worked! In a minute that red wine had disappeared down my gullet, chasing the egg roll. Then came that feeling I sometimes get at a party or reading, that I'd really rather be washing my hair, so I looked around for a medicine cabinet just in case someone had left some shampoo lying around. In the very back bowels of the bookstore I discovered a private apartment, complete with a bathroom deluxe. None of that bathtub-in-the-kitchen nonsense you see in so many Manhattan studio flats. I swung open the mirror to continue my obsessive quest. Not a drop of shampoo within, but disappointment was allayed by finding hundreds of pills there—Probably Ted's also. A treasure trove. Red, yellow, pink, coral, midnight blue—it was like *Valley of the Dolls*! I looked both ways—no one had followed me—so I took most of the pills and rationed them out into the various pockets of my green windbreaker and khaki shorts. Then I left New York without regret and continued west on Route 66.

I spun the wheels of the *Cruisemobile* up Broadway all the way across the Major Deegan Expressway; on either side of me the huge buildings, black with dingy paintjobs, oppressively tall, made me long for the open spaces of the Pacific Coast Highway. I had miles to go before I reached California, but hope sang in my heart, and my pockets, stuffed as they were with Berrigan's rainbow of pills, banged against my thighs like the saddlebags men must have used on some other, historic Western journey.

NEGATIVE

I.

Since 1980 I've lived in San Francisco. Again and again I've tried, without success, to relate my experience of the sensual world to the facts that surround me.

At SF International, there's an airport bar called the "Fillmore," which capitalizes on this city's '60s fame with a decor of psychedelic posters and black lighting. A video machine set high into one mylar wall plays, non-stop, scratchy cinema of the historic Airplane, the Dead, Quicksilver. Travellers rest their elbows atop tiny round black formica tables like 45s, and gold 45s hang from the ceiling, spinning from nylon threads above our heads. The waitresses are flip and bouffant. I love it there and you would, too.

Sometimes I take the Airport Shuttle even if I don't have to take a plane or pick anyone up, just for the chance to relax and hoist a few at the "Fillmore" bar.

So there I was, about six months ago, relaxing and hoisting, when Nicky Denham got off a plane and wandered into the place. Struggling under the burden of garment bags, Tom Cruise aviator glasses, he looked lost and frightened in the purple haze of the strip lighting. He pushed the Ray-Bans upside his forehead; that's when I had him pegged.

Out of all the brokendown gin joints in the world he had to pick the one where the wallpaper boasts a repeated pattern of Robert Indiana's l-o-v-e logo.

"Hey!" I said to him. "I remember you! You're Carter Denham's son, right?"

He was looking at me like he'd never seen me before in his life, but friendly enough, as though he could be wrong.

He wasn't wrong. We'd never met. I only recognized him from photos, the snapshots and formal portraits his dad had shown me all those long years ago. I told him a lie. Well, what would you have done? I told him, "I worked with your dad at the Morgan Guaranty Trust."

"He's still there," Nick said.

"How's he doing?" I asked. "I haven't seen him in fifteen years."

Nick shrugged, let his overnight bag slide to the floor. "Okay, I guess."

"He still married to Anita?"

"Yeah, sure. What's your name again?"

"Kevin," I said firmly, writing it on a cocktail napkin. "Kevin Killian." Under the name I wrote down my phone number and stuffed it into the breast pocket of Nick's leather bomber jacket, close to his heart, take away that lost suspicious look from his green, yellow-flecked eyes. "It's an Irish name, what do you do, Nick?"

"Systems analyst," he said.

"Fascinating!" I cried. The waitress, in go-go boots and miniskirt, slid a $10.00 daiquiri under Nick's elbow. "Absolutely fascinating. Silicon Valley stuff, right?"

Since that afternoon I've asked myself how I could have blown my opportunity. My ass is sore I've kicked it so often.

2.

Carey and Anita live on. One day Carey answers a personal ad in a sex paper, and within a week he's met Travis Santucci, a nice young man who's nineteen and hardly shows it. In certain lights Travis looks about twelve, the way nowadays all young boys look any age at all, depending on haircut and attitude.

As Carey gets older his behavior becomes settled. Like sediment in a rock pool. He's always been dignified, but today his dignity wears a collar of ivory round it. When he thinks back to the stunts he used to pull in the '60s his pulse races with worry, he starts migraining. He's antibody-negative: but he's not sure how. On the one hand he thinks it's due to dumb luck. In another more sober mood he attributes it to having limited his sex life to the young. He frowns, and his face turns cold as his wife's. His affair with Travis Santucci satisfies most of his needs, which have stratified with time.

He's got other needs, too, but Heaven can wait. When I came into his life he was in the midst of a professional crisis. Therapy wasn't working out. He took out his car and picked up hitchhikers to slake some of his painful identity, like a snake shedding its skin. When I reached fourteen, like gray Gibraltar rock, Carey lounged before me in a hotel room, furnished flats on the railroad's edge. He put his hand into my lap and found my cock underneath a twist of white fabric, turned me out. As I grew older he couldn't love me, composed as he was out of what chemical fluids. So *finis*. He was, he realizes, crazy then. At any time I could have blown the whistle on him and his whole life would've come tumbling down like Grenada investiture. Yet my thin little lips and high nipples intrigued him for a while; for six or seven years my love of toys, my fondness for him lulled him to a dreamy sleep, for which I was to blame. Who, me? He drinks more now than he used to, but isn't that natural? I used to walk through my days with the imprint of his kiss burning my lips.

Like chapstick—in reverse—

Travis doesn't know why there's so much fuss made about *safe sex*, but he goes along with it anyway, and sometimes when Carey says, "In the old days we could do anything *and we did*," Travis feels the pull of nostalgia for a time that was never his own, a tooth missing in another's head. He and Carey have a '90s kind of relationship, and that means missing out on large chunks of one another's life, but that's cool because it gives them each so much space.

His ad read simply. "Dad: I've been bad." He received 75 replies and, stumped by their sheer number, chose to answer Carey's only because he was the oldest to have replied to him. He remembers thinking this is as good a way as any to get someone mature and really well-off, because if you haven't made your mint by age fifty, there's not much sense trying to support a young artist is there.

His real name is Tim, but, dissatisfied with "Tim," he took the name "Travis" from a jeans commercial that had been big when he was 10 or 11.

A woman's voice calls out on the soundtrack, "Travis, you're years too late!" A Packard pulls up to a solitary gas pump in the middle of the American desert. In the background stands the Benedict house from George Stevens' film of *Giant*. Out the Packard window her expensive boots gleam in the sun. Her lazy legs are tightly encased in the brand of jeans the TV ad is selling. All this is in the past and to view the ad today you'd have to ring up the Broadcasting Museum on East 57th and ask them for a special viewing.

Travis has been very bad and, alone in a room, opens the closet door and finds an adequate knock-off of one of Christian Lacroix's pouffe cocktail dresses. Black bodice, red and pink ruffled skirt. This he pulls down over his naked body. Its cinched waist sits askew, like a broken toilet seat, on his jutting hipbones and his impertinent buttocks. In the next room Carey waits for him, idling away the hours with a big scotch and soda and a copy of *Forbes* magazine.

Travis and his friends from art school are staging a psycho-drama, *Needles and Pins*, based on the marital woes of Cher and Gregg Allman. Travis plays their son, Elijah Blue, and doubles in the part of a hospital nurse. When the lights go down Travis feels like a completely different, much more insouciant person, and often makes up his lines as the performance goes on, which is fine with most of the cast except for the bitch who plays Cher. One night after the show the Cher guy goes berserk and hits Travis in the temple with a heavy glass bottle that's supposed to represent "Uninhibited" perfume. There's blood all over the sidewalk and all over the collar of the nurse's uniform.

Dennis writes that "AIDS ruined death." It hasn't done much for memory, either. One night *Needles and Pins* raises its ticket price to $50.00 as a benefit for the NAMES Project. The actors don't know whether or not to expect a big crowd. Maybe no one will show up at all. This uncertainty persists until the curtain parts in the middle. Then it's discovered that only four patrons sit in the audience. But the show must go on and, indeed, each actor gives the performance of his life. The four men in the audience turn out to be Cher's attorneys.

The naughtier Travis is, the more Carey seems to appreciate him, and yet Anita treats him shabbily, as though she weren't part of a *menage à trois* she has only to put the kibosh on to end. It's she who lets him in, then she who has a key made at Geletti's Hardware, then she who fixes him endless *rancho nuevos* and breakfast in bed. Travis isn't having a very good day, out on the street the weather's oppressive and some bum dies on the subway ride over, and so Travis decides to throw Carey's little Sony Trinitron out the airwell window, and the shit hits the fan then as far as *she's* concerned. Turns out she likes Oprah at three and her Donahue at four, and nix on that.

Travis reaches behind him and pulls up the layers of petticoated cotton as he walks down the carpet runner through the hall that leads to Carey's den. The air conditioning's on and the sweat cools on his wet balls, turns to steam I guess, evaporates into the fabric. His cock sticks out about a mile, I mean it looks like the Avenue of the Americas poking up. He's coming to a place he knows so well he could be blind and still reach it. His legs are bare, and his feet are wedged into '70s platform shoes, six inches high, that tilt his pelvis out and give him a little pot belly it looks like, kind of. An opera purse dangles from his elbow, a blue satin shell, there's nothing in it but a phony driver's license, a glass bead of coke and a can of mace, almost empty.

Then before he knocks he smooths down the dress, then sighs to the ceiling. Knock knock. *I remember*: he made me drink coffee, said I'd shoot up faster, at the wet shot hot zone age of fourteen. Something floated, unmixed, atop the coffee: only Cremora or some kind of bachelors' sex dust? "Spanish fly" went buzzing in my head; *this is so grown up*. Lying like Hell I shook my head. I walked around a potted palm on the floor that looked like a bed that he watered with coffee.

With some of the guys, Travis goes to the Mapplethorpe show at the Whitney. Afterwards he acts out some of its startling photos for Carey.

"Now I'm not all black and white," he warns ahead of time, "so you'll be getting some color values the pictures don't have."

Carey's body has thickened over the years, but he can still fit into the suits he wore at both his weddings. There's one small strip of flesh that seems to have knotted above his hips, that no amount of diet or exercise will remove. It spoils, a little, his look in a Speedo, but he's still a well-built man. The worst thing that's happened to him is that one day while shaving, he noticed a hair growing in the delicate outer ridges and lobes of his ears. *This happens to old people*, he thought. The shaving brush, wet with white foam, fell from his hand and landed in the basin with a click and a slither. Fright. *Not to me, not to me.*

He stood before the mirror and flexed muscles in his arms and chest, folding his fists above his head like Mickey Mouse ears. A dab of shaving cream gleamed under one nipple. His bath towel slid to the floor in a red ribbon around his bare feet. The apartment was very quiet.

After an unsuccessful bout with tweezers, Carey confides in his barber downtown. The barber stares at his left ear with sad eyes. "You should have told me, Mr. Denham, let me know much sooner. We've been clipping ear hair for years, it's one of our specialties, you might say. The painless way."

The barber shop is crowded, but subdued. On every square of lilac enamel wall tile a hook holds an electrical instrument. "Painless?" Carey repeats.

"Guaranteed, or your money back," says the barber. "It's the thing today. No one wants to walk around looking old. Bad for business. Old or dishevelled, and ear hair brings out the worst of both. The way other men look at you, businessmen, relatives, friends."

"Don't they look at the shoes first any more?"

"Fraid not, Mr. D. Today it's the ears, ears all the way. Haven't you read Mr. Trump's best-seller *The Art of the Deal?*"

Guiltily Carey remembers the Trump book that's sat untouched for a month on his nightstand under an ashtray. He shakes his head. No.

"Well, read it, please, Mr. Denham, read it for your own sake. Now there's a man who always makes a nice impression; and you know why?"

"I'm beginning to get the picture. Smooth inner ears."

"Now on some men, a little ear hair looks good. Some— European men. And in Tokyo, I understand, it's a sign of virility."

"But I'm not European, am I?" Carey supplies. The colorful pages of *Playboy* sigh in his lap, a statuesque former rock star, 42, proves she's still got what it takes in black satin lingerie. Reminds him of Brooklyn Harbor. A dark foreign freighter stirs slightly, waves ripple from its hull in silky black undulations. The woman rises to her knees and the black satin puffs out around her. She's wrapped in a cloud of perfume. Reminds him of sex, or the way "sex" comes at you in big bold letters when you're salivating for it. "And no way I'm Japanese."

"No, you're the all-American type, I'd say," the barber says regretfully, applying a swatch of linen, dipped in astringent, to the tiny cuts inside Carey's right ear. "Mom, apple pie, the flag."

I used to lick inside that ear, my tongue darting and plunging, down to the lobe, where I'd hang like a ruby from an Ethiop's ear. "Hang there like fruit, my soul, till the tree die."

I'd move my tongue to say the words of love and passion he lived upon.

"Daddy," I'd tell him. Just that one word at first, then a string of imperatives long as the night. On Sunday morning the sun rises above the harbor, gulls swoop, the air is filled with pink and red gleams. The fog lifts from the blue-green water, and motley patterns of oil and refuse glitter in the dawn's cold. He snores with his mouth and nose pressed into the pillow. *Repression* I think wisely, nodding to myself, pleased with myself and my bedroom psychoanalysis. His ear lies open, open and clear. Reminds me of a shell you'd find on the sands. "Anemone," I say to myself. That was his paradigm: one side turned to deep sleep, the other to the open air and to delight. A divided nature.

"Like father, like son," I'd tell him, when we'd match erections under a restaurant table at lunch. A bottle of wine stood in straw between us. I'd chew on some straw with my teeth and tongue prominent, mimicking fellatio.

"Don't," he said sharply. "What if someone sees?"

Afterwards we went to the Whitney to the Mapplethorpe show. When you walked in a large self-portrait greeted you, the artist almost naked, grinning over his shoulder at you, cheerful, a greasy, medium-sized bullwhip dangling at his feet, its handle prodded sideways up his ass. Carey, bewildered, averted his eyes. There was too much cheer in his picture, too great a lack of prophecy. "You can take the boy out of Wilkes-Barre," he said, exaggerating his naivete. "But you can't take the Wilkes-Barre out of the boy."

When I turned fourteen there he was, a ditch so wide, so filled with white sluggish life, I said, "Hope I pass out before I puke," to someone unseen.

When we took the train to double back to Long Island, the conductor stepped on Carey's shoe, and Carey took him to task. "There's a small rip in my shoe," he said firmly. "You'll be hearing from me with my shoemaker's bill." I was so embarrassed. "Give me your badge number, sir."

"We don't have badge numbers, we're conductors."

"What kind of organization is this anyhow?"

"Carey, would you cool it," I hissed. "You're on the LIRR, not at FBI headquarters." I was so embarrassed. I wanted to steal away from him, away from the small, encloistered void he provided.

It was exactly as though he were my real father, and everything one dislikes about one's father, at that age, and in that relation of power and death.

Travis speaks softly yet firmly. "Undo me."

With a shaky hand, Carey touches the top button of the black dress, a button covered in black velvet, and wedges it out of the imprisoning buttonhole. The hairs on the nape of Travis' head stand on end.

"Undo me," Travis repeats. I take his speech as an invite to a sexual deconstruction. What our bodies do, not for love or pleasure, but towards a more highly qualified social structure. One by one, each plump button becomes disengaged and the frock falls apart on either side of Travis's spine. He's "undone" now, but his voice, little louder than a breath, hardly betrays it. Around his waist a sash of black silk baffles the boss. There isn't a button there; after some fumbling he finds the tiny pair of hooks. Travis steps out of the dress with grace; it slinks to the floor like an angry rebuked pet.

From his asshole a phallic weapon protrudes, greased with some white oily wax. Is he man or woman, boy or girl, animal or neutral calendar? His dates are written across his hips, round the reddened fixture of his anus. He moves, whip handle moves with him. One step falters, and the handle bobs too, bobbing the whip's long tail in an unpredictable flurry that catches a leg of the big bed.

Leaves a mark there. Nice apartment. It's late afternoon. From a train going off somewhere out of this century out towards smoky New Jersey, they hear whistles and vamps. Travis swings his hips like a burlesque stripper, but Carey doesn't notice. He's not looking anywhere but downward, and after a moment his eyes close. A segment of the bullwhip—coarse and veiny—he clamps between his jaws. He presses black velvet to his groin, humping it on his knees.

Whistles from stockyards and the weasely cry of cows, getting their insides sucked out near his house. Kind of a Chicago story out there.

"Pull the curtains," Travis breathes.

Anita's red geraniums are wilting in the windowbox.

"Pull the curtains."

3.

And half a world away, George Grey is HIV-negative too. His philosophy: if you don't think there's AIDS, you won't get AIDS. Simple as that! As evening falls, the silver waters of Pearl Harbor darken. Above his head George hears the whispering of the brackish-colored palm leaves as he stands on his lanai. Each of those leaves as long as his body, at its longest point.

Karoll comes to a halt behind him, slips her arm through his. He feels the point of her chin wedge into his shoulder.

"What're you thinking, George?"

"Nothing much, just lucky I guess."

"I saw Tom Selleck today."

"Oh please, Tom Selleck's common as pig-tracks round here. Tell me something new, etonnez-moi, Karoll!"

"What's with the French!" she yells in his ear. She's tickled to be here. "You know I don't know French worth a damn."

"Just lucky I guess." Down in the harbor the big black freighter stirs slightly, waves ripple from its hull in silky black undulations. Reminds him of the "black hole" theory, in a vague way, nothing you could really shout about. Reminds him of sex, too, or the way "sex" comes at you in big bold letters when you're primed for it.

Karoll and George enjoy the lifestyle they've always wanted, from the moment they put their heads together. A tropical home, a pitcher filled with Mai Tai, a lucrative business giving guided tours of the sin spots of Hawaii to American and Japanese tourists, both straight and gay. A cold volcano hangs serenely in the background, miles away from their condo.

Karoll plucks again at George's sleeve. She wants to exit the terrace, stage left, to where the color TV is playing her favorite show, *Golden Girls*. About 18 months before, she had the great honor to meet Bea Arthur and Betty White when they came to Pearl Harbor to promote *Golden Girls* and to do some charity work for animals. They're both great women. Good sports too. At the Hilton they willingly posed for photos as Karoll stood between them, arms linked and orchids everywhere. An anonymous hotel employee held Timmy up so he could be in the picture too—Timmy, Karoll's ancient cocker spaniel. When guests come to visit George and Karoll, the first thing they see is the photo, it stands on top of the TV like an antenna of good will and intergenerational sympathy. The one Karoll really wants to meet is Estelle Getty, who plays Bea Arthur's mother on the show. Getty is actually the youngest of all the Golden Girls. "Did you know that?"

"*She's* the *youngest*?" Incredulous.

"Marvellous makeup, isn't it?"

"My God, yes, you'd think she was eighty!" George pretends he enjoys *Golden Girls*, and watches it alongside Karoll in bed, but Karoll's not sure how he feels deep down inside. Sometimes she suspects he's just going through the motions, to please her. The Girls may be saying the most uproarious things, or cutting up, outrageous shtick, and George just sits there like a lump, propped up on his elbows, his tan face an empty place, his bright blue eyes somewhere else, absent in a way she knows doesn't relate to the show, to TV, to Hawaii, to the world we all live in.

"You okay?" she whispers. She passes her hand in front of his eyes, and he blinks, and starts back to life again with the suddenness and verve of Frankenstein's monster, after the electric clamp is pressed that gives him the divine spark.

"You're okay, I'm okay," George jokes. "Betty's good tonight," he adds carefully and sincerely.

Reassured, Karoll drifts away again and zeroes in on the set, and on the color photo above it. She remembers the tenderness and awe with which Betty White, regal in a vivid purple print pantsuit, patted Timmy's head and scratched his quivering ears. At that moment she felt beyond privilege; she'd been touched by some of the abundance God wishes for all His creatures, great and small.

I don't know where George is now. He is lost to me, like the wife and kids the amnesiac doesn't remember. They crowd round his bedside in the hospital room, but he's helpless—he turns to the nurse for advice. He knows her kind ruddy face better than the faces of these demanding possessive strangers. She brings him pills and juice; they bring him nothing but rigor, question marks, demands.

Know us.

Love us . . . We're talking *Phil Spector* here . . . I read about this service called "Friend-Find," and wrote to them asking their help tracking George down. I wanted to touch him again. "Friend-Find" wrote me asking for more information. What was his Social Security number, for instance? I had to say I don't know. It would have been so easy to obtain it, if I could have guessed I'd need it one day! At any time, on any day, I could have turned to him and asked him what it was. "One thing I do know is his mother's address," I wrote. "You could write to her and see if she has any news." They did, but she refused to cooperate when she found out who was behind the inquiry. They couldn't even find out if he was dead or alive. Yet this is the same firm which advertises, among its past successes, reunions of POW platoons and adoptive mothers and children!

Believe you me, as we say back in Smithtown, I was mighty let down.

If he reads this book, he may reach for me.

I may hear from him via my publisher, a call may come late at night, his voice on the wire. Wondering. "How did you know I'm still in Hawaii?"

"I didn't—I just guessed."

"You were right about that, but wrong about Karoll. She hates *The Golden Girls*."

Or, "Karoll's dead!"

Oh, gee, I'm really sorry to hear that! I'll say.

"That's all right," he'll say dryly. "We all have our crosses to bear."

I may hear from him, or I may not. They may find a cure for AIDS tomorrow, or they may not. My boss may divest his holdings in corporations that deal with South Africa; or he may not. Maybe Elvis Presley's alive. "We buried her at Graceland," George may say. "We misspelled her name out of ignorance and impatience. And Timmy lies beside her, paws crossed under his snout."

Alone, George spins through the channels, the TV's warm, the night's cool. The green iris of the VCR stares him into submission. Click, rewind.

Kevin leans forward, bare to the waist, and whispers into a man's ear. *Anemone*.

Click. Rewind.

"Kevin leans forward," George says. "Whispers into a man's ear. *My enemy.*"

The sheets onscreen are rumpled, toyed with, stained. Sleeping head buried to the cheek in dreck and come. Carey's ear, open to the New York night. He's been in a dreamy sleep for seven years. My vocabulary did this to me, I attest. Jiggle the vertical, horizon, definition. I can't get it straight. Bang the box. I can't get it straight.

Neither can George. At his feet Timmy shuffles his front paws nervously in sleep, he ruffles the invisible blond hairs along George's tan calves. Poor Timmy, his hair's matted with some moist oil. Heat dog. His tongue lolls from his open mouth, flickering now and again as the image shifts on the TV. Good boy.

On the videotape Kevin looks about seventeen. George squints. It's Kevin's body all right. He's whispering something the audio's fucked up on. "Anemone? My enemy?" George can't make it out. He thinks: Kevin looks hot and bothered about it. Wonder what it is. Timmy shuffles and snorts. Maybe it's one of those things a dog can hear, and people can't.

GEORGE (squinting)

When I taught Kevin to write I knew he'd turn on me, turn my teachings inward, eventually, why not now? We wrote a "book" together, *Bedrooms have Windows*, the story of a tormented soul, its growth and development, fated collapse, head transplant with Susan Hayward. Once we peered ass-deep in ivy through the slatted wooden blinds of a country cottage. Two men and a woman stood naked within, slathering themselves with food by-products. It was two in the morning in our middle-class suburb, Smithtown. Kevin's eyes were bugging right out of his head. I envied him his interest in these people, whose bodies weren't svelte and whose clothes, strewn about the room dotted with lard and oil, showed they shopped at the Mall. We grew up in Smithtown, a suburb of New York, a town so invidious we still speak of it in Miltonic terms. Paradise we're evicted from. Smithtown, Long Island, kind of an MGM Norman Rockwell hometown, a place so boring they gave it a boring name . . .

BACHELORS GET LONELY

CHAIN OF FOOLS

Again I approach the Church, St. Joseph's at Howard and Tenth, south of Market in San Francisco. It's a disconcerting structure, in late Mission style, but capped with two gold domed towers out of some Russian Orthodox dream. I'm following two uniformed cops, in the late afternoon this October, we're followed by the sun as we mount the steps to the big brass doors and enter into the darkness of the nave. I see the pastor, Filipino, short and shambling, approach us from the altar, where two nuns remain, arranging fall flowers around the vestibule. I fall back while the cops detain the priest. They're passing him a sheaf of legal papers regarding the closing of the church, which has been damaged beyond repair by the earthquake of '89. Anger crosses the priest's handsome face, then he shakes the hands of the two policemen; all shrug as if to say, *shit happens.* I glance up at the enormous crucifix where the image of Christ is sprawled from the ugly nails. His slender body, a rag floating over his dick. His face, white in the darkened upper reaches of the Church. His eyes closed, yet bulging with pain. Again I bend my knee and bow, the body's habitual response. Across my face and upper torso I trace the sign of the cross, the marks of this disputed passage. I'm dreaming again—again the dreaming self asserts its mastery of all of time, all of space.

Late in the '60s Mom and Dad enrolled me in a high school for boys, staffed by Franciscans. I was a scrawny, petulant kid with an exhibitionist streak that must have screamed trouble in every decibel known to God or man. My parents had tried to bring me up Catholic, but as I see myself today, I was really a pagan, with no God but experience, and no altar but my own confusing body. In a shadowy antebellum building high on a hill above us, the monks rang bells, said office, ate meals in the refectory, drank cases of beer. In the halls of St. A—, bustling with boys, I felt like the narrator in Ed White's *Forgetting Elena*, marooned in a society I could hardly understand except by dumb imitation. In every room a crucifix transfixed me with shame: I felt deeply compromised by my own falsity. My self was a lie, a sham, next to the essentialism of Christ, He who managed to maintain not only a human life but a divine one too. He *was* God, the Second Person of the Trinity.

But I talked a good game, as any bright student can, and did my best to get out of my schoolwork, so I'd have more time to develop my homosexuality. I spent a year in French class doing independent study, reading *Gone with the Wind* in French, while the other students around me mumbled "*Je ne parle pas*" to an implacable friar. Presently I was able to convince the history teacher that reading *Gone with the Wind* in French should satisfy his requirements too. Then I could go home and confront my appalled parents by saying, "This is something I have to read for school."

Later on, when I was a senior and drunk all the time, a friend and I invented an opera, a collaboration between Flaubert and Debussy, set in outer space and ancient Rome, that we called *Fenestella*. George Grey and I flogged this opera through French class, music class, World Literature, etc. We recounted its storyline, acted out its parts, noted the influence of *Fenestella* on Stravinsky, Gide, etc, you name it. Our teachers slowly tired of

Fenestella, but we never did. The heroine was an immortal bird—
a kind of pigeon—sent by St. Valentine out into Jupiter to
conquer space in the name of love—on the way to Jupiter she
sings the immortal "Clair de Lune." I must have thought I too
was some kind of immortal bird, like Fenestella, like Shelley's
skylark. None of our teachers pointed out the unlikelihood of
Flaubert (d. 1880) and Debussy (b. 1862) collaborating on anything elaborate. We had them quarrelling, reuniting, duelling,
taking bows at La Scala, arguing about everything from *le mot
juste* to the *Cathedrale engloutie*. Nobody said a word, just gave us
A's, praised us to the skies.

I had no respect for most of these dopes. In later life I was to
pay the piper by dallying with several teens who had no respect
for me. Nothing's worse than that upturned, scornful face, that
throws off youth's arrogance like laser rays. When I was 16 I had
the world by the tail. But in another light the world had already
made me what I was, a blind struggling creature like a mole,
nosing through dirt to find its light and food.

In religion class Brother Padraic had us bring in pop records
which we would play, then analyze like poetry. It was a conceit of
the era, that rock was a kind of poetry and a way to reach kids.
Other boys, I remember, brought in "poetic" records like "All
Along the Watchtower," "At the Zoo," "Chimes of Freedom."
The more daring played drug songs—"Sister Ray," "Eight Miles
High," "Sunshine Superman," or the vaguely scandalous—"Let's
Spend the Night Together." When it was my turn I brandished
my favorite original cast album—*My Fair Lady*—and played
"Wouldn't It be Loverly." Now, that's poetry, I would say expan-
sively, mincing from one black tile to a red tile, then sideways to
a white tile, arms stretched out appealingly. After the bell rang a
tall man dressed in black stepped out of the shadows between
lockers and said, "Have you considered psychological coun-
selling?" I should have been mortified, but I shook my head like

a friendly pup and, with purposeful tread, followed him to his office. Then the office got too small for his needs and he drove me to what I soon came to think of as *our place*, down by the river, down by the weeds and waterbirds.

Getting in and out of a VW bug in those long black robes must have been a bitch. Funny I didn't think of that till later. It happened in front of my eyes but I didn't really notice. I was too—oh, what's the word—ensorcelled. He—Brother Jim— wasn't exactly good-looking, but he had something that made up for any defect: he'd taken that precious vow of celibacy, though not, he confided, with his dick. First I felt for it through the robes, then found a deep slit pocket I was afraid to slip my hand into. Then he laughed and lifted the robe over his legs and over most of the steering wheel. And down by the gas pedal and the clutch he deposited these awful Bermuda shorts and evocative sandals. And his underwear. His black robe made a vast tent, then, dark in the day, a tent I wanted to wrap myself up in and hide in forever, with only his two bent legs and his shadowy sex for company. So I sucked him and sucked him, Brother Jim.

"Why don't you turn around?" he asked. "Pull those pants all the way down, I like to see beautiful bodies." He made my knees wobble as he licked behind them. Wobble, like I couldn't stand up. On the wind, the scents of sand cherry and silverweed, the brackish river. The squawk of a gull. Scents that burned as they moved across my face, like incense. After a while he told me how lonely his life was, that only a few of the other monks were queers, there was no one to talk to. "You can talk to me," I told him, moved. Every semester he and the few other queer monks judged the new students like Paris awarding the golden apple. Some of us had the staggering big-lipped beauty that April's made from; some of us were rejected out-of-hand, and some of us, like me, seemed available. Then they waited till they felt like it, till they felt like trying one of us out.

He made me feel his . . . dilemma, would you call it? Boys, after all, are tricky because they change from week to week. You might fancy a fresh complexion: act right away, for in a month that spotless face will have grown spotted, or bearded, or dull. You might reject me because I have no basket, well, too bad, because by Christmas I'll be sporting these new genitals Santa brought me, big, bad and boisterous. This was Jim's dilemma—when you're waiting for a perfect boy life's tough. So they traded us, more or less. Always hoping to trade up, I guess. "Don't trade me," I pleaded with him. "Oh never," he said, tracing the nape of my neck absently, while on the other side of the windshield darkness fell on a grove filled with oaks and wild hawthorn. "Never, never, never."

I wanted to know their names—who was queer, which of them—I *had* to know. He wouldn't say. *I* named names. How about the flamboyant arts teacher who insisted on us wearing tights, even when playing Arthur Miller? No. None of the effeminate monks, he told me, were gay. "They just play at it," he sneered. How about the gruff math teacher, who had been the protegé of Alan Turing and John von Neumann? If you answered wrong in class he'd summon you to his desk, bend you over his knee, and spank you. If you were especially dense you'd have to go to his disordered room in the evening and he'd penetrate you with an oily finger, sometimes two. "No," said Brother Jim, my new boyfriend. "Don't be absurd. None of those fellows are fags. You'd never guess unless I tell you." I told him I didn't really want to know, a lie, I told him I'd never done this with a man, a lie, I told him I would never tell another about the love that passed between us, a lie. And all these lies I paid for when June began and Jim got himself transferred to Virginia. But then another teacher stopped me in the hall. "Jim told me about your problem," he said, his glasses frosty, opaque. This was Brother Anselm. "He says you feel itchy round the groin area."

He's the one who took me to see *The Fantasticks* in Greenwich Village and bought me the record, "Try to Remember." If you're reading this, Anselm, try to remember that time in September when life was long and days were fucking mellow. As for you, Brother Jim, whatever happened to "never?" You said you'd "never" trade me, but when I turned 17 I was yesterday's papers. Thus I came to hate aging, to the point that even today I still pride myself on my "young attitude." Pathetic. I remember that our most famous alumnus was Billy Hayes, whose story was later made into a sensational film called *Midnight Express*. At that time he was mired in a Turkish prison for drug smuggling. We students had to raise funds for his legal defense, or for extra-legal terrorist acts designed to break him out. Students from *other* schools went door-to-door in elegant neighborhoods, selling chocolate bars to send their track teams to big meets, but we had to go around with jingling cans, asking for money for "The Billy Hayes Fund," and you know something, people gave! They didn't even want to know what it was, good thing too. Later when the film came out its vampy homoerotics gave me a chill. Later still, its leading man, Brad Davis, played *Querelle* in Fassbinder's film of the Genet novel. And even later still Davis died of AIDS and I conflated all these men into one unruly figure with a queer complaint against God.

Standing on the desert's edge, a man at the horizon, shaking a fist against an implacable empty sky.

At first I resented Jim and Anselm and the rest, their careless handling of this precious package, me. But after awhile I grew fond of them, even as they passed me around like a plate of canapes at a cocktail party. Anybody would have, especially a young person like myself who thought he was "different." I watch the E Channel and see all these parents of boys, parents who are suing Michael Jackson, and I want to tell them, your boys are saying two things, one out of each side of their mouth, or maybe three things, one of them being, "Let me go back to Neverland Ranch where at least I was *appreciated*."

Unlike Michael Jackson, the religious staff of St. A— wore ropes around their waists to remind themselves, and us, of the constant poverty of St. Francis of Assisi. One of them quoted St. Therese to me, to illustrate his humility: "I am the zero which, by itself, is of no value but put after a unit becomes useful." I pulled the rope from around his waist, teasing him. I took one home as a souvenir. These fat long ropes, wheaten color, thick as my penis and almost as sinuous. I believed in those ropes. I said to myself, why don't *you* become a monk, think of all the side benefits? I walked down to the grove of trees by the river's edge one April afternoon, thinking these grand thoughts of joining the seminary. Beneath my feet small pink flowers, a carpet of wood sorrel or wild hepatica, leading down to a marshy space tall with field horsetail, up to my waist. "God," I called out, "give me a sign I'm doing the right thing." I felt guilty that I had sinned in a car, guilty and stained, like a slide in a crime lab. I waited for His sign, but zilch. Above me a pair of laughing gulls, orange beaks, black heads, disappeared into the sun. *Is that my sign?* thought I, crestfallen. *How oblique.* But right around that time I began to realize that there was something stronger than a Franciscan brother.

Marijuana leads to heroin, they used to say. I don't know about that, but after awhile friars just don't cut it, you want something stronger, something that'll really *take you there*. You want a priest. Ever see *The Thorn Birds*, the way Rachel Ward longs for Richard Chamberlain? Or Preminger's *The Cardinal*, with Romy Schneider yearning for some other gay guy, it's a thrill to think, y'know, with a little luck, this man licking my cock could turn out to be the Prince of the Whole Church, the Supreme Pontiff, in ten or fifteen years and right now, you can almost see his soul shining right through his thinning blond hair, already he's godly—Again the dreaming self rises above the squalid air of the black back room, the hush of the confessional, breaking free into a world of pleasure and Eros and hope, all I continue to pray for and more. Out in the snowy East of Long Island I bent over Frank O'Hara's grave and traced his words with my tongue, the words carved into his stone there: "Grace to be born and to live as variously as possible." Another lapsed Catholic trying to align the divine with the human.

And because I was so willful, I made spoiling priests a kind of game, like Sadie Thompson does in *Rain*. Under those robes of black, I would think, are the white limbs of strong men. I trailed one priest, Fr. Carney, from assignment to assignment. I was his youth liaison—encouraged to inform on my peers' drug habits, I had first to increase my own. You have to be a little hard, a little speedy, to become what we then called a "narc." He also got me to bring along other youths to retreats staged on isolated Long Island mother houses. When I graduated from St. A— I continued to traipse after Fr. Carney, like Marlene Dietrich slinging her heels over her shoulder to brave the desert at the end of *Morocco*, all for Gary Cooper's ass. "You don't have to call me Father Carney," he would say to me. "Call me Paul." I felt like king of the hill, top of the heap. Oh, Paul, I would say, why am I being treated so well? "Because you are who you are," he told me. "You are someone special. You are Kevin Killian."

I grew more and more spoiled, and he must have enjoyed my ripeness, up to a point; and then he left me, in this valley of tears. I remember standing in his room watching the cold green spectacle of Long Island Sound, leaves of yellow acacia tapping into the window, with this pair of black gym shorts pulled down just under my buttocks, and thinking to myself, I'll bring him back to me with my hot skin and my healthy boy type sweat. And him, Paul, slouched on his king-size bed, turned away from me, bored, extinguished, his breviary pulled next to him like a teddy bear. "There's a list on my desk," he said. "Some of them may be calling you." So when I pulled up my pants I'd have this list to turn to, the names of other priests, *next!*—Like one of those chain letters, filled with the names of strangers, to whom you have to send five dollars each or Mother will go blind. "You're trading me too," I said, before the door hit me on the ass. Thump.

So the next guy called me, Father some Polish name, and he turned out to be—*really into the Rosary.* Around this time I got to thinking that despite what they told me, I was not someone special after all.

These men were connoisseurs all right. They pulled out my cork and took turns sniffing it. Meanwhile the *sommelier* stood by, a smile in his eyes, attentive, alert. Disillusioned, dejected, I began to read the whims of these men not as isolated quirks, but as signs of a larger system, one in which pleasure, desire endlessly fulfilled, *jouissance*, are given more value. Within the Church's apparently ascetic structure, the pursuit of pleasure has been more or less internalized. By and large, the pursuit (of violence, danger, beauty) *is* the structure. I had to hand it to them! Under their black robes those long legs were born to *can-can*. Pleasure, in a suburbia that understood only growth and money. Aretha Franklin said it best, singing on the radio while I moped from man to man. *"Chain-chain-chain,"* she chanted. *"Chain of fools."*

I met Dorothy Day in a private home in Brooklyn, when Father Paul took me to meet her. She was seventy then, and had been a legend for forty years, both in and out of the Church, for her activism, her sanctity, her saltiness. I had read all about her in *Time* magazine. She sat on a huge sofa almost dwarfed by these big Mario Buatta-style throw pillows, gold and pink and red. Her hands were folded neatly in her lap, as though she were groggy. The way to get closer to Christ, she asserted, is through work. Father Paul argued mildly, what about the Golden Rule? Isn't love the answer? No, she responded sharply,—work, not love. Last night on TV I watched *The Trouble with Angels*, in which mischievous

Hayley Mills raises holy hell at a Long Island girls' school, till she meets her match in imperious, suave Mother Superior Rosalind Russell. At the denouement she tells her plain girlfriend that she won't be going to Bryn Mawr or even back to England. She's decided to "stay on," become a nun, clip her own wings. I remember again wavering on the brink, of becoming a priest, saying to myself, why don't you do the—*Hayley Mills thing?* Saying it to myself from the back row of this cobwebbed movie house in a poky town on the North Shore of Long Island, fingering the beer between my legs, all alone in the dark.

Now I'm all grown, Dorothy Day is dead, and when I open *Time* magazine I read about altar boys and seminarians suing priests. One quarter of all pedophile priests, they say, live in New Mexico. I have no interest in pursuing my "case" in a tribunal, but I'd like to view such a trial—maybe on Court TV? Or sit in the public gallery, next to John Waters, while my teachers take the stand and confess under pressure or Prozac. I'd get out a little sketchpad and charcoal and draw their faces, older now, confused and guilty and perhaps a little crazy. Then their accusers would come to the stand, confused, guilty, crazy, and I could draw in my own eyes into their various faces, into the faces of my pals and brothers.

Oh how I envied them their privilege, their unflappable ease, the queers of the church. If they were as lonely as they claimed, weren't there enough of them? If their love lives were dangerous, surely they would always be protected by the hierarchy that enfolded them. I remember one monk who had been sent away years before to a special retreat in Taos and he said, *I didn't want to have to come back and see any boys. But then I wanted to come back, it must have been to meet you, Kevin.* And I pictured this empty desert sky with nothing in it but one of Georgia O'Keeffe's cow skulls staring at me through time. My face broke into a smile and I said, "That is so sweet."

I broke with the Church over its policies on abortion, women's rights, gay rights, just like you did. Perhaps its hypocrisy angered you, but that's just human nature, no? What scared me was its monolithic structure. It's too big either to fight or hide within, like the disconcerting house of the Addams Family. I tried to talk to It, but It just sat there, a big unresponsive sack of white sugar. So good-bye. And yet I suppose I'm a far better Catholic now than then. I dream of this god who took on the clothes of man and then stepped forward to strip them off at the moment of humiliation. This renunciation for a greater good remains with me an ideal of society and heaven. I try to get closer to Christ through work. I tried love for a long time but it only lengthened the distance between Him and me.

So I try to call the number of St. A— to see where the 20th high school reunion will be. So that's when I find out the school's now defunct, for the usual reasons: indifference, inflation, acedia. I continue to see the Church as the house of Eros, a place of pleasure and fun, and I continue to regard men in religious costume as possible sex partners, yearning to break free. Such was my training, my ritual life. I can't shake it off, I'm not a snake who can shed its skin. Every time I pass a crucifix I wonder, what if it had been me up there instead, could I have said, *Father, forgive them, for they know not what they do?* I don't think I'm so special, not any more. At the church here in San Francisco, I bow down and make the sign of the cross, the logo of the Church, an imprint deep within forces me to replicate this logo. Up, down, left, right, the hand that seeks, then pulls away frustrated. The hand tightens, becomes a fist, the fist is raised to the sky, on the desert's edge, angry and queer. Inside the Church burns incense, tricky and deep-penetrating, strong, perdurable, like the smells of sand cherry, silverweed, trillium.

HOT LIGHTS

for Clifford Hengst

For long stretches of time every day I kept my body inside my clothes, but sometimes it broke out and made a fool out of "me," the me I wanted to represent to the outside world. Hungry for heat and light, my body rolled itself out of hiding at the snap of a klieg light, and this scared me. It certainly ruined my chances for ever running for public office, and I suppose limited my options in other ways. For everything one's body does limits or directs the rest of one's future. I met Jig Johnson in the early seventies, when I was a college student, high as a kite but perpetually short on cash. Drugs were cheap then, so was liquor, but since I had only a job as a grocery clerk I was always on the make, trying to stay alive in New York. Four times a week I would sell my blood, traipsing from bank to blood bank all over midtown with a sprightly gait that tires me now just to think of it. A pal at school told me, sotto voce, of a man who paid students large sums for acting in porn loops. He said these loops, in primitive color, badly lit, could be seen in various raucous Times Square peep shows, where weirdos dropped a quarter in a slot and a lead shield shot up into the wall, unveiling a twist of naked limbs and cocks. At some random time, say, five minutes, the shield descended again implacably.

"Uh . . ." "Duh . . ." I weighed the pros and cons in my head like the figure of Libra on *Perry Mason*. Trying to figure out what would be right for me, but not thinking very clearly. I was naive to the nth degree. First of all, thanks to a steady diet of so-called "soft" porn, I didn't imagine that "acting" in porn would entail having sex in front of a camera. I had never actually seen a hard porn film. I had the suspicion that the actors might take off their clothes, might kiss, might pretend to have a kind of sex. Cynically I thought everything else was faked, as in Hollywood films. "Special effects." I remember, around that time, reading current discussions of gay representation in the media. I was taking "creative writing" at school, so I felt personally involved with the debate, and felt obliged to make all my gay characters positive images. Oh, amid what fog of delusion I walked Manhattan, straining my brains to think of ways to make everyone lovable . . . How would my appearance in a porn film affect the representation of my tribe? I couldn't work it out. When I called Jig Johnson from a public phone in the lobby of school, the line was busy so I went to my French class. After 90 minutes of Rimbaud and Verlaine I tried the number again. Ring. Ring. "Hello?" That's when I started to panic. Luckily Johnson was businesslike and really together, as if to compensate for the stupid qualms of the guys who were probably always calling him up to feed their habits. He asked me if I was ready to play with the big boys. "Sure." He asked if I was free that evening for my audition. There was a bottle of Southern Comfort in my pocket. Secretively I downed some, then sifted my little pile of thoughts like Brian Wilson playing in that sandbox. "What time?" I said, nodding out.

In his apartment he held my cock in his hands and watched it swell up, like one of those time-lapse photography miracles on public TV. I stared down too, feeling the simultaneous pride and shame of an unbidden erection. Presently, when I was hard as a bone, Johnson slapped my cock, told me to get down on my hands and knees on the floor. "Head on the side of the bed," he called out, from the other room, the room where my clothes were, I hoped. On the pinstriped gamy mattress, stained with a dozen men's come, I lay my head flat, praying I'd make it through my audition.

He dug a flash camera out of the hamper and dangled it close to my nose. God knows what I looked like, what distorted expression was frozen on my dumb face. Then the flash exploded and the chemical smell of the early Polaroid film filled the squalid room. As I remained there, stiff and blinking, he moved behind me to crouch down between my legs. I felt him trying to spread my knees, so I helped, trying to oblige. I don't know, did I do the right thing? I felt a wet hand slither down my butt, down its crack, and I wondered if he was going to screw me. I kept thinking, *I'm playing with the big boys now.*

But he told me he just wanted a picture of my asshole.

And there I was thinking, *what, no sex?* I remember being assaulted by my own thoughts and my feelings of unworthiness, while the Polaroid started to whirl. Presently he threw down two pictures in front of my face: grainy shots, in lurid color, of my demented face, and my tight little red hole, like a bullet hole in the middle of what seemed an absurdly overstated butt.

"You'll be perfect," he said, and I wondered what perfection meant, if such banal evidences gave me so much pause. "You can dress now," he said, in a gentler tone. I covered my crotch with my hands as I walked out of the room. Like a little boy surprised. Suddenly I realized that porn acting involved actual sex captured on film. It just came to me in a revelation like St. Paul on the way to Damascus—a blinding light. "Far out," I thought, for I was always ready to have sex with other guys, but at the same time the thought of film's perpetuity unnerved me. It's one thing to reflect that, no matter how much of a mess she became, we can always think of Judy Garland as sweet sixteen singing in the cornfield; it was another to consider that, in a certain sense, I would always be a nineteen-year-old nitwit with a cock up my ass and a pot-induced glaze in my eyes. I found my clothes, undisturbed, and jammed them on willy-nilly. Johnson produced a bent card, an address scribbled on the back. He tied my necktie for me, absently, helped me tuck in my shirt. He smelled of some lemony scent like the floor wax my mother used at home on her kitchen. He was indescribably dapper, everything I thought of when I thought of the words, "New York." Even the points of his collar were perfect white triangles, stiff, formal, like watercress sandwiches cut in half. I felt like a slob in front of him, could hardly look him in the eye. If I had, oh dear, what pity or contempt would I have seen there? Or was I his mirror, his younger self, a self without a single social grace, no ease? I steeled up my courage and insisted that I wouldn't play an effeminate hysterical hairdresser in his loop, a type gay activists were deploring in the great debate. "You won't be playing any type," he said—probably baffled. "You'll just be yourself." Swell, except I didn't know who that self could be. In looks I resembled a slightly beefed-up version of the Disney actress Hayley Mills—very androgynous, in the spirit of the times—and my voice had hardly broken, so I was still prone to embarrassing squeaks that made me wish the floor would open up. So—so whatever . . .

At the front door another guy waited, in old army fatigues, and as if on a whim, Johnson had me unbutton the guy's pants and suck his cock for a minute. I thought about it for maybe ten seconds, then agreed, for auditioning had made me horny, and until this possibility of contact, I felt utterly unattractive. "Hi," the guy said. "Hmhhrw!" said I. He was my age, nineteen, or just about, with chalky white skin and hair dyed orange as Tropicana. I massaged his muscled thighs as I bobbed up and down in his lap. "That's fine," said Jig Johnson. "You can stop now." My co-star, whose name turned out to be Guy, shot a pitying glance at Johnson. "Where you recruiting now, Jig?" he said shakily. "Port Authority?" Johnson smiled and caressed Guy's orange sideburn in an absent avuncular manner, while Guy yawned and gradually reeled his dick back in his khakis. "There'll be six of you tomorrow," Johnson said. "Meet us at ten o'clock, Kevin."

"Okay," I stuttered, "and thanks, Mr. Johnson."

Guy called after me, "You're too good for this son of a bitch." Right then I kind of fell in love a bit. I set my alarm over and over again, took a dozen showers.

Of the actual filming I recall very little. I mounted the stairs of a dilapidated building a block from Broadway—had the space once been a dance studio? Big quiet room, torn blinds drawn to the floor, a room scattered with the kind of furniture college students leave behind in their dorm rooms after they graduate. There was a steady roar in my head, a dull roar like a subway station, a roar which rose as I met my other co-stars and first saw the camera, a big box with a red light beaming underneath to show we were "on." Had they invented videotape back then? I don't think so. Here film itself was the precious, expensive thing, to be parcelled out in stingy dear bits. I asked for my script, to give me something to read, to give me something to look at instead of all those distracting bodies sliding out of street clothes. I did notice that one guy had a shorter dick than mine, so I butched it up in all our scenes together, I'm no fool, I thought, *one less thing to obsess about . . .*

"Jig, Kevin wants to take a look at the script." First a blank look, then a laugh, then everyone laughed at my naivete. Guy, my co-star, patted my back consolingly, long white pats that brought the sweat dripping down into the crack of my ass. Nice guy. None of us had scripts per se, but there were scratch marks all over the carpet, drawn with chalk I suppose, of where we would stand at various intervals, usually down on one knee.

Mystifying marks like the arbitrary symbols in the Lascaux caves. Johnson told us to make up all our dialogue, since another gang of boys would dub us over in a different situation, probably a different city. Everyone was hard, stiff, unbelievably so, and when the hot lights bore down on my erection it gleamed like topaz, under a light coating of mineral oil, and I said to myself, *I'd* take that home with me! *I'd* pay money to see that! *Who's* attached to this rod of steel?

It—my rod of steel—twitched; and great shadows leapt and fell across Guy's startled, tiny face underneath: he resembled a still from some excellent Maya Deren film like *Meshes in the Afternoon*.

One guy, Charles, long blond hair like Fabio's, touch of a blond goatee at the base of his spine, spent hours bent over the back of a large sofa, getting fucked over and over, and his only line was "Mount me,"—*that* stuck with me. In the morning his asshole was a thin slit, moist, exquisitely puckered, but by late afternoon it looked like a red rubber ball, torn in half, and pierced with blood, sunk deep within. Most of all I remember the heat of the lights, how huge lights two feet wide threatened to blow the fuses of the entire apartment building, and how when their shutters opened a giant click sound rocked the whole room. These white hot domes, trained on one's skin, were like the great eyes of God the poet Jack Spicer wrote of in *Imaginary Elegies*. They see everything, even under the skin where your thoughts are. Your dirty little thoughts. You can take off all your clothes and pretend to be "naked," but you are still Kevin Killian from Smithtown Long Island, with all the petty details that denotes. And yet at the same time the heat made me feel languorous, forgetful, like Maria Montez at the top of some Aztec staircase—dangerous, as though there were nothing beyond the circle of white—no audience, no society, only oneself and the red or purple or black hard-on that floats magically to the level of one's lips. I suppose all actors must feel the same way in some part of being—that the camera's eye represents the eye of God, which at the same time judges all and, threateningly, withholds all judgment till time turns off.

We poured out onto the street at sunset, tired and spent, yakking it up. We would never be stars I thought. No one would ever see this "loop." And I was glad, but sorry too. I asked if anyone knew the name of the picture. No one did. (Charlie said they should call it "Saddlesore.") It didn't really have a name, and as such, I thought, it had no real existence. Just six guys fucking and sucking. We said we would all meet in six months at a Times Square grindhouse for the premiere. Auld acquaintance. I tried visualizing our putative audience and words popped into my head: "a bunch of perverts"—shady men in black trenchcoats, visiting conventioneers touring the louche side of gay New York. Nobodies in fact. "Bye dudes." "Later." "Adios." I took away more money than I'd ever made in my life—a hundred dollars, except Johnson took back like three dollars because he bought us some lunch—beer and Kentucky Fried Chicken. At the same time I read some interview with Lou Reed: asked whether he thought homosexuality was increasing, he replied to the effect that, "It's a fad, but people will tire of it, because eventually you have to suck cock or get your ass fucked." I reflected that I had in one fell swoop ruined my chance to be President, earned $97.00, made a new boyfriend, kind of, solidified my connections with the entertainment world, had some great sex and still I felt utterly ashamed of my own specularity, my need to see and be seen. I came, onto the face and chest of a boy, and my semen seemed to spatter and fry, before my eyes, as though his body were the very skillet of love, such was the wattage of those hot lights.

I remember walking around Columbus Circle looking for things to buy with my money, and feeling disappointed there are no stores there, only pretzel vendors and hot dog carts, so I bought a pretzel and a hot dog, and stood with one foot curled around the ironwork fence at Central Park South, watching the crowd. Wondering if anyone could "tell." My wallet felt fat, expansive, as though my money might grow to enormous size and eat the whole fucking city. I was so filled up with energy I thought I could walk all the way uptown to Guy's neighborhood, then just kind of drop in, rekindle our newfound intimacy, lick that dead-white skin from the nape of his neck to the puncture wounds inside his arm . . .

I slid into a bar on Sixth Avenue, pondering desire, Guy, money and guilt. Had I let down my tribe by playing a part which wasn't actually a part per se, but couldn't therefore be a "positive" one? Wish I could go back and console my younger self, rub his young shoulders, explicate latter-day porn theory to cheer him up. And also get him to cut back on all that drinking! At once the most and least ironic of art forms, pornography undercuts the performative authenticity of penetration with oh, just lashes of mad camp. Its greatest stars, like those of performance art, are the biggest dopes in the world; its most discerning fans those, like my present-day self, who feel ourselves beyond representation for one imaginary reason or another. I stepped into a liquor store on 82nd for a bottle of Seagrams 7, knowing I'd find an answer in its rich musky depths. On the way out I saw a phone booth, and I called Guy, who had scrawled his number backwards up my thigh from the back of my knee to the juncture of my balls. "I know it's not six months yet," I said, "but I was thinking—"

"I can still taste your dick in my mouth," he said—an encouraging sign, or so I thought, but instead he hung up on me, and I felt a blush rise right up to my temples. I thought everyone was staring at the dumb boy on the dumb phone who just got the brushoff. The glare of judgment burning me like lasers through my cool.

I kept thinking, I'm wearing way too many clothes! And I fled. Finally night fell and I looked up at the moon that shone over Morningside Heights, its white soft beam so limpid, full of the poetry of Shakespeare and the Caribbean and George Eliot— the antithesis I suppose of the hot lights I had grown to need. How relaxed, how relieved I now felt, in the white moonlight. Relieved of the chore of playing with the big boys. My clothes seemed to fit again, I became myself. The moon's fleecy lambency corraled my pieces and re-linked us, we joined "hands" as it were and sang and danced in a circle, very Joseph Campbell, "me" regnant, manhood ceremonial. Birth of the hero. I became Kevin Killian. Did I make a mistake?

MAN AND BOY

On a deserted stage, a boy, Kevin Killian, age 20, sits facing the audience wearing a suede fringe jacket *a la* Joe Buck's in the film of *Midnight Cowboy*, except purple, to match the era of the '70s in which he lives. His long hair climbs halfway down the middle of his back, cut into luxuriant brown curls like the film actress Jacqueline Bisset or the rock star Jimmy Page; and his eyes are clear, though he's full of Scotch whiskey. He keeps pouring Scotch from a pint of Johnny Walker into the little hole in a can of Tab. The blue of his eyes, the shocking pink of the Tab can, the brown of the Johnny Walker, and the deep purple of his ridiculous suede jacket, make an unsettling stage picture. Onstage now walks a nondescript middle-aged man, Kevin Killian, 45, dressed in a suit. His hair, how flecked with gray, is cut short. He's twenty pounds heavier and perhaps an inch shorter than the boy he sees before him.

MAN: I woke up one morning with a stitch in my side; then it wouldn't leave me, it became part of my life, so I walked around tilted, compensating for my loss—a phantom pain, I didn't know what I had lost. Later I realized it was my youth. Since then I've continued to age but never as sharply. For all of us, a moment comes, sooner or later, when the feeling hits, when the years crowd too closely together. At some point the vertiginous drop begins.

BOY: It's so strange meeting you. I've been thinking about you my whole life. Would you like a drink?

MAN: How flattering.

BOY: Oh come on, have a drink.

MAN: No thanks. But you go ahead. Have one on me.

BOY: If you weren't "me," you know, I'd be trying to seduce you. For you're exactly the sort of quizzical older guy I'm always trying to make.

MAN: And you are just the sort of fucked-up 20 year old I find most attractive. Grist for my mill. The novelist, you know, must take his inspiration from real life.

BOY: Where did you get those bags under your eyes!

MAN: *You* gave them to me, I guess.

BOY: Big bags—deep luggage. I could smuggle drugs in them.

MAN: Enough already about my eyes.

BOY: I like your asperity, I don't have that. I'm naive, kind of a blank. All I want is to be cool. Like a diamond in a big refrigerator. All the same, I'm crestfallen, and it's you, Kevin. You've settled down, become a bore.

MAN: Maybe that's what happens once a person turns thirty.

BOY: Or forty.

MAN: Exactly! What nobody ever told me about aging is that I'd age both ways, past and future.

BOY: What the hell does that mean? Don't be cryptic.

MAN: I'll try and slow down, though that's not my forte. Okay, you grow older and older—if you're lucky, but that's another story—

BOY: Then tell it another time.

MAN: —And so you try to preserve what little currency you've got; at the same time, you're losing track of things—no longer can identify the bands heavy in rotation on *120 Minutes*. That's one part of it. But at the same time you find yourself with a craving for the things you used to hate: you wind up liking the things your parents used to like. John Wayne movies for example.

BOY: Oh, how I hate John Wayne.

MAN: Schoenberg. Ella Fitzgerald. Perry Mason. Ten years ago I couldn't have carried around these wants in my basket. There wasn't room I suppose. All around me the taste for Henry Mancini and Ferrante & Teicher now blossoms like a sick rose. I feel myself growing older before and after, like the Push-Mi Pull-Yu animal in the Doctor Doolittle stories, or, or, or—

BOY: I think you've had enough caffeine for one evening. Come here and lie your head on my lap and tell me, show me a picture of what you're thinking.

MAN: *[lowering himself and lying down with his head in BOY's lap.]* Or picture a kind of Gumby with a flexible rubber waist so squashed in that his head and feet are heavy with rubber, his stomach a thin membrane like a rope of spit.

BOY: Uh-hunh. Say, are you seeing anybody?

MAN: That's what aging feels like.

BOY: Nobody? I have an absolute devotion to one man, an older man, maybe your age. He's so smart, smarter than either of us. Sometimes I lie at his feet and he reads to me, from books. Every kind of book, except interesting ones.

MAN: I remember. His name was Carey.

BOY: What do you mean, "was"? Don't we go on and on forever? *I know he's married, but—*

MAN: Oh Kevin grow up!

BOY: *—but he doesn't love her!*

MAN: No, don't grow up, what am I saying?

BOY: In *Alice in Wonderland*, Alice says that books should have either pictures or conversations. I'd like to put a picture in one of Carey's books—a picture of me—

MAN: And deep down you must know, you're not that important

to him. I remember asking him once about mutual funds. Have you done that yet?

BOY: No. Am I going to?

MAN: In about two months. His eyebrows will rise a little at that one. It will turn out you had them mixed up with mutual masturbation.

BOY: But I like watching his eyebrows rise, like two sleek humps, for his hair is the soft buttery color they call "camelshair," when you see it in coats; and I want to get him a coat made of camelshair.

MAN: You never will. *He's* the one with the money.

BOY: Most of the time however, we don't do much talking. Tell me, Kevin, what's *120 Minutes*, anyhow?

MAN: It's a show on MTV.

BOY: *(sarcastically).* Oh! That's crystal clear.

MAN: As I get older I dream less often, but what I lack in dreams I make up for in memories. When I wake up in the morning, squelching the alarm again and again, my head is fuzzy with thoughts, and fat, like a down pillow newly plumped. "What were you dreaming about?" All I see is a big black space—the absence of something that once really happened. Across that vast blackness I see two figures turn and cavort, me as a young man, and me as myself. The big person teaching the little person certain practices, and how to avoid stress. The little person saying, shaking his head sadly, "Let's get old together."

BOY: Do I get to be rich?

MAN: No.

BOY: Famous?

MAN: No.

BOY: How much grief am I supposed to swallow in our relation? Am I still a writer? Do I publish any books?

MAN: Several—all duds. I do have one piece of advice. Everyone you think is gay is straight, and everyone you think is straight is gay. *[To himself.]* That'll save me some time.

BOY: Even Lev Raphael? He's in my creative writing class in school and he is like Keir Dullea and Lou Reed wrapped into one! If he ever turned around and spoke to me I think I would die.

MAN: Even Lev Raphael.

BOY: But he can't be gay, I always see him with that girl.

MAN: Even Lev.

BOY: That awful girl who I hate, but now, if what you say is true, I'm registering strange feelings of empathy for her, she's not so bad, she's just misguided perhaps? Let's drink to her.

MAN: Make it a stiff one. But none for me, none for me.

BOY: Did you guess that you'd be married by the time you turned 40?

MAN: To a woman no less! I always thought I'd live on Cape Cod with the sea breeze splashing my face and four or five faceless kind of stud men of all nations would be running in and out of the surf in daring bathing suits, building world peace with candles and soda crackers.

But instead I live in San Francisco with a woman. When I fell in love with her it was with an abrupt kind of violence—a hook in my heart, like *The Texas Chainsaw Massacre*. Love does funny things, violent things, to all kinds of people, and I should not have expected to be immune.

BOY: I'm nervous about that. Look at me! I'm not the type to have sex with a woman.

MAN: Well, this will all be in the 1990s when you can have sex with *packages of Kraft swiss cheese* and there will be support groups to tell your struggles to.

BOY: I better have a drink first.

MAN: For years I've been writing a biography, of Jack Spicer, the San Francisco poet who died, quite young, in 1965 of alcoholism. Survived by most whom he cared about, Spicer, like Frank O'Hara on the East Coast, was the center of a cult, or school of younger poets who idolized him, and his own peers, whose feelings were more mixed. I tracked down dozens who had known Jack Spicer, and I kept asking them, in different ways, how it felt to be a gay writer in the middle of the twentieth century? And how disgruntled I was when they couldn't remember. I felt furious when they'd refer to events that clearly took place after Stonewall, for example. "But he died in 1965!" I would insist, politely as I could, gripping a pencil so hard one snapped. "Contain your memories to one period!"

Then a young woman called me on the phone, said she was writing a paper on the life and work of Sam D'Allesandro—a young writer who died several years ago. She knew I knew him and had found me on the internet. "Of course I'll answer all your questions," I cried, "and I'll be frank, honest and direct," I added, thinking darkly of my age-befuddled respondents. "I won't hold anything back." She must have been thrilled. But then when push came to shove (and it always does) I was such a flop. The big thing was I couldn't remember. She asked, "When did you meet him?" I said it was in the spring of 1985. Dodie said, it was the summer of 1984. He was wearing a brown leather jacket. I said, he never owned a leather jacket in his life. On and on it went until we were both numb. And yet how could I ever forget the animal attraction he shot out from every pore of his body, nor the way my cock felt hardening in his mouth, and his pink lips around its shaft like a rubber ring.

BOY: —Like me and Gary Ross. When I woke up I felt a sugary ring around the base of my cock, and a heavy unfamiliar weight bobbing up and down atop my thighs. His chin, tucking into my balls. "Get it on, bang a gong."

MAN: I don't remember Gary Ross.

BOY: *(furiously)*. How can you forget! He is the *Falcon Maltese*, the hottest man on the whole lower West Side!

MAN: And I guess I was stoned.

BOY: And what's the internet?

MAN: Um, wait and see.

BOY: You're hard on yourself and that means, hard on me.

MAN: I remember.

BOY: I don't want to know about all the things that are going to happen to me in your life, I don't want to know about AIDS or anything like that. I just have one question, it's about Christopher Isherwood.

MAN: *[dumbfounded]. ????*

BOY: See, it's kind of dumb but I have this thing for Christopher Isherwood. I've read all his books and I know he lives in California and my question is, do I ever get to go to Santa Monica and *meet* him? I know he lives with a younger guy, a painter, or something, and I was thinking, maybe I could go and somehow get rid of the other guy and move in with Christopher Isherwood. So does that happen?

MAN: I forgot about this part of my life.

BOY: Do I? I know it's eccentric of me, to have this fantasy, where somehow Don Bachardy falls off a cliff into the Pacific, but I'm there to console Isherwood, whisper in his ear it's time to lie down now, life is a cabaret old chum, my young arms and hands will massage you to sleep while my cock wobbles in your face, Mr. Isherwood. Your cute little blue-eyed face while you sleep, forget about Don Bachardy, he was just a nothing. So Kevin, do I ever go there?

MAN: God, how embarrassing!

BOY: I'll be strong, I'll put off my schoolgirl crush like a second skin, and be me, me, Kevin. Oh, but how can I when I don't even have the right to be myself? Which of us is the "real" Kevin Killian?

MAN: I don't want to spoil your party by telling you about your future, Kevin. I want to keep you just the way you are, a halo of idiocy around your head, your hair reeking of sweet Moroccan hash, your knobby knees, your big hands and your erection that sticks straight out 24 hours a day.

BOY: Feel it! I'm into exaggerated gestures just like my idol Christopher Isherwood—he who told the world, "You did not live in our time! Be sorry!" Ah, Kevin, if I *don't* get to push Don Bachardy off a redwood deck in Santa Monica, and I *don't* get to fuck Helmut Berger, what happens to me and where's the fun in life?

MAN: I must be a sad disappointment to you.

BOY: Oh, no!

MAN: You sure?

BOY: I've grown to like the "me" I became. Your wrinkles, your crinkly hair like Brillo, are dear to me now, like tiramisu of the damned. But how about you, Kevin? Will you ever care for me? Are you too old to have erotic feelings towards the boy you once were?

MAN: I'm speechless as vinyl. Have you grabbed the wrong end of the shtick?

BOY: Will I grow into that sexy body like a hand between your legs? If you had teeth I would bite me.

MAN: I don't remember being so bold. But I must have been.

BOY: One of these days I'll remember this encounter, and I'll write about it and when I do I'll be cruel. Solipsistic and cruel. Grrrr!

MAN: I must have kissed my ancient body with your young turbulent lips—

BOY: —At one time or another.

SPURT

The blood jet/ Is poetry.
—Sylvia Plath

My little car vibrated under me, as though its engine were announcing exciting plans to fall apart, but I didn't pay much attention. Tears were drying on my face. I was preoccupied, you might say; I simply hadn't the time for car trouble. For a week the temperature had stayed high above ninety degrees, and the radio announcers kept saying it was going to rain. Even at night the heat was thick and hot, like a soup, but I kept driving, for when you're drunk, no challenge is quite beyond you. Traffic was light on the Long Island Expressway. Full moon, and moonlight revealing huge purple clouds scudding east, always before me, moving faster than I could. Squinting, I tried to read the hands of the dashboard clock. It was either 4:00 a.m. or 4:00 p.m. I was driving east, into the moonlight, away from the belt of lights that surround New York, and I was so drunk I could hardly keep my eyes open. My lids felt heavy, as though while I were crying some evil genie had implanted them with iron filings. My face felt like one of those castiron spigots that pour water into old-time zinc-lined, claw-footed bathtubs.

"I'm spent," I mumbled—that seemed dramatic. For luck I grabbed the bottle of Glenlivet that stood propped between my thighs, its long glass neck tapping the vibrating steering wheel. Single malt whiskey that had lain undisturbed in some Scottish cavern for more years than I'd been alive, and now, glug glug glug. Created just for me, on my dumb day of grief. On Monday morning I'd start cracking the books and really put my nose to the grindstone and work on the dissertation. You must keep going, I said to myself, like a coach giving a pep talk to a reluctant player. All the same, tonight, I would try to imagine that I wasn't returning to school—that I was done with writing and thinking—that I'd never met Tim Baillie.

Something magical about really flogging your car, and the clear stretch of highway ahead; and feeling the motor and its complex accoutrements shudder under your heavy foot. And dipping an elbow out into the hot summer night and watching towns go by like reflections in shop windows—whole towns and neighborhoods, gone, gone, gone. You lose touch with the world—a car is an island all its own, another world; a world from which, perhaps, you might never return. The radio, staticky and shrill, burst out with bass-heavy Motown, then the abrupt, insinuating guitars of the Eagles. A low-slung, dark car passed me on the right, gleaming like a streak of phosphoresence under a Jamaican sea. Sucker must be doing a hundred easy. Lotus. Then the driver seemed to slack in speed and I was passing him. I saw his face—couldn't help it, he was staring right at me.

Cute guy, in a sleeveless T-shirt, blond, tanned, beach boy look, shock of curly blond hair on top of his head, big pink rubbery lips and dark eyes staring at me. Like he'd seen a ghost.

One hand rested on top of the wheel, lazily, as though he could drive without looking ahead. I sped up, and he sped up too. Cruise control. I caught him looking at me, again and again, and he flicked on the driver's seat light, a plastic dome that filled his car—

for a brief moment—with a thin plastic light, like cheap statuary of the Church. I guess he knew how hot he was. His lips parted. I could see him trying to speak, or signal. Eighty miles an hour and his mouth was saying, "Wanna fuck?" I nodded, he nodded, I got hard, I shifted the bottle, the Eagles wailed, over and over, about how dangerous life was in California. What drips. Glug. Our cars kept passing each other, and the driver's image faded in and out of the open passenger seat window. "Let's," I heard him call, and my car leapt ahead a length or two. Then he was beside me again. A sheen of sweat made his upper body look wet, as though someone had pulled him out of the shower and thrown him into a moving car and said, "Drive!" He was my dumb guide race car stud boy, come to lift the cover off this hot sultry night and show me love's underside. Or something.

I swung in behind the tail of the Lotus and we slowed down to a sedate 65 mph, into the right-hand lane, and a few interchanges later fishtailed out onto an exit, by a gas station and a diner. Under the purple neon lights of the diner we parked side-by-side. The Lotus was a gorgeous lime-green, a color that the purple neon and the purple clouds overhead kept remarking on, whispering among themselves. Buzzing about. Bzzzzzzz. "Where we going?" I asked—don't even know if I asked in words. When I jumped out of the car, the air smelled of burning rubber, and he was pulling off leather driving gloves. He was six feet tall, dishevelled, with long ropy arms, supple with muscles and fading tattoos. Steam covered the parking lot to a level of about four feet high, up to our chests. The net result was I couldn't see if he was hard, but knew he was. A thick white steam like dry ice, or the hot air that pushes up Marilyn's skirt in *The Seven Year Itch*.

"I'm Scott," said my new boyfriend. "You know where the Meadowbrook is?" "The motel?" Calculations spun in my head like the apples and oranges in a slot machine. He shrugged, and the muscles in his shoulders rippled. He said to follow him. But first he kissed me, his big lips pressed flat against mine. When he broke away my mouth was aflame. "How old are you?" Scott said, like a challenge. I couldn't think if he wanted me older or younger so I told the truth. "Twenty-five." One time in life when truth seemed to do the trick. "Grand," he said, sliding into the Lotus butt-first. "It's room 813," he said. "We've got it all night." Foolish me! I thought "we" meant me and him; boy did I ever get that one wrong! I got back into the Maverick and took another slug of Glenlivet, then checked my wallet, then followed Scott down an access road past strip malls, gas stations, and into the huge eerie, almost empty, motel lot. They should have called it "Salem's Lot" . . .

Any of you ever been to the Meadowbrook Motel? I don't even know if it's still standing. In 1978 it was a sex motel, catering to the needs of suburban adulterers who could steal an hour from the PTA and the IRS and rent by the hour—what my cop pals called a hot-sheet pad. The Meadowbrook reared up its proud head like some Vegas monstrosity, huge lobby studded with Italian crystal and a marble fountain. On either side of this lobby two endless wings extended, big rooms joined by a kind of faux-balcony with wrought-iron railings. Privacy and discretion a must.

I couldn't see the Lotus, but I saw room 813. The door was ajar, and bright light edged the crack of the doorway. "Hello?" I mumbled, tapping, and slowly the door swung open. I stepped into a dazzle of whiteness and was grabbed from behind by a big burly guy: a thrill shot through my lungs like pure oxygen. "Hi," said a voice, teasingly. Big arms like bolsters against my chest. "What's your name?" His voice was dark and low, like some underground stream choked with weeds. When he ordered me to shut my eyes his words came out in a gargle. He twisted my wrists behind my back and held them there with one tight fist. I suppose I helped a little. "Where's Scott?" I said.

"Shot," said my captor.

"What?"

"I call him Shot," he replied, pinching my nipples through my white Brooks Brothers shirt. "I guess his name is Scott, but I call him Shot."

I relaxed a little and surveyed the room. "Why?" The salient feature of the Meadowbrook rooms was, and maybe still is, their walls—every available wall surface covered with mirrors, like the end of *The Lady from Shanghai*. Mirrored ceiling, too, hung with the primitive track lighting of the '70s. Again and again my reflection gleamed back at me, and I could see the face of my captor. He shut the door with his bare foot, slam. Even the back of the door was a mirror. I guess there was a thermostat on one wall, but other than that there was only me, him, a TV and a bed. Endlessly. And silent air conditioning—its thin metallic smell seemed to bounce back and forth between us. The TV was showing some closed channel sex film starring Marilyn Chambers. Marilyn was laughing her fool head off while jerking off one white guy and one black guy. The sound was turned down so I couldn't catch the dialogue.

"Because he's, like, well . . . he's shot," said the man behind me. "Didn't you see his eyes?" I'm thinking, God, I'm supposed to have sex with this guy? He was about fifty-five and must have weighed 300 pounds, wrapped in an oversized white terrycloth bathrobe, its sash underfoot on the red rug. "What is he, your scout?" "Ha ha ha," he laughed, as though I were joking. His unruly beard and jolly grin would mark him today as a Daddy type, a big bear, but back then we didn't have that type: to me he was just fat. But I was drunk enough to not really care. Weakly I held up the bottle of Glenlivet, waved it around. "Want a drink?"

"Shot's into bondage," said Bear Guy, making a face. "But not me, I'm only into eating beautiful ass, how about you?"

"Whatever," I said. The ruined king-sized bed looked good to me. On TV Marilyn's face beamed, dripping with cum on her temples, eyes, lips. Okay, the linen wasn't exactly pristine—a thin strip of blood streaked the top sheet. "First I just want a drink."

Suddenly solicitous, Bear Guy led me to the bed and vanished into the bathroom. "Don't run off now!" I sat on one edge of the bed, taking off my shoes and socks. Soon he reappeared with a glass of ice. Glug glug glug. He said his name was Schuyler but all his "friends" called him Sky. "You've been crying," he said. I wondered if he was some kind of counselor in regular life. His big kind brown eyes. "Yes," I said, as I helped him insert his big hand through the zipper of my pants. "I've just been to a wake."

Sky squeezed my balls in that tender way some big guys have. "Ah, one of those long drunken Irish wakes. You look Irish."

"Yes," I said. I could see my face in the mirror, and beyond that I could see my own back. Everywhere I looked I saw me, sipping this motel glass full of that wonderful Scotch. Sophisticated. My dick was hard. I saw it. I saw it in the mirrors. It was everywhere, sluicing up and down through his hand. "This'll make you feel better," said Sky. He grabbed some change from the nightstand and put a couple of quarters into the frame of the waterbed. Instantly the bed started sliding and shaking up and down, to and fro, like an ocean liner on stormy seas. "Whoa," I said. "Relax," said Sky. Obedient, I shut my eyes and rolled onto my stomach. I didn't want to see his belly, tons of flab folding over and reconstituting themselves as he bent to work. I lay slumped amid the big coverlets and stained sheets, hid my hot face in a pink satin pillow, ruffled with black lace. "Good night," I said sadly. I didn't want to puke. Sky tugged my pants down to my ankles, then peeled off my tight white underwear, oohing and aahing like a connoisseur, touching and nibbling. The bed kept shaking as he parted the cheeks and licked the crack. At his muffled request—"Mmmftlmm?"—I raised my hips. I imagined my legs sprawled, my bony ankles dull under the weight of his knees, his bearded face buried inside my butt, a buffet. Comfortable.

His tongue darted in and out, in time with the whirring vibrations of the waterbed, licking the walls of my asshole. Nothing could surprise me, so when I became aware there was another boy in the bed near me, already passed out, snoring, I wasn't shocked, only pleased. I held onto his waist, pressing my cock along his long thigh. Hispanic guy with nubbly little pubic hair surrounding this enormous flaccid organ. His body was warm, he was naked, zzzzzz. An hour later, when I came to, he was gone. I've always wondered who he was and what became of him. The bed was still. Sky's quarters had run out.

And Sky must have run out too. Inside my ass I felt a little stretched, but not much. My mouth was parched. Five-thirty a.m. Scott was sitting on the other end of the bed, fully dressed, making a phone call, by the mirrored nightstand. "You're up," he said to me, scratching the bridge of his nose. "Grand."

There was still about an inch of my drink left—thank God. Scott had two grams of cocaine that he said were worth a hundred dollars. "On me." This was his hint for me to fish them out of his clothes. They were in the right-hand pocket of his blue jeans. I slithered to his end of the bed, while he talked on the phone, I think to his girlfriend or wife. I patted him down to find them, to find the tiny lump the vials made in those slick blue pants. The inside of his pocket felt warm, greasy, like sticking a hand into a Joseph Beuys sculpture of fat. I looked over his shoulder and saw our two faces. I could barely make mine out; it looked like the mirror was melting it, like rain on spring snow. But his face glistened, tan and sweaty, brilliantly smiling. His eyes were blue, like mine, but darker, almost black. I pulled the stash out of his pocket and dropped the vials, lightly, on the big sloppy bed. He hung up and then we scarfed the coke. What the hell. After we kissed some more he jumped to his feet to remove the belt from the loops of his jeans. "You work in a garage or something?" I think I said. "Your clothes are dirty, man." Even his boxer shorts had grease stains, as though he worked on motors in his underwear, then wiped his hands on them.

Ever been really drunk, in a room full of mirrors? Liquor, brown and warm, slops down the side of your mouth. You can't swallow fast enough. Your kisses get sloppy, your vision too. All of a sudden there's a little click in your head, and the first person turns into the second person. That's you—Kevin. Have another drink. Don't mind if I do. You stroke the warm cock in your hand, you can't decide if it's yours or another's. Click. The second person slips into the third. Kevin rose suddenly, the chenille bedspread sticking to his butt, and made his way unsteadily toward the far end of the room, where a picture in a neo-Rosenquist style hung on the wall of mirrors. He thought it was marvelous.

Fine scars striped Scott's chest and back—thin shiny veins, like long gleaming tapeworms—and across both cheeks of his butt a thicker scar, of rough skin, as though he had backed into a hot pipe. Inside his head Kevin was, like, ????, but he kept grinning as though it was nothing out of the ordinary to see a guy whose outsides looked like insides. "So, you're into bondage?" Now it was Scott's turn to make a face. "Who told you that—Sky?" "Oh no," Kevin said sarcastically, "Lana Turner told me."

He wore Kevin's hands around his waist like a belt, but Kevin took them off and lit a Parliament, backwards, nonchalantly lighting its "recessed filter" so that acrid smoke filled the air of the mirrored room. Scott walked nude to the bathroom and flipped on the light. Blinking, he tipped a plastic glass sideways in his holder, one limp arm pointing at it, his fingers working, weakly, as though he wanted to grab it. "I'll take a drink too, you got any to spare." Like any other alcoholic, Kevin measured what was left in the bottle and tried to figure out if, indeed, there was any to "spare." Scott was naked in the threshold of the bathroom, and Kevin kept ogling him blearily. His body had the extraordinary angles of the junkie, the bumps and bones, the big thick red cock like a wind-up handle for the toy it set to motion. "Turn around," Kevin said. Scott complied. Kevin peered at his ass. It was big and full, a whole novel's worth. I could eat breakfast off that butt, thought Kevin, scar and all. He saw Scott's elbow working, moving like a piston from behind. Like, he's jerking off, kind of. When he turned again he had a hard-on bigger than a mackerel, and Kevin had seen a lot of fish. "Want another drink?" he said, pointing to the bottle that stood on the bedside. The alcohol sweat from Kevin's body gave him a chill on this hot humid night, just before dawn, and he shivered as though—as though, he thought, a goose was walking over my grave.

Brrrrr.

"Let's take a shower," Scott said. "I'm filthy." He told Kevin he liked being tied up to the shower pole—is it called a "pole?" Whatever it is that holds up a shower curtain—whatever it is that he was tapping like a woodpecker, in a rare burst of excitement. "Nah," Scott said flatly. "It's called, the rod!"—a word he seemed to find excitement in, as did Kevin: a phallic word, concealed yet radiant, like Poe's purloined letter, among the bathroom's pedestrian fittings. Then Scott further wanted Kevin to take the knife he held out, and slice him with it. "After that it can be your party." Trouble was there wasn't any rope in their mirrored motel room. On all four walls, on the ceiling, their faces, multiplied to infinity, represented an infinity of puzzlement, thousands of eyes darting around drunkenly to look for rope. Finally Scott gave up, shrugged, "No rope, let's improv." Improv? Very Second City, that boy! Very Lee Strasberg! For a few minutes Scott pretended he was tied, but that got tired. He stood facing away from Kevin, wrists crossed above his head clinging to the pole as though lashed on. He kept looking back over his shoulder, trying to panic. Trying to feel trapped.

"Hey," whined Scott. "I really could, you know, use some rope. And I'd like to do this before Sky comes back, if you don't mind."

There was a second click in Kevin's head—a click of clarity. He saw clearly, vividly, where he could find some rope—in the trunk of his Maverick. Viewed the mental image in 3-D. It was like getting sober. The third person vanished. The second person lasted only long enough for you to whip one of the motel towels around your waist and prop open the door with your pants. Then you were out in the parking lot, and pop! I opened the trunk, staring down at the rope Tim Baillie had hung himself with.

A tiny wind whistled under the thin cloth of the towel, tickling my balls. I bent over and took the extra rope. The leftover rope. Tim Baillie was dead now; I had just come back from his wake. He was my advisor in grad school, and I had slept with him to pass my orals. Do they still call them "orals"? I guess I used him, without many qualms: just did it, set him in my sights and knocked him down like a bowling pin with charm, Irish whiskey, and my big basket in the front row of Victorian Studies. "Kevin," he said, "you could have been a real scholar if you had anything in your mind." And now Tim Baillie—"Dr. Baillie, if you please!"—was dead.

Coiled loosely on the floor of the trunk, among pieces of an oily jack, the rope looked harmless enough. But just looking at it made me jittery, as though it concealed cobras. I remember fantasizing about an inquest where I would have to get up on the stand and some Perry Mason type would be snidely asking me, "Didn't you know he would use that rope to hang himself?"

"No! No! I've gone through this a thousand times! Dr. Baillie said he wanted to pack a trunk!" "A trunk to death?" "No, no, an ordinary trunk!" "Mr. Killian, may I remind you that you swore to tell the whole truth and nothing but the truth?" What could I say? I knew I didn't love him, but wasn't giving him all that head enough for Tim Baillie? He had been closeted for forty years or more; I thought I was bringing a little sunshine into his elderly life. I remembered lying in his bed in his awful condo in Rocky Point with all his books on Alfred, Lord Tennyson stacked sideways on the bookcase, as though he didn't care enough about them to stand them up straight. I remembered listening with him to Willie Nelson's doleful *Stardust* album again and again—his favorite album, whereas mine was either *Radio Ethiopia* or *Sexual Healing*. Maybe I should have loved him. But nobody respected him, why should I? He was just this flabby fool with spots on his face that might have been freckles. He left a note, they told me: "I can't stand this heat." I didn't know, when he asked me to get him some rope at Smithtown Hardware, what he'd use it for. I remember his pursed lips when I showed him all the rope I'd bought, saying to me, "I only need about 12 feet, it's just for a trunk, I'm not Christo wrapping the Eiffel Tower." He cut off what he needed with a pair of cooking shears. Least he paid me for the whole 100 feet. Always this sarcasm, always the mockery, the checkbook, the despair. I thought I drank a lot till I met him—his eyes were the color of grappa, all the way through, no white, just this sick luscious purple tinge color. Gulp.

When I heard about Tim Baillie's suicide, I was sitting at a table in a bar in Port Jefferson, reading a book, and nursing a bottle of beer and a glass of rum and Tab. The bottle kept leaving wet rings in the pages of the book. You know how Seurat worked? Placing millions of tiny dots of color into pointillistic masterpieces? I began to think, well, maybe you could do this with the wet rings of a beer bottle, and later Chuck Close took my insight and became way famous doing so. Oh Tim! If I made you feel second best, Tim, I am sorry I was blind. Maybe I didn't hold you, all those lonely lonely times. Little things I should have said and done, I just never took the time, et cetera!

Room 813, Scott was lying on the bed whacking off, keeping his dick hard and his heels cool. "Grand," he said when I showed him the rope, and mimicked lassoing him. Expertly he tied himself up, lashing his wrists to the shower rod and needing my help only for the last knots. The rod was L-shaped, to match the contours of the bathtub below; its two ends screwed into two different mirrored walls, and a sassy full-length shower curtain of hot pink vinyl hung from it dramatically, the drag queen of all shower curtains. I stood behind Scott, kissing and biting his neck and shoulders, my hard-on poking between his thighs, his big butt. I gripped the knife in one hand, my knuckles white around its heft. He was on tiptoes, arms braced tautly against the frail metal rod. I flipped a hand between the part in the pink vinyl curtain, and turned on the shower, a rush of cool water beating on the other side of us. "You know what you're doing?" he said sharply. "I'm not a piece of meat, I just want to let some blood out. You don't hack me like you're at some butcher's shop." I saw him full length in the mirror facing us, on the other side of the tub. The hair under his armpits was blond, darker than the thatch on his head. His nipples were brownish-red, spaced far apart on his magnificent chest. "Right under my ribs," he said, "Let's start there." I could see how hard he was. His erection lifted his balls right along with it—everything pointed to the knife. I just wanted to fuck him but thought, well, later, later it'll be my party.

I took a deep breath and lifted the knife to his skin. First I heard a kind of screech, like two cats fighting. Then another screech, more protracted, from above my head. The shower rod screws sprang half out of their sockets in a noise of splitting glass and metal. My instinct was to jump back, anywhere, but there was nowhere to jump to. The knife fell from my fist. I tightened my hold round Scott's middle, his skin a blur. Another screw flew out of its seating and the shower walls collapsed. "Uh-oh," whispered Scott, and we began to drop, he right on top of me, he getting the worst of it for sure. Splinters of glass shot through the air, then whole panes peeled from the steamy bathroom walls, sticky with glue, and loud with crackling and smashing. The room was imploding. With a sudden crack, the rod bent again, into three broken parts, and all the curtain rings fell to one end like poker chips clicking on a croupier's table. Scott's body, still knotted to the mangled metal rod, fell to the bathroom floor with a heavy thud, though I tried to cushion his fall. Hot pink vinyl fluttered and descended over our heads. Slumped to the floor, Scott's torso sprayed blood, pink mist erupting up the side of the bathtub, mist that grew red at its edges. His hands were still tethered, with the hemp now wet, swollen. I sat on the floor, afraid to move, for the glass was everywhere, on the rug, on the pink tiles, strewn across the tan of his naked body like sand. And also I was afraid of sitting on the knife I had let go.

Mirrors, with bright colors zigzagging across them, his dick seemed a thousand feet long, like a string of sausages in a Chuck Jones cartoon. I kept seeing him bleeding out the corner of my eye, the way you might think you're seeing something when you're really paranoid. Peripheral vision.

"Guy, you all right?" I said.

His eyelids pulled up to reveal blue irises swimming in twin seas of pink. His lashes were incredibly long and from overhead, the gaudy light of the motel's fluorescent tubes threw long shadows onto his picked-over cheekbones. One large shard of mirror stood, like Stonehenge, embedded directly into his stomach, about an inch above and to the left of his navel. Another shard toppled over on his right thigh, propelling a piece of pink flesh, that looked like dog food, across the rim of the bathtub. The blood was everywhere. I was covered with blood, spots, streaks, puddles. But somehow I hadn't been hurt. I ran back into the bedroom to grab a drink; also to fetch a pillow to staunch Scott's blood: I had the word tourniquet in my head.

"I'm all right," he gasped. "Wow, I just wanted a little cut, dude, you brought in the whole artillery, didn't you?" "FX," I said. "Now help me," he said. "Help me come now."

I sat back on my haunches and used one hand to stroke my cock. With the other I held his dick, which hardened and throbbed to a vivid red brightness—its natural pink intensified by desire. I studied it before I began to pump: it looked angry, swollen, as though stung by bees. Blood and pre-cum, greasy in my loose fist. The aroma of blood: stale, tangy, older than either of us. Scott stirred, smiling, moved his head across the wet shiny tile. Gently I placed the pink satin pillow between his head and the floor; its black lace ruffle grew instantly darker with blood and water. "This is like some Mario Bava film!" I thought, scared to death, but horny, too. Scott's dark blue eyes fixed on some point on the mirrored wall, from which another face gazed back at him, mine or his. His tongue protruded from his mouth, like a dog in summer lapping up water. "Cool," he said.

His tan flesh, which should have been lightly dusted in sand, his beach boy look, spoiled or accentuated in scars, and everything pricked with glass, like a St. Sebastian I felt so sorry for, yet couldn't help. All I could do was jerk him off. That's all he wanted from me. His tongue touched the tip of my dick as I labored over him. Lick. Rustle. Spurt.

Again. Spurt. Presently I straightened up, creaking from my knees, and tossed a towel into the bathtub, so I could stand in it without cutting my feet on the broken slices of mirror. Then I stepped over his body and into the shower, let cool water rinse the blood from my arms, hair, crotch, legs. Through a streaming veil I watched Scott sink into sleep, as blood continued to pool up in all the concave sites of his fading body. Was he sleeping? Unconscious? His blond hair matted red, brown, black; his smile gave no clue, his big lips slack, happy, purple and gray as the petals of a sterling silver rose. I nudged him with the Glenlivet. He didn't seem to want a drink, again I'm like—????? Then I dressed, found my keys, left the motel. I guess.

SANTA

I'll be writing two stories at the same time, but think of this as no "New Narrative" trick but as a kind of Victorian novel in miniature. Three stories really, because I've stretched out Brad Gooch's "Satan," as one might stretch a canvas before hitting the palette. In "Satan," a photographer, Eddie, so badly abuses his black model that even his rich white patrons, who like abuse to a certain point, start to drop him. This causes him to see the light and to change his ways. Reading the story you can't help but think you're getting a close-up of the home life of our dear Robert Mapplethorpe. "Eddie stands up. He walks through the cut-up loft, looking for something to photograph. But there's nothing. Except this white lily flower in a black onyx vase. He doesn't want to photograph it. Why not? But he breaks through that feeling and grabs the vase in his hand, feeling as if he's sticking his hand through a plate-glass window. Can't make any phonecalls. The switchboard in his head has stopped lighting up.

"Eddie walks slowly back with the vase into the studio room. Puts it on a wooden high stool. Takes its picture.

"The lily looks cool." I suppose the seduction of transparency, "sticking his hand through a plate-glass window," lured me into this web of sin in the first place. In September, 1988 I wrote to Whitley Strieber, the horror writer whose latest books detail his thesis that ordinary Americans, men and women like ourselves, have been the victims of sex experiments by alien creatures in UFOs.

After receiving my letter, Strieber wrote back consolingly, advising me of a support group for people in my area suffering from my problem. I learned one lesson from this exchange, there's help for everybody. As Joe Orton said, "Nature excuses no one on the freaks' roll call." And I'll copy in this space back and forth from my original letter:

> Dear Mr. Strieber,
>
> Twelve years ago, I was 23, a waiter in the North Shore town of Smithtown, Long Island. I'd been visiting my parents on my way to work, and as I drove away from their house a startling thing happened. As I made the left turn out of my folks' subdivision onto Route 25A, in a desolate, woodsy area, I noticed an ice cream truck farther ahead on the highway. One of those trucks like "Good Humor" that parades around suburban neighborhoods playing jingles with jingle bells. This sight, combined with the sound of those little bells, froze me in my tracks.
>
> This was summer, June 1, 1976, just before twilight. The setting sun seemed white and cold, a big ball of snow on the horizon above a line of blue trees. Suddenly I ceased to be an adult and became a child again, a child four or five years old.
>
> I was swimming in some kind of deja vu experience. That, at least, is the way I rationalized it afterwards.

In "Satan" the photographer torments his model by forcing him to listen for long stretches as he reads aloud from Melville's *Benito Cereno*. I saw so clearly how all our stories are piled up on one another now, the way you or I can think of two things at the same time but with a corresponding lack of definition. How often have I envied people who have two TVs, they can watch two shows at the same time, but then I always have second thoughts and say I really wouldn't enjoy that. When I was 23, though I had my epiphanic moment watching the ice cream truck, I never gave my feelings much credence, I think partially because I did own a car and thus could slink in and out of situations like the Pink Panther in the cartoons, and I want to give a cogent example here, my love affair with Ralph Isham. I don't know why I slept with him in the real sense, but I had my reasons. Two of my friends lived in the house next to mine, Ron and Becky, in a trial marriage, but almost from the week I met Ron I felt a crush on him so strong, so statutory that I didn't think of him as a friend but as a source of light and heat. That he was planning on marrying Becky I tried to put out of my mind even as I threw myself into their wedding plans ass over teakettle. Their house was even smaller than mine. You couldn't sit waiting for Ron to come out of the shower without a few drops of water passing the beaded curtain that served as a bathroom door, and hitting you on the arm or leg or head. His favorite TV show was the "Battle of the Network Stars," and to this day I'm fond of it too, and my favorite network is still ABC even though NBC has had far better shows, such as *Santa Barbara*, which I'll get to in a minute. I always root for ABC when the network stars do battle. "They film this at Pepperdine University in Malibu," Ron said. "It's a fantastic school, Kevin, you should go there, maybe they have a graduate program in English." Years later I went by Pepperdine on the bus to Hollywood, and I looked out into its silver beaches and its trimmed playing courts and Denise Venturi architecture and thought of Ron. But this story isn't about him, or hardly, it's about his uncle.

Ron's uncle Ralph was a caricature of a man, a twisted jumble of body parts, he walked and talked quickly, like he was trying to sell you something, and when he spoke he used a high voice like a tape whirring in super speed. I mean my own voice is high but his was the kind only dogs can hear. When we made dates on the phone it must have sounded like Yma Sumac talking to herself in some South American birdland. His wife was called Brooksy, by everyone, even the Mayor, and she collected replicas of the Statue of Liberty. Whenever any of Brooksy's friends wanted to please her, or say you knew her birthday was coming up, you were perfectly safe in buying her a replica of Lady Liberty, or a picture of it, or whatever, and she'd go bananas. Remember the hoopla when they restored the Statue of Liberty? I wished that she was still alive to enjoy it, when it began, when it was over, and now it's new and nice again like a phoenix.

The point is that Uncle Ralph used to delight neighborhood kids by dressing up as Santa, and as I was discussing this story of mine with other people, three of them told me the same thing—each was involved with a sick man who liked to dress up as Santa, so it started me wondering if there are any *normal* people who like to play Santa, and I decided, on the whole, probably not.

The salient thing about Santa is that he comes down the chimney and leaves these toys. One body of material places him in a workshop at the North Pole, lording it over elves and reindeer, but in my opinion these are corruptions of an original text in which this big man just comes out of nowhere, leaves you toys and takes some cookies and milk from a little plate, then vanishes.

And so I shall reflect in this manner. On *Santa Barbara* Mason and Julia were trapped in this snowstorm on Christmas Eve and they had to seek shelter so they knocked on the door of this ordinary suburban house and this man answered the door, and Dodie said, "I bet he'll turn out to be Santa," and I thought, "He looks just like Uncle Ralph." She was right, I was wrong, but it made me think, the first ingredient in any good soap.

I had met Ralph several times at family parties and get-togethers. I never thought he was gay. On the day of Ron's wedding I saw him again, dressed in a puffy powder-blue suit, a kind of tuxedo from the sixties, and I began to drink heavily at the country club where the reception took place. Out in the sun the planters' punch I was drinking went to my head first, then to my bladder. This compound of elegant facades and white stucco pillars had its share of charm and urinals, but I couldn't find either, not at first. "Excuse me, is there a bathroom around here?" "Men's locker room, that's closest." "How novel," I said, I mounted the stairs and started to climb, gripping the white bannister for dear life. Through the tight seam of my black pants I felt a few fingers up the crack of my ass. I looked back and attached to the hand, Ralph's face came gleaming up at me like this elderly Howdy Doody puppet's. He was grinning like he knew some kind of secret. "Going to the head?" he said.

"If I can find it," I said.

"You can piss right in my mouth," he told me. "Any old time you've got the notion." This bold way of speaking, coupled with the hand in my ass, convinced me there was more to this guy than a funny voice and a wife who was a collect-a-holic. I moved my hips in such a way that I led him up the stairs as if into a space capsule that has somehow landed on the White House lawn, or the end of *Close Encounters*. I don't have to tell you how he got my phone number and started calling me up every day and every night until Mickey started to get suspicious. Anyhow it's all water under the bridge like so much other memory and experience. I started to piss and he held open his mouth to swallow me up whole without a choke or gargle, I figured, "It's these old ones have the stamina," because Uncle Ralph was sixty Ron said.

Mr. Strieber, I told myself the sight of the ice cream truck had brought back, in the way of classic Freudian analysis, a buried childhood trauma. But this memory in turn I'm today convinced was nothing more than a screen memory. Yet this is what I remembered:

I was four or five, an ice cream truck rolled up to our house where I lived with my parents, and I was lured away by its driver and placed onto the passenger seat of the cab. I made no protest, my mouth was filled with ice cream. I was a self-possessed child. So long as my mouth stayed full I didn't care what happened to me. The driver of the truck was a large man in a white overall, wearing glasses with dark lenses. He kept driving, bells ringing and merrily jingling, farther and farther away from my home. Finally he pulled into a deserted forest clearing, at which time I was removed from the passenger seat and put inside the truck, into the refrigerated space where the ice cream pops are kept, and molested there.

All this came flooding back to me as I sat there behind the steering wheel, my eyes flooding with tears and my heart pounding a mile a minute.

I told myself that this buried memory must account for a lot of the troubles I'd had growing up. At that time, the mid-'70s, you were just beginning to hear about the apparently endless cycle of child abuse and sexual victimization of children. I counted myself one of them after this flashback. And although some of the details seemed bizarre, I chalked it up to the nature of the child/sex experience.

As the years went on, however, I began to doubt my own recollections of this event. For one thing, I couldn't make myself believe that a sex criminal, no matter how deranged, would climb into an ice cream truck freezer to do so. I dunno, what do you think? I realize you don't pose as an expert on sex crime, Mr. Strieber, but you're a man of the world, possibly of more than one world, right? Give me some feedback if you'd be so kind.

"Oh, God, I don't know why I get myself in these things," I told Mickey. Actually I knew very well, or sort of well, but it's more dramatic, I think, if you keep yourself out of it. "I have to meet Ralph tonight."

Mickey was this guy who, well, I guess you'd call him my boyfriend. He was from a wealthy family in Connecticut, and I had met him here in San Francisco, then he returned to Long Island to live with me and follow me around like a puppy dog's tail. His mom and dad were social climbers who would have preferred him to enter Yale after Choate instead of escaping to Polk Street and poppers. Mickey distressed them by preferring the seedy side of town, it didn't matter which town, out of a hankering for some real experience—what the French call *nostalgie de la boue*. Not that Smithtown has a real "seedy side," but it did have me and it did have Ralph, Ron's uncle, whom Mickey had never met. His name was Mickey Manzl, and this similarity to the name of the famous Yankee slugger made some people remember his name, and made others forget it. When I was in a bad mood, which in those days was often, I would carp at him, "Why not call yourself 'Michael' like every other homosexual?" Anyhow I went out with Ralph at least partially to keep Mickey aware he wasn't my only source of sex knowledge, sex comfort. Every time I left the house his eyes would darken and narrow till they resembled two dried up old peas. For he had come 3,000 miles, buoyed by my promises, to be treated instead like the dog's dinner. Still he kept saying, "yes," as if he really thought love could change me.

Bedstead:
From a knot of inch-thick rope the boy's hands dangle like dogs' paws. "No fair," Ralph thinks, elated. He wipes his palm on the bedsheet. Awkwardly Mickey's head tilts to one side, a block of bone and hair and sleep perched atop our tired flat pillow. One

hip lies atop the sheet, and out of tension the other stretches north by northwest. If the hips were hands, hands of a clock, his ass would say seven-fifteen. And if so, the time would be wrong, since it's only about one-thirty p.m. (EST).

Two thin lines in the boy's naked stomach tilt, diagonal to match his distorted frame, one under the nipple, the other just under the navel.

If these lines were the hands of a clock the time would be about ten to nine. Fuck this hands business, the boy's half-dressed in white underwear, and looks hapless enough even for Ralph. From the open fly pubic hair protrudes a little—cherry hair, with a bead of sweat glistening in it: sweat, or some other clear liquid? (Tears?) His long legs are bent at the knees like a stork's, and one hard heel digs for leverage into the soft thick mattress pad. There's a lot of confusion in his posture, but all Ralph can see is his allure. On a little side chair a cat crouches, filled with tension and thirst. Mickey feels the slightest bit of sex excitement he can possibly register, as though someone in another room were talking about sex. His throat feels tight and cold.

So there I was at Ralph's house one evening—Brooksy was visiting relatives in Milwaukee, and it must have been summer, but I remember vividly Ralph taking the Santa outfit out of a wardrobe and showing it to me, and I asked him to put it on for me. The radio was blasting, *Der Rosenkavalier*, the torrential renunciation of the Marschallin. "You want to see Santa?" Ralph repeated, his eyes lit up by happy flames. "I'll show you Santa."

Command performance? *Noblesse oblige?* First he showed me this awful nude body, then wrestled it into this girdle with attachments—he was into rubber in general—and then into the girdle's chain link he inserted the various pieces of durofilm padding that gave all his convex parts new contours of fat. As he swaggered through the house drawing the curtains, he looked like the victim of a terrible burn case. Then these long johns, with the crotch cut away, and the red flannel suit, trimmed with white fur. Around his false waist he wrapped the kind of wide, black, vinyl belt Edie Sedgwick once wore. He was padded all over, except at the groin. "Is that what all Santas wear," I asked, "their cocks and balls hanging out at the crotch?" "You ever sit in Santa's lap?" he said, waving his limp red hat. "Then you must have felt him through the red velvet." "Don't little kids mash you with their heels?" "So what?" he replied, as he pasted on the beard that completed his drag. "What if they do? It goes with the territory." His big black boots Sylvia Plath described in "Daddy," so picture them stamping and mincing in your direction while all you're trying to do is knock down enough Dewar's to stay sophisticated. In the first *Anniversary*, Donne says the body's a "poor Inn, a prison-house packed up in two yards of skin," and in Ralph's case that was true, except make it "three yards of skin." He was a cheater and, like all cheaters, had made a precious gift to himself—he was able to think of two things at the same time: his own safety, and his own pleasure.

<u>Want:</u>
Ralph wants to give Mickey a little of everything he's got, like a dim sum cart. One from Column A, two from Column B. Not a lot of any one thing, but generous. "Howdy." Ralph twists the body before him so that its ass swings around, upward, then with both hands grips the waistband of the undershorts. With an ease that appalls him, he splits the fabric in a V down to the thighs, so that both halves of the ass lie bare and undignified. This is what Ralph goes for, this sense of power and apathy. "Ready to roll?" he shouts. I watch his hand move up and down from a distance, trying to figure what Mickey is feeling. If I had just gone to prep school maybe I'd know.

Between the cheeks of Mickey's ass, the hand stops and looks around for five minutes, prodding and nibbling till it's been spread pretty far apart, maybe six inches. "I feel good?" Ralph asks, not to me, maybe to Mickey, though maybe to himself.

He sees this thing in there, this thing . . . makes him wince it's so repulsive. Still, it's what he goes for and has been for decades now. It's only about an inch long, and no wider than a paramecium. Slight hairs and puckers give it the unthinking look of a—caterpillar, or something else from the world of nature.

Ralph looks away from it for only an instant. The cat's observing him cautiously, intense interest plain in its pale green eyes. It's a warm day and my bedroom is hot with sun; the torn windowshade in a square yard of sun like a warm griddle mounted on one wall. Around Ralph's plump hand Mickey's warm skin blushes. Ralph's cock has the sheen of marble to it, I sit there wondering if all sixty-year old men stay so hard. Purple, pink marble, its base a flat place like a tombstone or relief. "It's the old ones," I think: *you know—Picasso—Chaplin—William O. Douglas* . . . Ralph ignores me, while Mickey stares in my direction without seeing. First his asshole seems tight as a seam, but once dug into it opens, irrevocably as a can of beer. Around its mouth the taut glossy skin weeps red and pink, like the fabric rain slickers are made from. Ralph watches as Mickey's knees slide further apart, helter-skelter, but slow, and his throat touches the pillow with a certain majesty of defeat. "I'm open," Mickey thinks. Like the wallet you find in the trash after the pickpocket's done with it.

"I'd like to meet your little friend sometime," he told me.

"He's not so little," I said. "He's taller than I am."

"You know what I mean," he said, staring past me. Oh, I knew. Mickey's green eyes and chestnut hair attracted all kinds of geezers, I used to think he reminded them of Joel McCrea or someone of a bygone era.

Ralph nodded, turned the radio low. "And I'd like to meet him in a very specific way," he said coolly. "Do you think he'd be into it?" He liked to get me drunk so I would piss more, often enough he'd buy me a case of Tab at a time, and a bottle of Johnnie Walker Red on top like the bow to a Christmas gift. I'd stand over him like the Statue of Liberty, give me your huddled masses, I'd say, yearning to breathe free. I'd see his little fists going up and down and I'd know I was pleasing. I said, "You are wrong, this is wrong," without taking the time to suss out what was wrong or right about my behavior or environment. I knew there was something kinky about this relationship, but whatever it was, there wasn't enough of it. "Something," the noun, was too vague: I wanted a whole novel to open like *Call me Ishmael*. "Let me tell you *how* I'd like to meet him—or is that too much to ask?"

Why these are the words every lover wants to hear, is this too much to ask! I was excited, it smelled like trouble.

Then two years ago another experience made me doubt my own sanity. I woke at six a.m., a strange white light covering my room. An intense chill filled the room, yet I was sweating. The walls were white like they'd been dipped in frost. It reminded me of the inside of a huge refrigerator.

Although I can't explain why, right then I knew that what had happened to me in my childhood had not been a case of sexual molestation, not in any ordinary sense anyhow. No, I can't explain how I knew. But some alien presence had been in my room!

The impression of a powerful force for evil remained with me for days.

I thought back to my mental picture of my molester. His eyes, hidden behind the almond-shaped lenses of his glasses;

his white suit, which I had thought part of a uniform, suddenly reassembled itself into the protective garments of a lab technician.

The frost that had surrounded me that day, and on the night I speak of now two years ago, I now re-vision as being part of a much larger space than the confines of a Good Humor truck. Bigger than any bedroom either. These spaces were only the recastings my mind had worked on the real space into which I was abducted, a space much vaster than I could take in at the time. His face didn't much resemble the face on the cover of your book *Communion*, although it shared the same blank black eyes and skinny lips, the elongated ears and the bulbous head. There was some kind of shiny metal apparatus dangling from a belt around his waist, which I misfigured as the kind of change dispenser ice-cream men wear on their rounds. But it was not meant for dispensing change: that I know now. It contained some kind of battery or Geiger counter, buzzing and whirring and emitting electrical impulses I took for sexual ones.

Inside the humid hole Ralph's thumb begins to revolve, a blade in a fan. Or "key in ignition" might be better. Mickey's breathing, so is Ralph. The air that expands their lungs beams a cold blue light, the color of peace and science. Ralph's stubby fingers touch the rags of underwear that dangle still from the boy's red thighs. Give them a little yank. Above frayed cotton the pink warm skin glows under the marks Ralph has made, pulsates white and yellow: pastoral colors. Without much finesse Ralph works his cock up to the vicinity of Mickey's ass and wriggles till he's pinpointed it. He leans over: his lips meet Mickey's ear. "I'll make you a star," he says, mouth dry. There's a ridge of muscle on the back of Mickey's neck Ralph now watches. He guesses it must come spontaneously to the skin of a boy who knows he's going to be fucked. Yet this same ridge, which Ralph likes in a way, suggests any number of dispiriting negative outcomes, as does the fog, clammy and cold, that seems to emanate from Mickey's shoulders and shoulderblades.

At Ron's parents' house, at Thanksgiving, I'm invited as a family friend, and when I got there Ralph and Brooksy were entertaining everyone with details of their latest day trip to Liberty Island. I felt ashamed that I was seeing him. He didn't make matters any easier by following me into the bathroom and trying to sit on the toilet bowl when I took a leak. "Get the hell away from me," I told him, "or I'll aim for your face instead of your mouth." Through the thin plywood door I heard the TV, an announcer announcing the holiday classic *Miracle on 34th Street*. "That's my movie," he said to me blithely, and he left. I stood there looking at the foggy mirror inhaling and exhaling me like cigarette smoke. "Two can play at this game," I thought, and I went out and ate two pounds of turkey and most of the oyster stuffing. When Santa comes down your chimney it's exactly how I feel when I get fucked. This enormous invasion. It doesn't happen any more, to me, so I think of it as a belief system, like the Great Chain of Being, once in everyday use but now an Elizabethan relique. I draw a window-shade over the events, every day I look up and wonder what happened to the last man who put his dick to me.

That's okay. It'll pass. Leaning over his prey, Ralph tries to come in, into Mickey's little clarinet hole. Mickey cranks back his head and blows a foul breath at him, and for his pains gets a poke to the jaw. Then Ralph takes both hands and shoves himself into the miniature hole. Like miniature golf, he thinks. "Pretend you don't like this," he says. His knees feel pleasantly warm with friction. He's beginning to work up a sweat, as you might from a nice morning set of tennis.

"Won't have to pretend much," Mickey thinks, hanging from his hands by the rope. The rope abrades his wrists and begins, ever so surely, to cut off the circulation of his arms. I watch his hands turning this pale shade of violet. Straight down point his cock and balls, swinging slightly clockwise. Maybe if we were south of the Equator they'd swing the other way. Ralph raises Mickey's body up, by the armpits: this alleviates the pain a bit, the kink, but this small plus is negated almost instantly. "There's a big thing," Mickey realizes, "in my anatomy."

"Blow into it," Ralph urges.

"Can't," Mickey says. "Take it out, it hurts."

"Can't stop now," Ralph grins. "Make me come, it'll get smaller, I swear. Blow into it, squeeze me."

The cameras explode and harsh white light bathes their bodies in sodium rays. These pictures are meant for Ralph's private reserve, the way his wife collects her Statues of Liberty on her sideboard and dashboard, he keeps these pictures in a tackle box in the basement. In another ten seconds a second set of flash-bulbs goes off, then a third, because I'm no Edward Weston and I need plenty of takes.

In the ebb and flow of light Mickey's face freezes into a rictus. Was that *the atom bomb* he wonders. Ralph sees Mickey's smile and reckons he's found his prostate. In Ralph's eyes Mickey's a silver mine, a Comstock Lode. With enough pioneer spirit, elbow grease, who knows what might be brought out of him? "Can I cut a little piece off your ear lobe," he says quickly. "No way," Mickey snorts. I jump out from behind the cameras and wouldn't you know it, the cat starts howling like it wants some Kitty-Os or other cat treats.

In our alien encounters, these creatures with triangles for faces and holes for eyes come to us at midnight. We don't object to their sex experiments, no matter how outre! Over and over Strieber outlines the shock and horror a good hypnosis produces, the subjects can't believe such outrages were performed right on their bodies without their consent or remembering them. In Strieber's own case a long metal tube was passed eighteen inches into his rectum to collect G-I specimens of the X description, yet he did not remember this. What about anesthesia in general? You're lying down on a silver table and figures pass by you with hands long as knives, fingers dextrous as Balinese dancers. The ceiling is studded with the whizzing blue panels of Nintendo games, and you play both victim and star. In your backyard the next morning a huge circle of scorched earth reveals the place of your trauma.

Earlier in the day I'd pressed Mickey's wrists together neatly, crossed them left over right, for that dog paw effect I wanted. "Why so tight, Kevin?"

"So it'll look natural," I said.

Natural? Well, "kidnapped," actually. "Ralph saw this one time in a skin magazine." In new white underwear I'd bought for him at the Army-Navy stores, I had to go all the way to Flatbush to buy just the right kind. *The things a mother will do!* "Bring your balls up," I suggested. My eye pictured a gourmand's feast of balls, big Brussels sprouts but tastier. Not these drab walnuts for goodness sake! "Make them big." "Can't oblige, I don't know how." I wasn't satisfied with the effect, but due to time pressure had to let it go. "Pretend you're in a movie," I said, "and you've been kidnapped. Or pretend you *have been* kidnapped. Whatever's easier." His studious face wrinkled in thought, trying to decide. Presently he brightened up. "I could pretend that I'm in this horror movie and I've been kidnapped by space aliens," he said. Taking a nail scissors, I snipped three fly buttons off the shorts, and slit along the cheap elastic of the waistband. You never know, do you? You try to prepare for every eventuality, but 'twixt the cup and the lip there's many a slip so what can you do? "I just want you to act terrified." Out from the fly I brushed his pubic hair so it would protrude a little, artistically as was feasible with seeming unplanned. Just like any other kidnapped kid, drowsy, scared, engorged with excitement.

I was in charge of his every motion. Even his stillnesses, which aped his death, were mine to chew on.

I thought there'd be drama in this tasted, sealed thing. Instead his taut body skewers my intention. I miss him now, like a shish-ka-bob you'd munch from, then put down, full. He moved away from me, decided to want another life. On a bed of rice I lay him out, and savory juices dripped brown and red to stain my white food starch. Food nauseatingly warm and viscous, sweetly rancid if sniffed at hard, otherwise the no-smell of water or nylon. He looks at me though these drawn eyelids, like peels of onion or non-seeing glaucoma. Narrative implies choice, it's a Miss America pageant readers pay to judge. In this story who's the best? Him or me? I say "me." I'm looking at him sideways, upside down, every which way: he's not to my liking—send him back to whatever kitchen he came from, sorry but *no appetite*. What future had Mickey with Ralph? Only a chiropractic problem, a taste of metal, a few bright sores some salve could soothe. I felt like Elizabeth Bennet in *Pride and Prejudice*: "How little of permanent happiness could belong to a couple who were only brought together because their passions were stronger than their virtue, she could easily conjecture."

Conjecture:
On Ralph's side I knew first, that he was a man deeply dissatisfied with life's lot. Life was too fast for him, and because I was young I believed sincerely I could slow it down to the sensual gift he gave me. I once asked Ralph if he had any idea why a bound boy excited him so. *And also that Latex!* His gaze shook a little, a tremor, then he faced me with an open glad smile. Turned out his

mother and sister used to tie him to a tree, when he was, say, five or six, when they went shopping downtown.

"That's it?" I said blankly.

"I like rope," he said. "I can still remember this old quarter-hemp twine they used."

"Did anything ever happen, I mean, when you were tied up?" *Maybe he'd been molested by some neighbors* I thought hopefully.

But apparently not.

A gag didn't really do it for him. He could have stuffed the cat down Mickey's throat and it really wouldn't have added to it. "Because they never shut me up," he said, with a reminiscent shake of the head. "No, sometimes I hollered so loud I got hoarse the next day."

Of Mickey's virtue I knew only that from the beginning of our intimacy he had been anxious to please, a white boy, with a heart of white gold. When I pushed the planes of his face downward, I saw both a long learning and a long forgetting. He pulled up his sleeve, to show me the empty space where boys in our neighborhood wore tattoos. Two square inches of flesh and tissue, blank as a circumcision. Two square inches where Ralph set his teethmarks in penetration. I poured him a glass of scotch and water, the world's flattest drink. "Welcome to Smithtown." For Mickey Manzl "passions" were the mediation we, the others in his life, placed between our knowledge of his body and our rejection of it. "Sorry there's no ice." I wanted to implant his body, toes first, into the ground and set him up a signpost, like the man going to St. Ives. He was the subject of my sentence, caught up in youth like a paper airplane caught in the wind, but unlike the paper plane he hadn't the skill to come down from his medium. As a "subject" he was thus perhaps *too supreme*, for alas, like all others my sentence needed a verb to keep going, and this his beauty would not allow. How then could he allow himself to be treated this way, on my behalf and on my say-so? This "act" of passive sodomy was the passage I predicated, this conjecture my predicate. I told Ralph one thing, Mickey another. That's my way. I am led through a corridor of gray metal, through my veins green bug juice or plasma is fed. As I walk a blank steel panel opens before me and inside my head grows a new space where a thought used to be, then another, soon I'm filled with enough air.

I'm content enough, like a bubble envelope. I lie down on my back and my hands are taped with black stickum gum, "relax now." I tell them where I live and how I used to watch *Santa Barbara* every day. And out from my mouth they extract my teeth, then begin their excavations. On the ceiling there's some famous stars or windows of the far night. I'm breathing in, not breathing out. The air's a faint blue, the color of speed and peace. Into my incision they feed a tickertape receipt imprinted with the false memories I'll afterwards connect to. I left out milk-and-cookies, not my missing diamond bracelets. I did not have that baby in high school, instead I spent the summer in Europe. I did not see that little chestnut boy, instead a man in a short white sportcoat sucked my cold little dick like gumdrops. I did not write this, this was my life, or vice versa. Me? I'm not from outer space, or even from out of your mind, I'm from the North Pole, Santa's Workshop, and I'm the eponymous Santa!

Every day I get up, get dressed, go to work, a little piece of me is dying, I quit drinking, quit cruising, I'm trying to quit smoking: still it comes on, I get afraid of Satan. I remember when I was a kid once, like six or seven: spying around I noticed a huge heap on top of a shelf in my parents' downstairs coat closet. I got a chair and stood on it and found a million presents, the chemistry set I wanted, the ViewMaster reels, the life of Merle Oberon. Also some other gifts that must have been meant for my brothers and sisters. What is going on I thought. Has the whole world gone crazy, *what about Santa?*

In the way of lovers, Dodie and I quizzed each other, "*What's the most unusual place you ever made love and to whom?*" My mind skittered over a dozen ugly places, finally settled on one, this old gray weather-beaten rowboat filled with fish, out in the middle of Long Island Sound on a cold April morning. Ralph and Kevin. Dead cold fish slithered up between our legs like Old Faithful sprouting, and some of them were still alive but cold, but that doesn't sound so unusual. It must have stuck in my head because of the gray of the bay, the gray of the sky, the gray of my skin, my little fish, my boat. All it felt like was semen, that is, the sticky wash of sex that goes on in one's head when one doesn't expect it to.

Ralph had stuffed his head with so much Eros it made him giddy, the way you feel swallowing the helium out of my party balloons. I couldn't get a grip on his thought about sex, I knew only what porn he'd read and seen. For him re-enactment was all, he was a book I guess, and at this I turned up my long beaklike nose deriding, with all youth's ferocity, his grievous lack of authenticity. What brought him out to this drunken boat? It wasn't the hunger for Life I prized. When I stretched out my hands fish, fat as stuffed sausages, crept under my fingernails. Hundreds of eyes and eggs. People eat this and I just fucked a birdbrain on it? "That was great," Ralph said. "Oh God," I told him, "you're so enthusiastic." "We have a group of guys, gets together," says Eddie, in "Satan." "You're supposed to recite the Latin Mass backwards. But most of these guys couldn't say their names backwards. So they say anything that comes into their heads. Dirty words. Curses. Spanish." I thought to myself, *boat. Fish. Unusual.* But the more I think about it, this setting was less unusual than it was a paradigm.

Bill:

Recently a friend died, and his mother found my name in his address book, or on his computer, and called me up to tell me about it. Bill was the editor of the Natalie Wood Fan Club News and through our correspondence I'd gotten to like him a great deal. His mother, Sylvia, stayed with him in the hospital after all had fled, unnerved, I guess, by Bill's increasing lack of connection with this, our own world. At one point, she told me, he walked into the dream house from *Miracle on 34th Street* and told her, "There really is a Santa, Mom." In his last hours he saw her, Natalie, extending her hands to him across a wide blue border, like a ribbon of cloud, murmuring his name, *come to me, come to me Bill.* "I'm on my way, Natalie," he said, and his mother sat nearby and her heart broke in 2 two's. "I've been waiting for you," Natalie said. "I'm coming," Bill said. Natalie smiled, her intimate, glamorous smile, and the screen dissolved the way it does in *West Side Story* when Tony first sees Maria at the big teen dance. "We don't know much about life and death," Sylvia told me. "We don't know much about what keeps a person alive, do we, Mr. Killian?" "Don't call me Mr. Killian," I said, "Nobody ever calls me that, except, you know, telephone people who want to sell magazines." "She was his whole life," Sylvia said. "And now both of them are gone."—It certainly seems like a careless symmetry.

But here's a tip for getting rid of people who want to sell you magazines on the phone. "Have I reached Mr. Killian?" I always say, "Yes," because you never know. Then it turns out they will send you three years of *TV Guide, Car & Driver, Mademoiselle* and *Sports Illustrated* for the low low introductory price of only $49.99. "How does that sound to you, Mr. Killian?"

The trick is in sounding slow but thrilled at the same time. "It sounds great! But do you have *Radio Guide* instead of *TV Guide*? See, I'm blind and I don't watch any shows on TV."

"Well, I'll check with my supervisor. While I have you on the phone, are you married? Maybe your wife would like *Redbook* or *Cosmo*."

"Yeah, but my wife . . . she's retarded."

"Oh, I'm sorry to hear that."

"Yeah, well, you got *Highlights for Children*, she likes to color. And you say you got Braille *Car & Driver*?"

"I'll have to check with my supervisor. We'll get back to you."

"Oh please do," I say. "I've been looking everywhere for *Radio News* in Braille."

I wasn't out till three in the morning: that was a nightmare you were having. I did not pass that bum in the street; I made him ham and eggs from my own kitchen cabinet. That buoyant love, that vernal stock tender, I did not refute, from him I was not absent in the Spring. Me? *I am a woman of heart and mind.* I stick my hand through a plate-glass window, the lily looks cool. Writing this down I feel so relaxed, numbers spin out of my head, ball bearings on your DC-10. Me? I was his whole life, and now both of us are gone.

GHOST PARADE

In the minute after my eyelids close, when I'm flat on my back, I hear the rapid susurration of a stage curtain opening and I see the ghosts parade in front of darkness' black fuzzy backdrop. The ghosts of the people I knew, however briefly—the writers whom I admired and loved and worked with. They speak to me without my asking them to. I see four or five of them now, each kind of raising his hand like kindergarteners, me first, me first. The quiet persistent one is Steve Abbott. He was the type who would put down his pipe like Robert Young in *Father Knows Best* and give an earnest answer to whatever was bothering Kitten, Bud or Princess.

Steve was a poet, or maybe better yet, a poetry enthusiast, in San Francisco when I first moved there and started to write in a large community. There was no stopping Steve, he was everywhere, and everything one had thought about doing he had already done. His great gift was a peculiar one, that is, he could forecast the future, ahead of the trend, he could see what would be interesting five years ahead of time, and write and speak cogently about it. He was the first to tell us about Bataille, for example. He knew all about Pascal Quignard years before I ever heard anyone else speak that name. He was an early supporter of Kathy Acker's work— Dennis Cooper's too. Although at heart a latter-day Beat poet, Steve wrote generously and well about Language Poetry. He admired Harry Mathews, Georges Perec, and others of the Oulipo School. In addition, he paired Jack Spicer and William Burroughs as twins at the same business, though I don't know if he succeeded in convincing Burroughs of the case. Whenever you visited him at his apartment—which was charmingly situated at the corner of Haight and Ashbury—he was involved in something new that one had never heard of. Today's interest in comics as literature would be old news to Steve, who was accomplished at comic art himself, though most of this material was lost or dispersed, like extra ballast, in the wreckage of his last days. And of course he kind of nourished New Narrative, at any rate he named it, devoted his magazine *Soup* to it, and attempted to theorize his perceptions in one of the essays in his book *View Askew*.

When he died we organized a memorial reading in his honor, and Allen Ginsberg who could not come asked if someone could read from his poem *Wichita Vortex Sutra*, really one of the great Ginsberg poems of the '60s. Why that poem, I asked. Ginsberg replied that Steve had caused it to be made, in the sense that, when he'd been a young student at the University of Nebraska in the spring of 1966, he had asked Ginsberg to come to the heart of the Midwest; so began the epochal voyage that Ginsberg describes in the poem. I wonder if future generations will recall his name as an appendage of Ginsberg's. His problem was, as I see it, a critical problem: his own shall we say "creative writing" had to it a certain—oh, I should just say it—he was not a particularly distinctive poet or fiction writer. It was as though he knew what he should do, and tried to do it, but "it" just wasn't there. When *Men on Men* appeared, George Stambolian's anthology of gay writers, in 1986, it was a shock, I think, to Steve, one from which he never really recovered, that he who had recommended all these guys to George—all these guys he had nurtured and discovered—that he had been excluded, rejected. Today I see it rather differently, for the way things have panned out, it's not enough to be good, all of my students, for example, are good, but you have to have the balls to keep trying new things and this Steve did every time he got up in the morning. In recent years our heroes have become what we used to think of as failures. And though his books are all out of print, each one is incomparably better than 99 per cent of the books that rule the marketplace.

Steve loved the movies, didn't matter which kind, he was an enthusiast. Long after Steve died, David Trinidad sent me an e-mail, "Remember when you and Steve Abbott and I went to see *Aliens*? I was so scared!" Guess that was 1986. I didn't remember, I was probably drunk. Steve was the man I turned to, calling him up late one night in November, asking him, is it easy to stop drinking? And finally thanks to him I stopped cold turkey December 1—I forget which year.

Bob Flanagan and I were born two days apart, on either side of Christmas, so I always knew how old he was to the day, until he died, when it didn't seem to make much difference. We enjoyed spending our birthday together if possible, but then we had to stop because of his cystic fibrosis. I remember thinking that he was the bravest guy I had ever known, until AIDS came along knocking everyone down like ten pins and it stopped mattering who was the bravest, there wasn't time for that. One year Dodie and I went to LA and for our birthday Bob arranged for us all to go on the Grave Line Tour of Hollywood, where you get into a hearse and go around LA and see all the places where the stars died. He brought his video camera and made a tape of our day, and I'm sure I overacted. The driver told us, as if it were a fact that everyone knew, that Natalie Wood had been murdered by Wagner and Walken to cover up an illicit affair. We went by Alan Ladd's house and the driver said all the rooms were super tiny with extremely low ceilings and miniature furniture so fan magazines could photograph him at home looking large. Next door was Johnny Weissmuller's house, a marshy lagoon at its side with vines he could swing from like Tarzan.

When I first met Bob, he was a poet, he had been a comedian I think, or an actor, in the Groundlings, an improv group with some kind of underground reputation? He couldn't figure out where to take his talents, and opted for the world of conceptual art, body art, which was then uber-chic, maybe even a hair "over." A year would go by, then two, and he'd say, I have to start writing again, and presently he did, while bedridden. He liked walking into a place and hearing people whisper that there goes Bob Flanagan, the super masochist. He really got off on the buzz of being his image, and was that a mistake? I couldn't decide. Surely there were some parts of him that didn't fit into the image. Sometimes I thought, well, now he'll have to top himself, like any star; it never seems fair; at least in writing the self can (sometimes) dissolve for a while so one gets some peace. But when you make yourself the showpiece of your art it has to be maintained. Even while the body is constantly under attack by the disease it suffers from, the image prevails, floats up from the body. It was the irony of his approach to sickness and disease that undercut, for me, the foolish conceptualism that fed it. For no matter how close he came to death, his public wanted more.

I wouldn't go to see him get nails punched through his dick. At Southern Exposure people fainted from his act. He would sit on our couch and tell us how pleased this made him, till the steps got the better of him and he couldn't come up any more. That's when they put the oxygen tube up his nose and he had to go everywhere with a tube up his nose and an oxygen tank strapped to his back. He kind of looked like Gary Oldman playing Sid Vicious in *Sid and Nancy*. I don't know where he ever found peace except, of course, in the kind of deep bottom space true masochists know. One time Bob read at Small Press Traffic and somehow, a group of the counselors or campers he had once known at a Bay Area CF camp heard about his reading and came to see him read. They were appalled to hear his poetry, which was filled with sexual explicitness of the XXX kind. I felt bad for him in a way. It's hard to juggle people who know you in different lives. He had a picture of himself as a teen with Jerry Lewis, acting out the part of being one of Jerry's kids. And he had a reel of himself and Sheree on different TV talk shows like what's her name, Jenny Jones.

I remember him coming to the Lab, a performance space on Divisadero Street, and showing his "Home Movies," clips from films that had impressed him as a child. Like the flogging scene in *Mutiny on the Bounty,* but some weren't that obvious. The longest sequences were Audrey Hepburn's travails in *The Nun's Story,* and the excruciating *Cinderfella* where put-upon Jerry Lewis must scramble and wait on his rich relatives—Judith Anderson haughty at the head of a mile-long table. All well and good except that, for some reason, few people came to see the show, and Bob couldn't understand why. "In LA we turned them away!" he said, scratching his head. He had little sick bags printed up—or popcorn bags, possibly could be used for both. I opened a folder the other day and one slid out, with Bob's face grinning on it. When I saw *Starship Troopers* there's a long sequence where Casper Van Dien gets whipped raw and I thought, how much Bob would have enjoyed that, if it had come out in 1962 instead of now.

Jack Spicer wrote, "What is seen in the distance when the murmurings of some defeated ideas, or lives, or even dreams are suddenly manifest? A ghost.

"Ghosts are not shrewd people. History begins with shrewd people and ends with ghosts."

Kathy Acker, prowling around the tile floor in the rehearsal space at John Woodall's studio, investing the lines she had been given with enormous flair and savagery, like a white tiger. Her little body pumped up like an inflatable cushion, like Dali's couch made up of Mae West's lips. When I hear the expression, larger than life, I think of Kathy, who could actually seem big through sheer presence. Well, presence is never actually sheer, it's opaque, a complex mechanism with a hundred different factors and parts. Mostly she was in control, and it wasn't always pretty. We were rehearsing Carla Harryman's theater piece *Memory Play*, in which we were all charged with playing animals of one sort or another, and Kathy had it all down from Day One. Rehearsals lasted so long—ten months or so—that eventually Kathy dropped out, but her spirit continued to animate the production. I learned a lot about stage presence from aping her.

She came over and sat on our gray futon and talked about how people in the Bay Area thought she was made out of money, how they were always pestering her to give readings for free, even though her fee was ten thousand dollars an appearance. "Gigs," she called them. Did anyone ever pay her ten thousand dollars, or was that just a catchy round number? I felt like paying her money just to continue talking. We went to the Thai restaurant around the corner on Howard, and she told me about Dario Argento's films, about which she was writing for her novel, *My Mother: Demonology*. She was curious about Robin Blaser, and his relationship with Spicer. She could be convincing, bending her body from the waist right into your face, turning those enormous eyes on you, making you feel—not listened to, exactly—but talked at in a most extraordinarily personal way, as though by being her audience of one you were fulfilling an important destiny you hadn't even, until this moment, known was yours. Always, though, her eyes drifted away over your shoulder for her next fuck, or on the lookout for someone she had offended. Someone she was embarrassed by. I think she had a thin skin and was easily hurt. She would be astounded if you didn't remember every single page of every one of her books, which, love her or hate her, are all pretty much the same. (That's not true, but you can't remember everything.) And sometimes what seemed a perfectly grand friendship from the outside went up in flames overnight. He or she (and her mother of course) "suicided," a neologism never far from her thoughts.

From my office I had free tickets to see some Steven Soderbergh film so we went out, me, Dodie, Kathy and her boyfriend the monk, she was always anxious to see the latest films, preferably in a sneak preview like this one, and or if they were free. She would walk out on any event if she were not on the guest list. The film was a zoo, we got there late and easily a hundred more people had been let in than they had seats for. It was *Kafka* (1991). A year or so later we were supposed to see *Evil Dead III Army of Darkness* and Dodie flipped on the answering machine to hear Kathy's breathy voice, "You guys, I can't go tonight, sorry, I met this *guy* and he's *fucking* me and I'm getting *majorly distracted* . . ." her voice trailing off as though she had dropped the phone into a bath of warm water. Minutes later the voice reappeared, again to whisper, "Sorry, how about Monday?" Then click, beep. I should have saved that tape that's for sure, sent it to Duke University to be with the rest of her papers.

She had never been invited to Naropa—and then one day the call came, and she was thrilled about the possibility of more promotion and more sex. (For Naropa had had a wild reputation for what we might now call sexual harassment.) "They've scheduled me for 26 interviews!" she crowed. A few weeks later I asked her how it had gone. "You know those interviews?" Kathy growled. "What they mean by interview is that you *meet with the students!* And I had to meet with 26 of them! After eight or so I called them off. And I never got laid—not once. All the action was down the hall, in Steven Taylor's room. He and Lee Ann's door was like the revolving door at Macy's Herald Square." She was disgruntled, unexpectedly puritanical. "Don't those two have anything else on their minds but sex, sex, sex?"

"How was the scenery?"

She gave me a look. "Like you really want to know."

"It's supposed to be beautiful, the Rockies."

That look doubled in skepticism. "I didn't notice. Who would? Not with all those 'interviews.'"

Glen Helfand wrote something she didn't like—perhaps a favorable review of that novel Gary Indiana wrote that contains a hilarious parody of Kathy. At a club a few days later she walked up to him and dashed her drink in his face. This had never happened to him before. This gesture, familiar from the movies or from day-time soap opera, brought itself to life, expanding outward like the petals of some miraculous flower. People said she had burned all her bridges in New York, then in London, and now in San Francisco the same patterns of behavior were becoming evident. And then she disappeared and the other stories I remember about her are O. Henry sentimental. "Ghosts are not shrewd people. History begins with shrewd people and ends with ghosts."

"Sam D'Allesandro" wasn't his real name—he wore this badge, this false badge of identity, with a disarming take-it-or-leave-it irony—but it wasn't until after he died that I found out he had been born "Richard Anderson." Surely the plainest name of an American author, ever? At his Hugo Street apartment, after the funeral, his parents and family showing us pictures of him growing up on the farm, and so forth, and they kept talking about "Richard" this and "Richard" that, and I must have looked bewildered enough that Fritz Schultz took me aside to one corner and whispered, "Sam's real name was Richard." Last month Sean Monohan showed me a series of drivers' licenses he keeps in a box, more pictures of Sam, with the name Richard Anderson eventually dying out, circa age 23? And the name "Sam D'Allesandro" taking over, supplanting the birth-name, the discarded name. And always the photos on the licenses radiant and luscious—he could have been modeling for George Platt Lynes. So that when he wanted to model and for some reason no photographer could really capture his beauty, he was disappointed of course. It's odd that there are people who are anti-photogenic, who look so much better in life than on film.

With a stricken look Sam would confide that he had been born the son of the '70s Warhol superstar Joe Dallesandro, and I believed him, though something about the chronology didn't gibe too well. Later on, this claim backfired, in Los Angeles, when a press listing of one of his readings there alluded to this famous dad who happened to be very much alive and living only a few miles away. Uh-oh! Maybe Sam identified with Joe Dallesandro's working-class values, his diamond in the rough appeal, his integrity or his allure? Joe played the addict, the hustler, the stud, the ambisexual whose lack of affect had its own, powerful affect—Sam did too.

When one met him, he proffered this fake name as if only he and you were in on the joke, as a shortcut to intimacy. Another part of him wanted to be famous, so he could get to meet and know as equals his idols—Patti Smith, Yoko Ono, Andy Warhol, David Bowie, Nina Simone, Bob Dylan, Kathy Acker. Did he ever meet any of them? I don't think so, but such was his tact that I don't really know.

But he did get to meet us—the writers of San Francisco who were busy working on a "New Narrative," a community-based project in which we, the prose writers of San Francisco, would recuperate narrative from the trap of modernism by rearticulating it as a postmodern conceptual art, wise to the precepts of Language poetry. We took Sam to our hearts, and learned of his potential quick, thanks to the untiring efforts of the late Steve Abbott. Immediately Sam took up the pose of a besieged Nijinsky fending off the imperious advances of a haughty Diaghilev. (Steve, Sam told us, wanted to spank his ass with a slab of bacon.

Or vice versa. And, you know, it did sort of sound like something Steve would say.) Yet Sam depended on Steve, and took to his teenage daughter Alysia as well, and after his death Steve did a yeomanlike job of editing *The Zombie Pit* for Crossing Press, when they had a brief fling with publishing gay fiction.

I first met Sam in late summer, 1983 when Bryan Monte introduced me to him after their reading at Intersection, in those days a leading artists' run space in San Francisco. His book *Slippery Sins* had appeared, and its potential intrigued me although I disliked the poetry. That is, it seemed like performance poetry. Later, he said he had taken the performance texts he had written and performed and chopped them up so they'd look like poetry, but also he'd written some "real" poems. Over the years, with the encouragement of his long-time friend, and former lover Fritz Schultz, Sam's work grew in power and authority. If the too-beautiful poems of *Slippery Sins* were vague about sex, vague about gender and the body, the prose he started to write now broke these boundaries down—flattened them out, in a series of bulldozing maneuvers, risky with enormity. His writing became "edgy," edgy enough to match his personality. And his willingness to revise, his attempts to improve every sentence became clear.

He would re-write a paragraph endlessly, often to mixed results. Even if it were "perfect" he might throw it away. I imagine he did the same thing with his attitudes, his feelings, with the various lives he led. This creation, revision, perfection and dismissal links his work in a mysterious way to God's, or what I imagine is God's. His stories attempt a religious philosophy they don't achieve, for what actuates them is his own desire, then its absence. His book comes to us as a phallocentric model of writing, the power and the exhaustion endlessly renewable. It's no accident, I suppose, that each story seemed less like a re-write of his last than a mirror image of it.

Sam and I met only rarely. I retain, however, an indelible picture of his looks, reinforced by the skill with which he was able to make them one of the central themes of his writing. I've known three or four writers with more glamour, and three or four with more sex appeal—but Sam's personal beauty was astonishing. At first it formed a screen behind which one could hardly see his work. One day he came over to visit and we watched the John Huston film of *Reflections in a Golden Eye*. Elizabeth Taylor and Marlon Brando. (On a then-new VCR; funny to think they're so ubiquitous now, but back then people would make dates to see one.) In a just world, I thought, Taylor and Brando would be sitting in my living room watching Sam and me on the screen.

Personally I took great interest in his development because it seemed to me, at that time, that we were experiencing another "San Francisco Renaissance," new narrative subdivision. My own work seemed inextricably tied to that of Bob Glück, Bruce Boone, Dodie, Sam, Steve, Dennis Cooper, Kathy, Carla Harryman, Francesca Rosa, Camille Roy. We were all in this "thing" together. I can hardly expand on that any further without getting weird. When he got sick, he wrote, "I'm terminal and that seems to make me important, no longer answerable for my bills or attitudes, my refused meals a sign of increasing power, withdrawal a symptom of bravery. No one will say so but I'm terminal. I don't care about politics or the old lovers I'd wanted to see on my deathbed. I've forgotten the meaning of everything except my medication. Buried beneath layers of thin tissue, a refugee on a field of darkness, I am isolated, confused, as white noise fills my ears. Only the world inside my imploding body is real, like watching on film as I disintegrate. I clap my hands at this new game that already bores me. I'm a pumpkin caving in, in a tunnel without return that grows narrower all the time."

WHO IS KEVIN KILLIAN?

. . . I'm always reading the *Chronicle*, every morning, at work, and I saw how the guy died, the guy who invented sodium pentathol. And you know, I felt bad for him. Didn't realize he was still alive.

Did you know him?

No, as a matter of fact I didn't. I mean, sodium pentathol's been around so long—part of my consciousness, you might say—I never realized any one person actually must have invented it. Like last year when the obit columns said the man who invented the Tequila Sunrise died. Same thing. And two years ago this old Swiss nut who had thought up Velcro. But with this sodium pentathol guy—maybe he was in Chicago, maybe it was some kind of offshoot of the Manhattan Project—I really felt bad, not because of anything pertinent to my life—I just got swept away with thinking how pathetic life is, that you could do something and nobody would know it, and how eventually you die and eventually everyone alive who remembers you will die—then you really don't exist any more. I remember Jerry Ackerman telling me he had written the life of Gerôme, the French painter, and he found one ancient old woman who had actually met him—and she was, like, three-and-a-half and she'd sat on his lap for 15 minutes.

I found that so pathetic. After she goes—and, who knows, she's probably dead now, because this was some time ago Ackerman met her.

Well, but his work remains—although I don't know it myself.

Yeah, I guess so. That's a nice tie you have on. No, I mean it. One doesn't often see fabric like that, is it naugahyde? But anyway that's when you said you had some pentathol I said, Hell, why not, let's do it in memory of this *guy*. Shitty thing is I don't even remember his name. But I'm almost sure he worked in Chicago.

I don't know Gerôme either. He's one of those big, blowsy French romantic painters, Ackerman's the expert on him. I guess they all have one expert on each of them. It's funny that here in the City there's this painter, Jerome Caja, they just call him "Jerome,"—just like the French guy! He's got this show now at Southern Exposure. Jerome does all his pictures from makeup— he's into drag and shit. Anyhow—oh, and all the pictures are real little, like a few inches square, because I guess, because of the price of cosmetics. So at Southern Exposure he had this show with this other man, Charles Sexton—and Sexton died—and he said to Jerome to have him cremated and give the ashes to Jerome, and make pictures out of them. And one of the pieces there is this ashtray—like that—filled with Charles' ashes and Jerome painted this little tiny picture of Charles at the tip of one of the cigarette butts in the ashtray. Isn't that gross? I don't know why, it gave me the creeps.

I really like that tie. It's very sensuous. My dad had a chair like that. Who gave it to you?

It's silk.

Did somebody give it to you who loved you, must have been, it has that feeling coming through it. I like the blue and the yellow. Steve Abbott had a few of Jerome's pictures, and Bruce and I were talking about, well!—about what will happen when Steve dies—because we have to sell his stuff for Alysia; and gee,

I guess all he really had are books—*and* these two Jerome pictures. So we were so depressed thinking about the day coming wow, Steve will actually die. And you know how when you're down in the dumps, brooding, sometimes one of you says something absolutely tacky and you both crack up. Well, we said we would charge the estate the rental of a helicopter—because we'd have to fly the books to Berkeley—and then each take one of the Jerome pictures, and we'd tell Alicia, *gee, I guess those books weren't worth all that much but here's ten dollars.* Oh, it was awful, but we were cracking up. Don't tell Alysia.

I don't know her. Otherwise I would.

Oh, she's really sweet. I guess I always say that, about people. Doesn't give you much sense of her character, does it? I'm a jerk. No, not a jerk, but sometimes I feel very inarticulate. The people I admire speak well: speak rapidly, firmly. They use intellectual precepts. But isn't kindness the important thing? You know what Cat Stevens said, we're only here for a short while. You don't get love without you give love back.

So in your heart of hearts you're kind of a drip?

Well, I'm sentimental, "drip" is in dispute. I cry a lot, these tears well up constantly, especially when I see *West Side Story.* When Natalie's on the fire escape and says, "Te amo, Tony," that's when I start to spout, like a geyser or a—I don't know—widower or something. There's always this displacement between the characters of my fantasy and the sentence I'm stomping around in, wild, big-footed, like Lucy and that Italian woman turning grapes to wine.

There's not much I want to know about you.

There is something I want to get out of my system, as long as I'm feeling this pink—way . . . I remember Lynne Tillman has this analyst for so many years she was totally transferred—I mean this woman was like her mother. And one evening after she got home Lynne did this double-take, her key in the latch—

remembering the funny look on this old analyst's face right when they said goodbye. It was the same look Lynne's father had had one night when he went to bed and he had this tremendous stroke. So Lynne rushed to the phone and all night long started calling her analyst, no answer, finally she took a cab all the way uptown or wherever and there was the ambulance, pulling away, and sure enough, she had had a stroke and—you could predict it from an expression? . . . It's not only your tie, it's your whole ensemble, the finish of your package. Henry James could have invented you—no, Abel Gance; but your gilding, the embonpoint, *those* Henry James might have supplied.

Thanks. In your stories there's a recurring figure—a drugged or otherwise helpless male, married off, without his consent. Does this have anything to do with your own marriage, to Dodie Bellamy?

Hey, I—gee, I wonder . . . never thought of it like that. Maybe. I guess. You know, that's the writer's unconsciousness bubbling up, like goat's head soup, right? But hey, I'm forty years old, I've been on drugs all my life. Every day I remember less, it's like dissolving. So life is like a drug, my consciousness has always been impaired, but also magnified I suppose. What happened is I fell in love with her, I know it's odd and everyone said it wouldn't last, not to my face of course.

Although people say such mean things to one's face I'm surprised that wasn't one of them. It's just that I'm gay, why get married?

Maybe you're afraid of AIDS.

Yeah well sure. I was really frightened, for myself, then after those tests less frightened for me, more frightened for the—whole fabric of society. You know. I felt this funny twinge of fear when Anthony Perkins died. I saw myself as one of those pathetic figures in the *Midnight Tattler* who say Richard Simmons paid them money to spank him. Or Merv Griffin had them dress in cellophane on Easter Sunday and pelt him with painted eggs.

When he died I got the cold shivers. I met him on an elevator, in a hotel in midtown Manhattan. A winter afternoon, not too cold. I was all agog, fairly bursting with excitement. Of course I thought of him as Norman Bates. He was taller than most people in the crowded elevator. This was during the MLA Convention, of course. That's where all of us sexual deviants went every year during the '70s. It was like—the Mineshaft and the MLA.

It was one of those cases where one thing led to another, but it was definitely my chasing that did it. Now when I see him on television, which is like always, I really get cold. Not that he was so good-looking to begin with. He kind of looked like a tortoise face, like the happy turtle who played a guitar they used to have on cartoons when I was a boy, I can't remember the name—like "Touche Turtle" or someone. And he always plays this weirdo, like Jim Pearsall or whoever, I mean Norman Bates was the least of his problems. He was a busy man, there to see his old friend Ingrid Bergman. Who I also got to meet. She was raddled with cancer, but still luminous—a Mexican lantern you plant in the sand.

Why do you love the stars so much?

. . . . I can't really answer that. I don't know. That's a side issue. I guess the worst thing I did was this one star, I wanted his autograph terrrible, and nothing seemed to help—I mean I wrote letter after letter, pleading for this autograph, and then I caved in on myself and said I had the HIV virus, and right away, snap, he sent me this long letter, saying to me, don't give up, a cure's right around the corner. I felt so guilty. Also it seemed like such bad karma, know what I mean? I had to take another test right away. It just seems like a miracle. I remember telling Nayland about this incident, and how bad I felt, and he was saying, "Oh that wasn't such a heinous," you know, "thing to do, Kevin," but his eyes were just shocked and all the color drained out of his face no matter what his mouth was saying. I mean I remember being on top of that bar, so drunk I couldn't see, with the bartender straddling the bar . . . Couldn't remember if he'd had his dick in me or not but I assume he did, I assume he came. I remember him jamming this thing up my ass, this crazy thing you squirt different mixes with, ginger ale, Coke, etc., this long wily thing lives at the end of a metallic kind of telephone cord, and it was like—whoosh! Ginger ale, whoosh! Lemon-lime or whatever—water I guess—and him saying, can you tell what this is when he'd press each button. And drunk as I was three times out of four I could guess right.

Like those Russian ESP experiments when they hold spades and hearts behind their hands up to their heads real hard like they're concentrating—anyway, you can see why I was nervous, especially because within six months this man was dead, dead of AIDS, and I was trying to stay sedate, not to panic.

Or that Argento picture that opens with the psychic, seated in front of an audience in one of those grand European halls that looks like an opera house. Suddenly she calls out, "There's someone in this room with 'danger' attached to him!" She starts mumbling about this child with a knife, a Christmas tree, this terrible danger and blood—the crowd goes wild. Oh I know, it's *Deep Red—Profondo Rosso* in Italian. It figures with Argento it's a gay guy who does it in this one, no it's not, it's his mother, that's right, well, what's worse? Me and Dodie were at Just Thai with Kathy, Acker who was telling us all about Argento and how marvelous and sick he is, this led us to watch oh, all his shows, they're so disturbed and sick and luscious.

Do you have sex with a lot of men?

It's like, she thinks of it as being faithful. I don't, but I do it anyhow, because I don't want to hurt her. That's the only reason. She says, you're in love with that boy, or that man, and I say, like, no. I'm not. Why aren't you? she says. You're gay! I say I don't know, I'm in love with you. She says, it's not natural, how can I satisfy you, you're gay! So I'm gay, doesn't mean I'm a cheater.

That makes it sound like I think I'm better than cheaters, I'm not. I used to depend on cheaters. I liked nothing more than playing *back street girl* to some married man. They're safe. They don't want to rock the boat, yet they're torn by these tremendous longings. And now I'm one of them myself but I learned from their example. I guess you could say I'm the new improved model. Oh and Kathy's new book has this huge incredible section that re-tells the plot of *Suspiria*, the weirdest of all the Argento films, only she calls it *Clit City*. Am I talking too fast?

No—I'm getting it all down. Did you really see those pictures by Jerome Caja?

No—but Rex Ray and Glen Helfand told me 'bout them. Isn't that the same thing? I mean, Southern Exposure's not on my *route*.

And then Dodie and Bob went, with this visiting priest from Italy. The jet set priest who told Dodie she looked like the young Iris Murdoch.

This sent her to the bookshelves and she read *Nuns and Soldiers* and *The Italian Girl*—gobbled them down like candy.

And this priest is so charming. We were sitting around this white garden table at lunch, him sitting there with this urbane smile as if to say, "I know everyone who's anyone, try me," but I couldn't think of anyone Italian, off hand, and I said, "Do you know Dario?"—Argento—and what d'you think, he says, "Yes, he was one of my students." like in high school, "and so was Cicciolina." Can you top that?

But why do you lie?

It's not lying, it's a—an attempt . . . to do something about my life. Before Steve's death we would go to the movies, or rather he would come by in a cab, just this one fleet that took those voucher tickets—his eyes were so bad he could only watch movies not TV. He said he was having this one dream, over and over, took place in London, where Mama Cass Elliott died, and he was this flake of ham lodged in her throat. And we were watching *Encino Man?* And he was too tired to get up after the picture was over, and so we just sat there, and I saw this big bucket of popcorn that these people left—they had hardly touched a bite—so we sat there and he told me about this one time, he had gone to New York, there was one person he wanted to meet, to make a pilgrimage to, and this was Helen Adam, the poet. And she was about eighty-five at the time—but still spry—it must have been ten years ago. And Steve says, "Kevin I thought I'd tell my grandchildren about meeting Helen Adam and now it looks like just the opposite," and I said, "Well, I'll tell your grandchildren if you can't. Or she can tell them about meeting you, Steve. Because she'll outlive us all if she's such a diva."

You eat food other people leave behind?

It just doesn't seem as important as the show. *I* have this one recurring dream that my fingernails keep growing—they grow all around the world, and stab me in the back. What's that about? In another I'm walking across this rickety bridge of life, and knives are flying everywhere, and some people are stabbed by them, some get to live. It was Halloween, I think, and David Rattray came to town. I had never met him but Eileen gave him my phone number, well, he was awfully nice, and he came to town and read at the store, he was like this weird spaced-out cross between Dario Argento and Anne Bancroft—I wonder if he was Italian. Afterwards me and Avery went to have a drink with him, he was telling us about all these drugs he spent the sixties doing—oh first he said he'd written this story about this very chic '20s lesbian in Paris, like Natalie Barney, killing her girlfriend, did I think it would upset the lesbian community here, in San Francisco! His head was large, and his eyes were these—pools of darkness, though he spoke very sweetly. He was from Long

Island like me. Then Dennis came around a month ago and said Rattray fell down in front of his house and he has this brain tumor, and what can be done?

And then Kush over there called up and said, "I have sad news to report, David Rattray is dead." You know, he was courteous. Michael Palmer said he visited Rattray in the early sixties, and he scared Michael, but by now all the fierce wild horror stuff had burned out of him except inside his brain I guess. I'm glad I got him to sign my autograph book, but that sounds so shallow, doesn't it?

I'm not here to pass judgment, though tradition says I should.

When I was young I had this friend, who was very powerful in my life. He made me do these things I wouldn't want anyone to know about. Things I hated myself for doing. But when I did them I got sexually stimulated.

Should I stay or should I go?

Oh that's okay, you go and sit down, but I want you to come back, you hear? I need you to imitate this powerful friend of mine later. "Now you take Philip Mandel," said my powerful friend. "The kid's a clown, but he's not all bad. Lives in the Bronx, right, he's got nothing going for him. Lives with his Mom or some shit, she's an immigrant I guess, she's fucking got garlic and cabbage on the stove all day. Works at the Museum which is no job for a man. Sometimes he shows up in the office smothered in some fairy Chanel perfume, and you know why? and you know why? To try to hide the immigrant cooking smells, but like covering up shit with sugar, some things a man can't hide! Christ, no wonder the kid's a mess. Envy eating him up. Just like it's eating you, Kevin.

"I know. I know. Because like, I used to sit there in Hammond, Indiana, only thing I had was hot nuts. I felt that I'd never get out of that house. Fucking *Chicago* seemed like Paradise. House filled with tubs of laundry—other people's underwear my

Mom had to scrub the comestains out of, and why? To put groceries on our fucking table, and I tell you, Kevin, I wanted to kill all the lousy motherfuckers. The rich folks from Hammond Heights in their Caddies, I wanted to tear their heads off, shit down their necks.

"Mom, she had to kiss the ass of every one of them, otherwise hey! Hammond's got other *laundresses.*

"So why," he said evenly, "why don't you go up there and schmooze with him. He's just asking for it and although he's not my type, I wouldn't mind watching the two of you, you know?"

"Fuck *you.*"

"No honestly Kevin!"

I'm a friend of Philip's, I told the woman who came to the door. Bits of vegetables clung to her damp pale forearms, I guess vegetables just kind of cling to one. Face to face we stood there for a long moment, before she recollected herself.

"I'm his ma," she explained. "Fixing dinner." In the humid air, just as my friend had foretold, hung garlic and cabbage, and another odor, too, tangy and bitter. Herring perhaps. Goldie Mandel seemed overwhelmed by my car, a 68 Mustang with nothing to live for. As I came into the house, I had the chance to study her further, a chance I welcomed, since my policy was "Know the opposition." In profile her face seemed doughy, irregular, in that her chin was slung back under her jaw like a bridle, and her rough, orange-tinged skin had some of the hard sheen of a ripening pumpkin, but her sharp velvety eyes missed nothing: she should have been a reconnaissance gunner instead of a mother. "Phil's taking a nap. I see to it he gets his rest."

So saying, she ushered me into a parlor which shared some of the traits of the waiting room of a doctor's office: low ceiling, subdued lighting, three or four glossy, but out-of-date magazines spread across a black, square table in front of two straightback chairs—Frank Gehry kind of chairs. "Philly works good and hard you know."

I remembered his languid impassivity at the museum office and marvelled once again at how easily the young seem to be able to deceive their parents. "Indeed he does," I hastened to agree.

Soothed, Mrs. M. favored me with a slight smile. "Sit, Mister? I fetch the boy."

"Thank you," I said, and busied myself with an old copy of "Modern Romance." *I Gave Myself to my Doctor*, I read. *I Needed "Crack" to Keep my Husband Free from Pain.*

"Mother, please, you *know* about my beauty sleep."

Philip's mother, her marrowlike face flushed with excitement, burst into his bedroom breathing hard. Her hands poked into his side under the blanket. Shaking him, she took inventory of the dark room. What had to be straightened up before I could be allowed to see it? She didn't want me to think she kept a sloppy house—that would never do. While Philip rose from his dreams, she began systematically to pick up the clothes that lay strewn across the bookcases and the armchair, meanwhile humming a popular song.

"Sit down to dinner, it's hot and ready. Look, Phil, look at the flowers your friend bought for me."

"They're beautiful," Philip allowed.

"My mother always told me, don't come to visit with empty arms."

"That's a Hungarian expression, was your mother a woman of Hungary?"

"No," I said. "She was an Irish colleen."

"Like Maureen O'Hara," said Mrs. Mandel.

"Or Sinead O'Connor," I said. Dinner was tasty as anything you'd ever eaten at the UN Embassy or somewhere. Who knows

what it was, some kind of Eastern European airlift vine mush.—
I'm not too good with food if it isn't what I'm used to. People
laugh at me for drinking Tab, that's okay, at first I started doing
it for an affectation, because it was a girl type drink.

*Over and over again these affectations and not much sense of a
real personality underneath them.*

Well anyway—Philip's mom kept shaking her head with happiness watching me eat and I got a queer kind of loser feeling in
my stomach. For I'm just this phony nut boy and you'd think she
was serving the Duchess of Windsor. I wanted to be noticed, I
think; to feel *different* somehow, so I did a lot of stupid things, I
remember in graduate school all us grad students had these
offices in the English Department and the other students put up
posters in theirs, oh, these dull things, D H Lawrence or Virginia
Woolf, and I had my posters of Farrah and Raquel Welch, and
this one guy comes into my office and says, "God, how jejune!"
After dinner I remark on how dark it 's getting outside. "Can I
stay over?" I asked Philip, all bright-eyed and bushy-tailed, this
phony garbage.

"Sure, if you want. It's no palace, but—sure."

Goldie Mandel dried her hands on her apron and joined in
the fun of digging out the old cot from the basement storage
room. The cot they used for when relatives came to visit. Must
have been rats in it all summer though. No, this is no good. The
three of us stared sadly at the discolored chewed cot like relatives
at a funeral.

"You'll have to sleep in Phil's bed," she said. "Philly can sleep
with me."

"I don't mind sharing," I said demurely. "Philip and I can
sleep together."

"He goes downtown, they call him 'Philip.' Look at his angry
face, you know, in my mind he's still my baby. I guess mothers
will never learn. Sorry, Phil!"

Philip was dying a million agonies of chagrin. Any minute now she'd be hauling down the photo albums from the vulgar, *glassed-in* sideboard in her dining room. The photos of him crying at his circumcision they all found such knee-slappers. Or how about when he played Hamlet in PS 23 in Goldie's stockings taped tight to his ass with electrical tape, for tights? But finally, with many additional expressions of gratitude and wonder, his mother turned away, and retired to her part of the flat, I hope for good, even Yma Sumac retired, why can't she! "Goodnight, Philly, good night, Mr. Killian, thanks ever so for the mums."

"They're not mums," Phil said.

"Listen to Mr. Luther Burbank with his wide flower experience," I heard her snort in the darkness.

"Do you *have* wide flower experience?" I asked him, and when I saw him blush I knew he was thinking of me.

In bed he was careful to turn away as I stripped to the skin. "There's some extra pajamas," he ventured, "in the dresser."

"You sound like your mother," I replied. As I turned to examine his posters and souvenirs, I felt him gaze on my body, and casually enough I picked up my balls with both hands, as if to scratch around them, and I tickled the smoother vein that kind of separates them, feeling the heat and throb, as the quiet stillness of the night pushed through the room, a deep lush quiet that was broken only by the ominous rumble of a motorbike down below. "Nice room," I said.

"It's not a nice room," he replied, in a low fervent voice. "How can you be so patronizing of me."

"Okay," I said. "It's not what you want. But it's okay."

"Why did you come here, don't you want to leave me any pride?"

"I want to be your friend," I said, ingenuous as a china doll. Naked I approached the bed and stood beside it, my elbows close in to my sides, my hands outstretched. "There's this gap between us I want to close over. That's why I came. Hey, this looks plenty big enough for two," I added, lifting myself by the cock into the bed. "Shove over, Philip, don't be a hog."

How old were you when this happened?

Oh real young, like twenty something, or yes. Philip was older than I, but to me he seemed like a boy to me. His long smooth body like a field of new snow, in his immaculate blue pajamas, striped with thin lines of black, buttoned up to the very top of the neck. "Aren't you warm in those?" I asked.

"Why are you here?" he kept asking me, just like an ignorant tourist or something. "You and all the rest of you treat me like dirt under your feet."

"I want to make it up to you," I told him, honestly. Then I lied, "You and me just got off on the wrong foot, that's all."

"What do you mean, wrong foot? What are you implying?" Like I wasn't supposed to know he was queer as Cole Porter.

"Listen!" I cried out. I shoved my pillow and face near to his, and lowered my lashes. Demure. Oh, I thought of this story about what I'm afraid of, I mean besides AIDS, and also being homeless and so forth. But Dodie and I went to lunch or something with Leslie Dick and Peter Wollen and for some reason, maybe a dog passed by, and he said he's afraid of large dogs, ever since he was a child in his native country, which I'm pretty sure is England. Then it turned out that Leslie is afraid of rats. I forget why, it was something about she had a rat in her cradle or something. But anyway she was working at CalArts, and had to inspect the art projects of the students, and this one girl disliked her and she had to go into this girl's room, this big warehouse type dorm like a cave, and this girl had put all kinds of wood up to make a fort, and vegetation, I mean like barrels of rotting food in this awful warren of spores and—

And rats.

It was like this installation like Joseph fucking Beuys she was making, this awful girl. And this was at night, too. In what little light there was she wore this malicious grin—it was as though she somehow knew ahead of time that Leslie hated rats. Well anyway there I was and I was saying to Philip, "I—feel funny saying this, but—ever since we met I've been fighting this strange attraction, to you, Philip . . . No, wait, don't get up, I just have to get this out of my system," and I told him of all the lonely nights I fought my strange attraction to him, and how I went to analysts for help, but how it was just too strong to deny any longer, and believe me, Phil was lapping this up. His eyes widened, narrowed, did every trick thing under the sun. His breath grew short, then he made himself hold still. "You'll think I'm crazy but hell, so do I, I just had to let you know, I don't know why."

"I don't know what to say," he brought forth finally.

"I know. I'm a pervert."

"No, it's not that. I understand."

"You do?"

His dark eyes closed and opened again. "I have some of the same—feelings, I guess," he told me. Gosh, scoop of the fucking century, but I put surprise and joy all over my face and gulped at him. Then I waited, then I whispered.

"You want to do anything? Philip? I'm right here." So saying, I reached out in the dark and put my hand to his smooth face, feeling the blush in his cheek, in the dark, unable to see his expression except for the fright in his tired, confused eyes. Something within me weakened my resolve, a variation on the feeling you get watching *60 Minutes* show Canadian trappers crushing minks in steel traps. "Relax now, this won't hurt a bit, and Philip? No one will know."

"Kevin," he said slowly, in little chunks, so I could barely make out my own name. Under my hand his mouth moved, jittery, alive.

"Don't worry," I told him, as though he'd been in a terrible car crash and help was on its way. "No one will ever know. Kiss me," I said. "I want you to, it's okay."

His whole head was shaking on the embroidered pillowcase, as he faced me. I slid closer to his body, and waited until he got his breath. I continued to probe his face, his ear, his nose, his moving mouth that trembled but made no sound. In the night a succulent tenderness dislodged itself from my brain to take an eerie shape between us, like a third person we had both loved very much. But there was no such person, as far as I knew. Philip finally spoke. But only to say he couldn't breathe. "I used to have asthma," he said, downcast. "As a *child*. Maybe it's coming back."

"I don't think so. You're just surprised."

"No, seriously, I can't swallow." He pointed to his throat and his nose with the exaggerated fright of Harpo Marx, a dumbshow to convince me.

"I won't make you swallow," I promised, and I lowered my hand to find the hole in the front of his pajamas, and I found it, while Philip protested his asthma, in weak lost syllables. I clutched part of his dick in my hand, felt it warm and hard, its slick surface dry and smooth, like slate warmed in the sun. Gave him a squeeze, he liked it. He tried to say no, with his voice, and my finger slid down the length of his cock to his balls, poking them a bit as if to say, anyone home, and out of nowhere Philip stopped demurring and laughed a laugh of pure pleasure, his head thrown back and his mouth open to the big world.

"I can't believe this!" he shouted.

"Quiet, now, you'll wake your mother."

"I can't fucking believe this," Philip yelled, a little less loudly. He seized my head and made me face him, and face to face we cracked up, in the blackness of the night his face was alight with joy. In a minute I had him naked and adoring below me as I pressed his shoulders down with my weight, his mouth smiling into the mattress, I tugged on his ears and brought his neck and head up high, riding his back like a jockey, his thin strong waist my saddle. "Now you'll get that wide flower experience." His pajamas lay crumpled on the rug like a blue and black candy wrapper after a fair.

And then careful to face him, I lowered myself onto Philip's face, felt him suck all the rich juices out, while his hands crept up along my legs like cunning cloths. I saw the whites of his eyes gleam in the dark, his head thrown back in excitement, his lips wrapped around the shaft of my cock. I guess I was trying to give him something back . . . He swallowed me up, I felt the walls of the room come in close for a minute like anxious spectators—; then they retreated to their proper place, made corners again, yanking the books and furniture back to themselves, realigned.

In the morning when I awoke he was awake already. Biting his nails and so forth. He was very nervous. I wasn't really thinking about him that much, no, just more about my friend and what next. You know, we were kids. Thom Gunn told me—you know I'm writing this book with Lew, this book about Jack Spicer's life—anyway Duncan and Spicer and all these gay Berkeley guys were living in this one house, and somehow so was Philip K. Dick. And Thom Gunn once asked Duncan what it was like to be a roommate of Philip K. Dick. And one night Duncan thought he was all alone, reading and writing in his room, and he looked up and there in the open doorway Philip K. Dick is just standing there you know, jerking off, or getting ready to come. And he made this one, you know, motion of his hips, like Nijinsky in the Spectre of the Rose, and came onto the floor, and Duncan was too astonished to say a word. And Philip K. Dick just turned around and went back to his room and they never talked about it, or nothing.

But why did he do that?

I don't know—Duncan said, years later, that it was just the pressure cooker atmosphere, this steam heat . . .

So Philip was biting his nails—my Philip, nervous, you know. "Everything's going good," I said, stroking the soft length of his prick. Skittish at first, Philip began smiling halfway through, like a kid at the circus. In daylight his skin shone as though the sun was trapped into it. "Yeah everything's working," I said. "But the thing is, I have this friend and I was wondering, could he come over sometime—he's real nice." Now here's where I want you to be my powerful friend.

Okay.

At his look instantly I realized I'd outsmarted myself. In a violent motion, as if stung by bees, Philip slid his hips further down the mattress. "What *friend*?"

"Just this guy."

"What his name?"

"He's sharp, real sharp."

"Real sharp, eh? Name wouldn't happen to be George Dorset, would it, Kevin?"

"Yeah, so what about it? Do you want to?"

"Is that why you came here? To be his pimp?"

Philip vaulted up out of bed, pulled the bedspread round his waist. He wouldn't look at me. "The fabulous George Dorset who gets under everyone's skin like *cocaine!*"

I wondered if his mother had knitted the spread, large splashy patches of green, blue, orange and zebra, like a Mondrian crossed with a traffic signal. "Your mother knit that quilt, Phil?"

Furiously he struggled into a pair of pants, under the blanket, with the usual success.

"Is she *Amish?*" I persisted. "They do wonderful work down in Pennsylvania Dutch country."

"What's the matter?" I said. "I'll pay you, American money."

"What do you think is the *matter*," said Philip. His whole bearing stiff, his shoulderblades pointed and flaring, he stood at the opposite side of the room by his open closet door. Inside the closet, hanging from a bare horizontal pole, hung his familiar blue suit with the shiny patches at the knee.

I leaned back against the pillow. It was then that a wild desperate knocking thundered and rattled through the house. I must have jumped a foot. "Jesus Christ, what's that?"

"My mother—that's her broom."

"You boys up? Want some French toast or Cheerios?"

"What's the matter? You gave me a big present, then you took it all away, that's the *matter, Kevin.*—No, Ma!"

"What's that?"

"Oh, fuck it."

"I'm not used to being treated like this." I arose from the bed and, made an invisible camera with my hands and thumbs, held it to my eyes, and pressed the invisible shutter. Phil flinched and held the blanket tighter, cowering by his closet door. I took the blanket and whipped it off his waist, and brought my mouth close to his ear so I could whisper, "You're *still* hard, Philly boy. Don't act like I raped you because we both know different. Look at it, wriggling like an animal. Don't hide it with your hands, look for a change!"

"I'm not just waltzing into your life and slumming, if you think so, you're all wet!"

"I suppose we had this date from the beginning," Phil said. "Don't get me wrong, I like American money."

He was weakening, well, who wouldn't? I didn't hold it against him. My hand tightened around his balls, pleasurably, so he couldn't help but gasp a little, in a goony way that recalled the heroines of my favorite romance comic books. I traced the line of his lips with one finger, hushing him. Then I traced a circle around his nipple, my arm over his shoulder, and circled again, tighter and closer, feeling him relax against my hip, backing into me weakly, as though overpowered by a super-serum or chloroform. I pinched the nipple between two knuckles and bit the side of his taut neck, till he caved in completely, fallen apart, his hardon a tool for operating like the gearshift of a car I could swerve in and out of first and second. "My boy," I said to him.

So I got on the phone. "George? This is Kevin. Guess where I am."

I don't know where you are, how should I know, am I supposed to be like Kreskin to you, where are you, at home?

"No, I'm at the Mandel residence. Philip's here too. His mother's out at the market."

And where is Philip, tell me Kevin.

"Phil? He's down on the floor, sucking my cock. Want to watch?"

Uh-huh, uh-huh.

"My big hairy red hard dick."

Yes, Kevin, yes, Kevin.

"Want to watch?"

YOUNG GOODMAN BROWN EFFECT

In Hawthorne's 1835 fable of Puritan guilt, Young Goodman Brown leaves Salem Village and his whitewashed cottage at sunset, the pleasant voice of his young wife, Faith, lilting through the air while she scrubs dishes or churns butter . . . Alone he sets out on a path narrowing into the forest, red leaves crunching underneath and the last rays of the sun disappearing overhead as he trudges on, one doesn't know why yet . . . He meets a distinguished stranger who agrees to walk with him a ways, and little by little we discover that this kindly old man is really the devil, guiding Brown to a witches' Sabbath. Brown's had the intellectual curiosity, perhaps, to wonder what evil feels like; but he didn't know the experience was going to be so universal, large enough to envelop just about everyone he's ever known. As he proceeds into the heart of night, the exalted status of his companion impresses all those they encounter: the "good" people of the town, teachers, ministers, jolly grandpas, mothers and virgins: all are on this pilgrimage together, and all of them are hooked on evil. It's that thing where what you thought you knew is different once the lights go out. Brown's feeling ill and horrified, but then they get to the clearing and who's there, in a bridal gown, but Faith his wife, eager to marry her Satanic lord at midnight, while the graves creak open to reveal the souls of the damned. "The husband cast one look at his pale wife, and Faith at him. What polluted wretches would the next glance show them to each other, shuddering alike at what they disclosed and what they saw! 'Faith! Faith!' cried the husband, 'look up to heaven, and resist the wicked one.'" Our young hero blacks out and when he comes to, in the morning, all seems well in the village and Faith seems innocent, but how can he believe his senses? I guess we've all had those days where our wits give us opposite accounts of the "real," but in the supermediated age we live in, the Young Goodman Brown effect, if I may isolate it with a name, has increased geometrically. Let me tell you a little story about a boy I know, and how I became aware of his double life and how I felt when it found me out.

My downfall, like Goodman Brown's, stemmed from pride. I always thought that being a novelist necessarily entails sharp wits and better yet, a good working knowledge of men and women's ways. As a novelist I should be able to see more accurately other people's relationships, know their innermost thoughts. I'm usually wrong, so wrong in fact that I have been questioning whether the novel in fact does know any more about human relationships than, say, that abandoned pair of sneakers, knotted and dangling over the telephone wires at the foot of my alley. For too long the novel has privileged itself, and the joke may very well be that it is clueless. At least insofar as I am a practitioner, I confess I don't have all the answers, in fact I have never had one. But my modesty, false modesty or whatever, jumped up and bit me in the ass a few months back. This anecdote will show you how, I don't know life, but video does. Fall, 2007, another semester teaching at the art school, and having the strangest feeling that one of my students, a young man of exceptional talent, looked somehow familiar, as though I had known him, known him intimately.

This was Jason Marais, who had come to San Francisco from Delaware, back East, landed like a refugee with a broken wing.

Delaware's the one US state that I'd never met anyone from before—that I know of, unless it's a guilty secret in the shadowy background of some of my friends, but why cover it up? Why not just look me straight in the eye and say, "I'm from Delaware?" I'd look at him over my clipboard with what must have been, had a third party been watching us, a strange expression of suspicion crossed with guilt, lining my face. I'd continue talking about how to write an essay, and I give myself credit that not once did I actually stop talking, but I came damn close. I looked down and the clipboard was shaking in my hands, betraying a—I couldn't figure it out, but some sort of deconstruction was taking place right before my eyes, like it was Michael J. Fox was holding up that clipboard in that wobbly way he has that's actually quite charming. Or a scene from *The Exorcist*, the 1973 movie adapted from the controversial bestseller of the same name, Linda Blair plays disturbed adolescent Regan, who hasn't been herself lately. "She's acting like she's fucking out of her mind, psychotic, like a . . . split personality," says Ellen Burstyn, her equally distraught mother. At night, the words HELP ME appear across Regan's stomach. During the day, she levitates, taunts the young priest sent to help her, and beats mother Burstyn senseless, stabbing herself with a crucifix. Yes, that's rather how I felt when I talked with Jason, wobbly and self-conscious, only I didn't know it with my "mind," only my hands knew.

What my mind knew was that my young student, as it happens, is a superb stylist masquerading as a writer. Some of us who burn bright at age 23 may burn out by the time we're 30, but it might be that this Jason, my Jason, has it in him to write something great and to keep up with it. In other areas his life, as I tried to piece it together, seemed makeshift, his background blurry and partial, a smudged fingerprint. He'd throw out enough back story that you could just about piece together into one master narrative, but there'd be leftover pieces that seemed to fit nowhere. (But that would be true were I to tell you about my life, wouldn't it? It's not as though we each have one story, one life to live.)—Jason's family had some money, or had lost their money through the generations. I got the picture that the father was a withholding, disapproving type, but sometimes I thought he was dead, other times alive. The mother was more visible, hovering around Jason's broad shoulders like a fog of charm, cellophane crinkling in the sun. She was more permissive, didn't mind him being gay, wasn't trying to get him to go straight. But she was no angel either. She had a series of flower shops all throughout Delaware. I wanted to meet her, then I thought, well, it's always weird when writers' parents turn out to be my age or even a bit younger, and they look at me thinking in horror, this bohemian man might be what my boy or girl becomes most like! I could ask her what the state flower of Delaware is and if she found it more popular than ordinary flowers, like roses.

At my office I was asking people about Delaware, for it's funny how many people will confess things at an office that they won't in the outside world. There's a French expression for the phenomenon I'm about to describe, it's a version of our "open secret," a fact about someone so obvious that it's never mentioned and thus becomes invisible to those not in the loop. In France they call it a "secret de Polichinelle," a secret that's known to all the world, except for the person who doesn't know it. Polichinelle was "Punch," in the Punch and Judy puppet shows of France, and his secrets were "stage whispered" by the narrator to the entire audience, though he remained his benighted, wooden-headed self. I started asking people if they had a twin, and what d'you know, many acknowledged this straight out. In fact one girl at my office is one of three triplets! This was the dominant fact of her young life up till now and yet I would never have known it because it was exactly too obvious. Strange Chestertonian paradox, you have made my life more interesting than it deserves! "Are you adopted?" produces a few reactions, though there's something more charged about this question, and people get skittish when they're asked. This woman in our accounting department, Elena, was adopted, and with a girlish moue she said that as a child she'd fantasized about having royal blood like Princess Diana. In her sharp three piece suits and Cuban heels, Elena does look a little like Diana, though a dark-haired version of her. And I could picture her kissing AIDS patients or walking through landmines like Diana, she's pretty rad. The scenarios are endless. I suppose the truth of it is, almost any of us could be adopted and not know it. But Delaware you would think one would remember, and one wouldn't be ashamed to have hailed from any particular state, and yet no one copped to Delaware—not a soul.

At school functions Jason would return my gaze with an utter lack of curiosity, rather the way a cat will look at you, those impenetrable eyes flat and inexpressive. Thus I couldn't read him, couldn't read him reading me. Did he know I found him sort of sexy? That isn't to say I wanted to fuck him. —Which, I will say, I sort of did, but I sort of didn't for all sorts of reasons. It wouldn't really be cool because of liability issues, as well as the outright prohibition of sexual congress between teacher and student. I'm always reading on the web of the tidal wave of pretty, 20 some-thing high school teachers who give themselves to their junior high students, texting them, "U were a stud last nt, A plus," and wondering, how did these women let themselves go like that? Often as not they have husbands and toddlers themselves, yet they're going down on their 15 year olds in the broad daylight of Smithtown Middle School. Why, how, what happened to the proprieties? Could it be that every time you make a new rule, whatever you're condemning just grows dearer to those who now can't do it freely? How did boys become men in the long huts of Margaret Mead's Samoa? Anyhow that's the reason I didn't want to go there, I just shudder at being perceived as "one of the crowd."

He surveyed me with what I came to think of as his Delaware look.

He was used to the gaze, that was obvious, and yet he'd go red at the oddest times, blushing a hot red all up and down his face, even the patch of forehead that peeked through his thatched blond fringe. For on top he sort of resembled one of those old time thatched cottages you sometimes see in old prints of medieval France. He's not a big guy, he's slightly built but with long legs that allow him to run faster (I would think) than the ordinary man.

Afterwards dissecting particularly purple patches of writing by Joan Didion, around the seminar table we would sit, thinking and Jason would be squirming in such a way that if he were your dog, you'd be thinking he must have worms. Really rubbing his ass into the hard purple plastic of the chair. This was a wonderful sign to me, that his cool surface could agitate where writing was in question. He could be positively expansive when it came to his own ambitions in that direction.

I remember at Walzwerk, an East German restaurant near my apartment, with wonderful pot roast and wiener schnitzel and pear soup, the waiter was even more attentive when I brought my class in as a special treat. We had a table for six and Jason sat on the very far end from me, he got drunk really fast and started talking about how much he loved Samuel Fuller movies. How he wanted to be the gay Sam Fuller, except in writing, that he would join the spirit of Denton Welch with that of Sam Fuller. My waiter, Mauritz, was all like, that boy you are with is famous on line. Big porn star him.

"Oh really?" I murmured, automatically, not really thinking.

Then he dropped his voice, dropped the clue. "Why don't look you at Extreme Remedies the web site? Look up under

'Scottt.' Scott with three T's," said Mauritz, handing me back my credit card.

"Okay I will."

"Why isn't there a gay Vollmann," shouted Jason, imitating the famous author firing two guns over his own head like Yosemite Sam capturing your attention. "A gay fucking Vollmann, *with balls* and not just, you know, a quaint French cottage in the Lorraine."

"Be prepared for another side to your friend," whispered Mauritz. I didn't know what he meant but, of course, it was the secret de Polichinelle. At home I clicked open the laptop, meaning to write something else, but my guilty fingers found themselves spelling out "Extreme Remedies." A site of vast capacity, "Extreme Remedies" isn't free, but with dozens of free tours, you could easily spend hours on it I suppose without having to enter your credit card number once.

My cat, Sylvia, prowled around my ankles, hoping to rouse me from my detective activity, give her some food. But in fact I couldn't say if she ever ate again. Such considerations seemed utterly distant when I typed in the single name, "Scottt" with three T's, and then presto, in an instant, I was transported as though by a genie, to the very site of Jason's other life. The picture moved and bulged, occasionally some pixels blurred and burned together but all in all it was a remarkably sharp image of the boy, Jason my student, in profile, on his knees. He was naked but for a wristwatch, like one of Colter Jacobsen's drawings, bent along a bench, his head touching the bench, his face turned to the camera, thus to me. His cheek mashed against the wooden width of the bench, as though an invisible boot was pinning him by the throat.

I could see his face appealing to me for help, his mouth mumbling some words or stentorian breaths. Hard to make out what he was "saying," but it was the sort of thing you yourself might mumble if it was your ass up in the air and being spread and pounded by what looked like an enormous grease gun. At my kitchen table I looked this way, that, hastily, for what I was seeing seemed so raw it seemed wrong of me to see, and of course we feel implicated when the moving image, relentless as the piston-fueled dildo machine manipulating his butt, moves into our line of vision. A ring of dampness rose inside my collar.

I can't believe he did this, I thought, and then: or let himself be filmed like this, for anyone—I suppose!—might want to try a fucking machine if you thought you could actually accommodate the dildo at its working end. In private, in the spirit of scientific inquiry, one might put it in an inch—an inch and a half—then slide it out gingerly, saying no thanks, too ornate. But in porn you can't say no thanks; there might be "safe words" but no thanks isn't among them. Onscreen Jason's tongue flickered all around his lips and he drew up one hand from the floor—was it supposed to be a garage or auto body shop?—and his mouth sucked in his thumb, as though for comfort. Spittle glued his blond hair to the bench beneath his cheek; his eyes had gone blank, flat buttons of blue and white, through which you might delude yourself into thinking you were reading messages of hurt or lust. Meanwhile the thing, nearly alive, like a Giger maquette from *Alien*, or a Sten gun re-engineered into a pile driver, made further assaults on his smooth, oscillating ass. His chest heaved, rattling like a torn muffler. I could see his cock, dangling down from his elevated hips, nothing special there, a glistened red-brown tube good for shaking, responding, quivering, but he didn't seem hard. Not hard-hard. Oh whatever. You can go and judge for yourself, is one of the most talented young writers around hard or soft in his video clip? It's moving so fast it's hard to tell, but to me what I saw was beyond phenomenology. His appearance in this video threatened to explain some aspects of Jason, but otherwise it only complicated him, made my knowledge of him more fleecy, the way you might dissolve the picture you had painstakingly etched on "Etch-a-Sketch" by shaking the red square toy with your hands. The connecting lines disappear and only grains remain.

I guess Jason's secret life explained that peculiar dog thing he does in class, rubbing his ass along the chair, as though it were sore, as though it were raw or wet. Poor guy, and yet, if this intrusion was so awful, why then did he return and make a sequel a little while later? And a second sequel, not a solo this time but a duet with a second, more vocal boy on the far end of the bench, a boy called Willie. Where "Scott" suffers in silence, Willie's panicked screams ring through the dungeon, glissando, like Joan Sutherland in one of those Rossini rôles, imprisoned for a crime she did not commit and yet free as the air at the same time, for her voice could part bars. And this boy's voice is like a pair of hands that pulled himself out of danger with the solace of musical theater. The tape is called "Scottt and Willie Meet Mr. Machine." Meanwhile Jason just kneels in perfect silence while, this time, an electrical charge is mounted to the oscillating dildo inside him, and you can register the sudden shifts in voltage only by his abruptly shocked and numbed eyeballs, glistening, unblinking. He is the lizard, to the other boy's lark. Jason can't talk, for the sheer mass inside him preempts his thought, indeed his identity. But Willie finds surcease in sound, in moving into a realm of spiritual and physical bird noise.

Well, you couldn't stay all day watching the same brief clips over and over, you had to pony up if you wanted more of this spectacle—this series of mini-spectacles—so I became a member of course. You could have DVDs mailed to your home or just have these full-length videos "streaming" (and was there ever a better word!) down one's screen from morning to night all month. Something like thirty dollars a month? At the time it seemed very reasonable. The devil had brought me to this place, but I was curious. And then when I wanted to look away something in the very transactional fact of my gaze made that a no can do. I had given myself up for good. It did remind me of the days when, when the internet was brand new for us, and me and Dodie would go on and look up sites, and the first thing I looked up was the "Anagram Generator." We tried making anagrams out of our names, and then when that palled, we thought of our cats, Blanche and Stanley, who were playing on the rug nearby. And when I typed in "BLANCHE AND STANLEY" the program spat back hundreds, thousands of combinations but oddly—horribly—the first one that came back, lo, leading all the rest—was "CHANNELLED BY SATAN." I looked down at the cats and they seemed to pause in their play and stare at me with those flat cat eyes as if to say, *you have reached the subhuman, how may we help you?*

I couldn't tell whether or not "Scottt" was a star within the confines of the Extreme Remedies world, or whether he was but a featured player. He had made a sizeable number of punishment videos, but five or six boys on the site had made more. And in fact in some clips he appears in the background, almost as an extra, like Harry Carey Jr. in the later John Ford films. In some he doesn't even take off his clothes but sits there in his "Jason" clothes, outfits I recognized, looking sullen or bored—that "Delaware look"—while some other twink like Willie takes it for the team. And just as he was sometimes not where you thought he would be, he could sometimes be found where one didn't expect him—as a sort of guest star in other people's videos. It wasn't just a gay site, it was open to anyone with $29.99 a month and the taste for discipline. In fact counting it up, there were probably more girls than boys being punished, some of them with credits long as my arm.

You could flick from here to there on thumbnails, and in one of them I thought I saw Jason in the background of an otherwise all girls orgy, set in a hospital ward with cheerful white hospital screens, yards of rubber tubing, cold steel stethoscopes, and what looked like real knives. In the center of the action was the star, "Diana," on her back, resplendent in what apparently was actual electroshock treatment mode, electrodes glued to her the sides of her head and you, the viewer, could control how many volts she was going to get, for the video was apparently at some previous time a live experience, now presented as sort of a souvenir of good times gone by. "I can't believe people pay for this shit," said I—the hypocrite, the distasteful spectator. Jason was dressed as a doctor in operating room gear with big pale green gloves of rubber, and seated on what looked like a metal bar stool in the corner of the operating theater. While the camera focused on Diana's jaw and eyes, and the sizzling burns of wire just above her temples, Jason extended his gloved hands slightly and looked at them with that goofy grin of the stoned, as if to say, what are these plastic things on my hands? Diana's screams filled my kitchen, and then I realized, she was Elena, the girl from my office. I had just never seen her lying down. Elena, the one who looked like Princess Diana except a brunette, the one who was adopted, she said. I saw her every day, her nimble fingers massaging a calculator or flicking the coffee machine to decaf.

And you know, ever since that weekend I spent as a member of Extreme Remedies, I haven't really been able to trust my own senses. I call it the Young Goodman Brown Effect. It's where from the time your alarm clock wakes you in the morning, to the dark hours of the night where sleep mercifully releases you from concern, you don't know who your fellow beings are. They all seem normal on the outside—most of them, that is: I mean you always have characters!—but the moment you turn your back, they're getting plugged from behind for all the world to see; it was only you their demure smile was meant to fool. And maybe I'm the same way, a polluted wretch who shudders to disclose his own sin. Shakes you up it does, when you see something out of the way. Of course God invented porn, and probably the entire concept of cinema, to drill this lesson in us. Those on screen aren't exactly real people, of course, they're simulacra and thus shouldn't be asked to meet ordinary standards of humanity. Meanwhile I see Jason from time to time at poetry readings and he was there tonight at Scott Heim's San Francisco launch for his new novel. Elena from my office is getting married in September, from what I understand—I out five dollars in the office pool to buy her a shower present. I can't really look either of them in the eye—I've seen too much of them and I resent them, giving away to a mass audience what should have been kept for me. Behind every good secret, resentment lurks: no wonder Punch and Judy were always batting each other over the head with those rubbery phallic bats. At the end of my days, when I'm borne to my grave a hoary corpse, they will carve no hopeful verse upon my tombstone, for my dying hours were gloom.

TRIANGLES IN THE SAND

I'm not on top the way I used to be, and late in middle age I let things flutter by; even events and faces I thought I'd never forget end up in a blind alley bricked up to the sky. This sad brain lapse is counterbalanced however by people and places returning to me after many years—full-blown memories emerging from cold storage still with the original dew fresh on them, or apparently so.

And in other ways I can see myself more clearly now, and as I look back I see that I had a ruthless streak; I could be horrifyingly manipulative. Funny I didn't see it that way back then, when, in my twenties I was a grad student and an ardent homosexual, an aspiring writer and a heavy drinker. I was quiet quite a bit, and bored, and resentful. But I always believed in myself, and told myself I was a misunderstood genius who'd been forced by circumstance, lack of dough, and general homophobia to walk a crooked path through life. I've written a book about my early search for homosexuality on the North Shore, a collection of memoirs published in 1989 by Amethyst Press; it was called *Bedrooms Have Windows*, after a '40s pulp noir novel by Erle Stanley Gardner, who wrote it under the pseudonym A.A. Fair. In the present book I tell a story it never occurred to me would interest anyone, if only because it was so inconclusive. But perhaps inconclusivity has become a watchword for our era; we don't trust people with totalizing answers. The best I can say is that it did happen, and the more I think about it the more I realize, that I was the only dick in the picture, everyone else was just doing their best pretty much.

I lacked compassion, like everyone else in the 1970s. Tom Wolfe wrote about the '70s as the "Me Decade," a horrid slur, but he got to something real we didn't want to think about.

I had a therapist once, in college, who got terrifically angry with me constantly, like full-bore furious. Today I watch *Mr. Robot* and marvel at how sweet and understanding and forgiving Gloria Reuben is to our hero Rami Malek. My college therapist was always shrieking at me, "Why can't you follow my diagnosis? The reason you will never be happy is because you want too much! Settle for something—learn to do one thing well—and maybe you'll become a man. You give in when you know you should be strong."

"I still give in, even though I know it's wrong," I admitted. "I'm like that boy in the Glen Campbell song. 'I guess I'm dumb, but I don't care.'"

Beyond the therapist's window I could see the snow drifting in billowy flakes, twenty stories above Fifty-Seventh Street, flakes that got smaller as they neared the busy sidewalks of Manhattan. My guy was a fierce old blowhard from the school of Anna Freud, and he never saw a faggot he didn't want to cure. I don't know that he cared about me personally, I was just some piece of pro bono work his clinic had asked him to participate in. I'd dyed my hair in blue, purple, green and gold streaks to match the look of my idol, musician Todd Rundgren, and it looked rad, or maybe we would have said it looked far out. With my stringy Technicolor hair spread out across the bolster on the head of his couch, I wondered what it would be like to have sex with this therapist, the way I wondered about all the men I met, all men I passed on the street or bumped into at Gristede's—and even the men I did have sex with I wondered what sex would have been like if they had loved me. It was the '70s and the culmination of a sex revolution long in coming, so one was always trying to make up for lost time. Maybe before the internet we had time for sexual pursuit that we don't have now, though we always complained how we didn't have time to enjoy the changing of the leaves or to do enough acid. We felt frantic about time in the '70s. (Maybe that's why durational work became hot in art in that decade, as opposed to being merely the province of those who couldn't paint or draw or whatever?) Yoko told us, "Try not to say anything negative about anybody a) for three days b) for forty-five days c) for three months." Wow, that was taking the long view. "See what happens with your life." I had *Grapefruit* sitting on my nightstand at home, I think all gay guys with long hair did, at least on the East Coast. I taped the sound of the moon fading at dawn and, as Yoko suggested, I advised my mother to listen to it if she ever got sorrowful.

I met musician Arthur Russell courtesy of the poet Allen Ginsberg in 1978 at SUNY Stony Brook, where I was grinding through the PhD program, the English Department, sigh. Our campus was a wooded "Colonial" suburb about sixty miles outside of Manhattan on Long Island's North Shore. In this privileged sector of Long Island, the university sat like a blight, its sixties buildings Bauhaus craters in what had once been the world's largest, most idyllic meadow. The Gay Student Alliance took up one and a half rooms, largely glass and carpet, in the hideous structure that the campus guidebook called the Student Union. From any direction on campus you could turn around and point at the Student Union, the ugliest building of them all, the one distinguished by a "post-modern" feature—a bridge leading from the building's rooftop to—well, it didn't lead anywhere, just broke off halfway through, thus lending the new building a touch of the "folly." Visitors looked at it blankly, while student guides explained either that the money ran out to complete this bridge, or that it had been intended this way all along, a whimsical extravaganza in the bleakest of gray concrete. We took it to be allegorical, it was the "bridge to nowhere," and there was a student literary magazine with the same name. I was 25 and pretty vacant, and I had been trapped in suburbia my whole life. All of us in the Gay Students Alliance felt the same, even the actual New Yorkers who had come to us from Manhattan, Brooklyn, the Bronx.

We all of us went aflutter, like yellow moths surprised by a hummingbird, when anyone "famous" visited us on campus. Like the ambitious stenographers in *The Best of Everything* (Twentieth Century Fox, 1959), we were all waiting for our main chance, trading on our youth and beauty to land Mr. Right. For me, Allen Ginsberg was going to be my ticket out of my papier-mâché nightmare of whiteness and blankness and hollow meaningless suburban living. I had gone through a long period of enslavement to David Bowie and was only now waking from my dream and realizing that I would never meet him in real life: but now the older, shorter, schlubbier Ginsberg was in fact almost within the realms of possibility.

I got this idea from a fellow gay student, William, a boy I'd gone to high school with. Two or three years my junior, Will was humiliatingly enough so much hipper about gay life. I'd gone trawling for a lot of sex, and that part was cool, but I didn't know how to date, and Will was infinitely at ease with romance and relationships. He had an easy, flirtatious way about him, and he mentioned casually that he had slept with Allen Ginsberg several times. It was sort of gross, Will said, but on the bright side he had never had so much first class attention paid his ass. And since he, Will, had been put in charge of the entertainment committee of the Gay Students Union, he could bring in whoever he wanted as speakers. In this way, in fact, I later got to meet the poets Eileen Myles, Michael Lally, and Tim Dlugos, for they came to entertain us gay and lesbian students. Tim eventually succumbed to AIDS, I saw Michael Lally last month at an old timers party in New York, though we never grew close. I'm still friends with Eileen. Just the other day we were talking about how *gay money* brought us together, but the committee must have spent a bundle to get Allen Ginsberg and Arthur Russell to come all the way east to Suffolk County.

Ginsberg was perhaps not the household word he had been ten years before, but he was still the most famous poet in America and possibly the most famous gay man, outside of Paul Lynde and Bayard Rustin. And during the '70s Ginsberg was particularly active and prolific as he sought new ways to deliver his message to the people, including a then-shocking shedding of his hippie clothes and aura to adapt three-piece suits, shorter hair, and a series of professional gigs that would culminate in a professorship at Brooklyn College, and the awards began to roll in; while he was growing closer to his guru, the wild man of the east, Trungpa Rinpoche, who played on Ginsberg's well-concealed attraction to obedience and blind devotion.

This was mid-May, 1978. A driver brought them out from Manhattan in a town car, to the university campus off of Long Island Expressway Exit 62. And that's a lot of exits. Even my own little town, Smithtown, was Exit 56. And as the Chrysler Imperial pulled up the driveway, Will was there to open the door and embrace Ginsberg, but the poet seemed to me to be avoiding his kiss for some reason. This was my big moment, I had humbly pleaded with Will to be allowed to be there at the greeting ceremony. Another GSA member stood nearby with some paperwork, but I clutched the flowers I had begged Will for the chance to present. The bouquet was what today you would call artisanal. There were two or three red roses threaded in it, but it was otherwise comprised of the native plants of Long Island— milkweed, goldenrod, violets, false indigo, verbena—*messy plants*, kind of RFD thrift store. A few feathers from the robin and the gull gave it even more Suffolk County humility: standing there to present my thoughtful, poetic gift, I must have looked like Lorine Niedecker, like the girl from the north country Bob Dylan and Johnny Cash sang about.

"Can somebody help my musician?" Ginsberg called out, in a brusque tone, the tone you would use were your wishes being ignored instead of catered to slavishly which was verifiably the case. Naturally we GSA guys tripped over ourselves trying to entangle Arthur Russell's limbs from his cello and the Imperial and get everyone out of the car and onto the outdoor stage safely. I still had the flowers in my hands so I couldn't really assist, but I caught his eye, the musician. He was awfully young, exactly my age I think, maybe a few months older. My mind dismissed him on one hand, but on the other something registered in another part of itself, an impression of a withheld energy that seemed very urban and refined, but not a giving nature. And also: *he'd be good looking except for that complexion.*

This was the first poetry reading I'd ever been to held out-doors, but it suited Ginsberg right down to the ground, he looked splendid and fit, while Arthur Russell, standing behind him about ten paces, like the wife of a Mohammedan leader, wore a pained scowl and always seemed in danger of toppling the straight-backed chair behind him right off the rear of the stage. Students crowded in a ring, it was a reading "in the round," but in practice Ginsberg delivered most of the work to the portion of the crowd gathered directly in front of his microphone. We stood on a lawn to the north side of the complicated Student Union, almost directly in front of the glazed portieres behind which lay our GSA office. To my mind Ginsberg was like a god come among us from Olympian heights, like those fifth acts in Shake-speare's late romance plays, as if he was going to resolve all the plots we tired and tormented humans had brought down upon ourselves. Was it just charisma I was responding to? He wore a white long-sleeved shirt and a large silk tie with diagonal stripes—it was an age in which men's ties could get really flared as they neared the navel, then cut back sharply approaching the home plate of the belt buckle. Overhead spring leaves splayed from maple branches, fluttering in the breeze like green and yellow pennants, and beyond the leaves, the late afternoon sky glowed pale gold and blue, like the inside of a Faberge egg, His reading brought down the house, or whatever the outdoor equivalent is for the house. His musician listened intently, tall and willowy, in a yellow and black flannel plaid shirt, untucked. From time to time he was called upon to apply his cello to Ginsberg's intonations in call and response format. Few could see his face, he seemed determined to hide that scowl under a mane of thick curtains of brown hair—though while playing, his expression changed into something less conscious of the suburban kids all around him. Restless, longing, I realized I still had my ignored bouquet in my hands, and this discovery embarrassed me so much I wanted to stow the thing into one of the green institutional trash cylinders featured everywhere on the campus; but a little bit of mad Ophelia infected me and, in time with the singsong poetry, I plucked a flower at a time and sailed them wildly over my head as if practicing for a new heaven and a new earth. Afterwards, I imagined, the boys and girls of the Gay Student Alliance would ask themselves, "What was Kevin muttering when he threw those hideous flowers up into the air?"

And one would report, one who stayed closest to me as I tore at my clothes and drooled and sang, "First he said there was fennel for you, and columbines. 'There was rue for you, Will, and here was some he would hold on to.' On Sunday, he said, it was a herb of grace."

"But it was only Tuesday."

"I know, that's what made him so scary and uncanny! He told me I should wear the rue with a difference."

"Like a *gay* difference?"

"I don't know, just a difference."

"I saw him toss some grody violets right at Allen Ginsberg's head."

"Yes! And he cried out, 'I would toss you some violets, Arthur Russell, but they withered, all of them did, as my love for Ginsberg crumpled and died.'"

Afterwards the question rose about how Arthur Russell—cello packed away in sturdy case—was going to get back to New York, since Ginsberg planned to stay in our neck of the woods visiting with the elderly poet Louis Zukofsky, who lived in Port Jefferson, the next town past Setauket, and Allen would need to keep the car. Surely that was all right with the Gay Students, who were paying for it? I could see my plan for charming Allen Ginsberg by having sex with him slipping away, like a drop of mercury. Was I surprised? Yeah! Was I surprised, no, not at all. "Anyone from the *Times* here?" Ginsberg shouted to the crowd, but the photographers were from *Newsday* and other Suffolk County papers. Click click click.

Hearing this non-response, Allen fixed his sad beautiful eyes on me, though, and kept them there. Then in a lower voice he asked if I had a car. Instantly my imagination bubbled and spouted, a geyser of new love dreams. Suddenly a beautiful evening loomed before me, the restoration of my hopes. I could see myself walking a pace behind my new boyfriend, Allen Ginsberg, to pay a visit to Port Jefferson to Louis and Celia Zukofsky, my hand grasping his as thoughtfully he held it out to me behind his back. Click click click, the world would see us together in the *Times*. Well, in the *Stony Brook Statesman*. And then, well, he'd come back to my place surely, or—"Yeah, I have a car!" I exclaimed. "That's great," he said, rising and wiping the remains of gay snacks from his lap. "Then can you give Arthur a ride back to the East Side?" "East side of what?" I responded, like an idiot. I felt sort of tricked into this and resented it, especially since my young twink friend Will said he would go along with Allen and the driver to Port Jefferson. (We didn't have that word "twink" then, so that's not quite right.)

I couldn't suss out how Arthur Russell felt, but all the way to New York I peppered him with questions about Allen Ginsberg. It was rather an effort for him to act chatty, but at some point on the L.I.E. he must have decided, if you have to ride with them, you might as well be nice to them. On stage, his severity worked with his music, and his strong, lean fingers flew up, then down, the neck of the instrument, and I was already thinking, he'd be kind of sexy if it wasn't for his acne. On the numbers in which he wasn't asked to play he sat there in what might have been a haze of Buddha, but supple and alert, and in the Blake duets he jumped up and his fingers worked that cello faster than I could see them. Was he an ideal collaborator with Ginsberg? Can't tell. I only saw Steven Taylor play with AG once, and he was more deft (and played different instruments, and provided a harmony vocal), and it seemed to me that Ginsberg cared for him more than he had Arthur Russell. But who can say? Anyhow what was the alternative, Allen alone with that horrid harmonium perched on his knee, never in tune? So when I dropped Arthur outside his building on the Lower East Side, I swallowed my pride to mumble, "What's your number?" And he slid the padded case from the backseat, rotated it to sit on the curb near a hydrant, leaned down and spoke to me through the passenger window. "I was just about to say," he began. "I don't know, we could hang out." Nodding I gave him the thumbs up sign and put on my blinker. Dark was coming on and I had a class to teach in the morning. He had one more thing to say. As I left East Twelfth Street he called after me, "You're a good driver." First and last compliment from him. And maybe the only time anyone's ever said that to me.

I drove home in the dark, morose, to my crazy apartment in Port Jefferson. I was grumbling and talking to myself like a Tom Waits character, and drinking from a little bottle of rock & rye. Do they even make rock & rye today? I wonder—since I stopped drinking in the '80s I don't keep up. But this was the '70s and I was a full-time lush and I was hurt I'd gotten the brush from Allen Ginsberg, and received the short end of the stick, as I saw it, an introduction to his cellist—his hired hand, his servant really—I was indignant as a mean Jane Austen character. I had gone to the reading with such hope, and now what did I have, nothing. Well, I had Arthur Russell's phone number, and maybe we would hang out. He had a dark Byronic look to him and big pillow lips, well, the lower was large, and great hair, but when I tried to call his face to memory I saw a hundred, two hundred, scars on it, so he was always in shadow. Hard to typecast such a man.

My apartment was hideous, like a joke. I know it's the style, and perhaps the strength of young people to see themselves living outside the pale, in unsuitable and unsafe structures. It makes us feel alive and iconoclastic. But I resented where I lived and would show it only to tricks, a hardscrabble lot, only the most hardcore of whom failed to bolt when they saw it. This is how I got in: a fellow grad student, Carl, drove his car into a telephone pole, and I took over his place. It seemed impossible that Carl himself, so quick, cute and funny a fellow, so heterosexual in fact, was now lying in a hospital bed swathed in plaster; so I moved into his place to propitiate Apollo, the god of healing, and Chiron his tutor. I wasn't there more than a year I'm sure—probably much less—but that apartment is one I can never forget.

I was working as a "waiter" in the Smithtown Sizzler Family Steak House, possibly the most ludicrous job I've ever held down (except for seven weeks as a rent boy; uh oh now I'm remembering performing secretarial duties for the late poet Harold Norse for a brief period, later, in San Francisco). I was almost twenty-six and a grad student studying Faulkner and George Eliot and allegory. I told myself these two things over and over for reassurance, for the pleasure of belief. Long Island is a jeweled bracelet flung out into the sea from Manhattan by a casual hand. Driving your car real fast at night down the Expressway from west to east produces the intimate, daring sensation of glamour in one, sexy because stolen, tragic somehow and yet profoundly real. Doesn't last long. My car was a 69 Maverick, so white it looked blue, so blue it looked smoky, intimate, like a crowded café. My little brother called it "the Cruisemobile" (I think he'd been watching *American Graffiti*). Writer's block had crushed every idea I had for my novel so many nights I'd drive from Port Jefferson to Montauk Point, then back, drunk on beer and playing the radio as loud as it would go. At that time Billy Joel, Long Island boy made good, was the only singer my radio would play and, despising him so, I would switch off the knob and roll down all the windows in the car and try to hear the surf from each shore, like stereo.

We hung out at a progressive bar in town up at the top of a hill overlooking the Harbor, where there were poetry readings every Friday night, next to the experimental theater space they called "Theater Three." You could bring in your own records and they would play them on the old hi-fi behind the bar. "Shut the light; go away; full of grace, you cover your face." Even our department's Pulitzer Prize-winning poet, Louis Simpson, was sometimes seen hanging out here, and if begged might take a turn behind the mic "trying out" something "new." Bending an elbow was considered democratic, and in my circles it was a gateway to otherwise unlikely sex; all of the professors I wound up having affairs with were brought in through alcohol's socially-approved lubrication, just as I, when a teenager in high school, had thrown away my doubts after a round of drinks offered by the religious order who taught us. I know for a fact I would never have been able to pass my orals if not for having managed to sleep with two fellows on my committee. (Louis Simpson never sat on my committee, and I never did bag the old Pulitzer Prize winner, who seemed resolutely straight.)

I drank Scotch and Tab pretty exclusively and was proud that I was known for my drink: only legendary boulevardiers, like Dylan Thomas or Anne Sexton, were known for their cocktail preferences, right? Once I took the Greyhound bus to Mardi Gras and in a bar at the French Quarter, this older guy offered to buy me a drink. "Sure," I told him, mentioning my preference. He winced but obligingly hobbled toward the bar. A few minutes later I hear a commotion at the bar, a uniformed bartender had leapt to the bar's long surface and was hollering out, "Is Kevin Killian here? Some asshole is ordering Scotch and Tab and who else could want that filth?" I was *known internationally*; it was one of the most gratifying moments in my life as a boy.

One woman used to float into the bar in Port Jeff every night exactly at midnight; she looked like if New Wave singer Deborah Harry had a younger sister. Her name was Bobbie Breath, and when I doubted it she proved her age with the birth certificate she carried in her Sprouse purse. Born 1921? I said, "You're so old and you look so young!" believing this to be a compliment. She smelled of cedar and lobster. Her boyfriend was a mailman my age and I always think of mailmen as so butch. "Cocktails, my dear," she whispered throatily. "My secret is cocktails."

Will called me and asked me what I thought about the Ginsberg event, and should the GSA have more cultural things, or did the kids just appreciate like live music and rock shows? I wanted to ask him how his trip to Port Jefferson in search of Zukofsky went, and if once again Allen gave his ass that first class attention he had bragged about in years past. But I was too proud. Will said he had a great idea that would make people forget about poetry. Some other trick, he said, was the agent for Divine, and next year Divine would come to the Gay Students Alliance and show us *Pink Flamingos*. And indeed that came to pass. "That's what the kids want," Will sighed. We talked of how gay culture was so various it had room for Ginsberg and Divine and Genet and David Bowie and . . . Janis Ian . . . Adrienne Rich, June Jordan (Jordan was actually teaching in our program, a gale force).

The night I met Sean was hot and airless and filled with music. Though I had this gut dislike for him I didn't connect it with the kind of sex we began to have on a regular basis. I wonder if the kind of sex people have when they love each other feels equally disconnected, related only inconsequentially to their emotions? Maybe. Sean was hitchhiking at four-thirty in the morning, leaning against a gray-white stump sailors must use to tie boats to, because seagulls perch on it. We drove for a few miles before it became apparent what he wanted and he was so drunk, it was awesome. I just asked him, when I let him into the car, if he wanted a superb rim job and also did he mind if a wee bit of mild spanking preceded it? He looked so happy, I perhaps took that for a yes. I poked around through his pants while I drove, adjudicating his interest, which was keen. But he was bordering on the line between yes and no. Between consciousness and dream. Between dream and pass-out. Occasionally he would jerk back to life again and holler at me, "I want to suck you off to the bottom of sea level!" and other loud protestations of love. In my grasping right hand, through the layers of cotton trousers and cotton underwear, his crotch was alert and interested—it all fit together in the ball of my fist. When I lit a cigarette I had to rake my hand away from this package, and already I felt a queer sense of loss— my palm had gotten used to his heat, his delight, his absence—his animal-like contentment in pleasure.

Back at my place a mattress took up most of the bedroom floor; a Tensor lamp close to the floor; thus a circle of almost white light on gray-and-white ticking in stripes so thin I found it hard to reproduce them on his skin, when I tried. Because he tried me. He told me his name but then clammed up; until the sun came up I didn't hear him say another word except for "Okay," "Ouch," and "Yes please." So I continued to strip him. He was a waiter too, like I, but where I wore brown and orange to work, in keeping with the perceived "California" ambience of the restaurant, he wore a black velvet bow tie, black pants, a silky white short, and a vest of scarlet—like Robin Hood, but I think it was supposed to look Italian. He was fair and tall, with the kind of body that seems perfect at twenty but will run to fat, which is even more perfect, so what the hey, right? I used him as my boy. I should have grown flowers in him, instead I bled him. His skin was so white it eluded the lamplight and crept out to the stars. A fountain of red blood ran underneath his loins as if in Xanadu. To wrangle a new meter on his butt, kind of an American alexandrine, I used a coat hanger. Also the tip of a sneaker. After a few hours it was over and I was so tired . . . How tired? I'll tell you how tired, it was awesome.

To reach the apartment from 25A one had to pull up the car to the tip of a bare ridge and abandon it before heading for the brush that surrounded a vacant, half-dug lot. Ten yards down a narrow set of footholds, a bridge made of rickety plywood steps afforded an uneasy footing, especially in the wind at night, or in the bleary morning with the sun in one's eyes or burning one's hair. Then the house began of which Carl's apartment was only a part, albeit the only inhabitable part. The rest of the vast house was empty. It looked like *Christina's World* in the famous painting. From the inside one felt one understood Howard Hughes and why he let his fingernails grow so long.

Or Jack Nicholson in that movie where he keeps trying to write that novel but the hotel starts to turn it against him. *The Shining*. All work and no play makes Jack a dull boy . . .

The small, dusty rooms of this house opened into each other like Ingrid Bergman's sex fantasies in *Spellbound*. As one tiptoed across floor after floor, one couldn't but notice that they grew progressively dingier and damper. I wonder if this too was true of Ingrid Bergman's fantasies. No one who walked through the house could imagine why it had been so haphazardly constructed, apparently at different periods but with a similar value placed, at all times, on the drab and distorted. Most rooms were barred from me by heavy wooden doors from the haps of which dangled broken padlocks. I flashed on the Bastille—Dickens' Bastille, I knew no other. One room had been set up as a laboratory; this made me wonder if the house had once been a school: *Dotheboys Hall*. But I wound up thinking of it as the Bates Motel, because I am essentially a cineaste not a man of letters.

He remained immobile throughout the operation, unless an obedient gradual raising of the hips can be seen as a kind of mobility. Only the progress of his prick along the dirty sheet gave him any kind of history.

I beat him slowly and wincingly; when I thought of it, when I wasn't distracted. Once I swerved and caught a face pressed against the double pane window. Was it a deer? No. I found out later whose face it was and boy oh boy did I get into hot water.

Once I found a used sanitary napkin perkily sitting atop the wet crumpled paper towels in the men's room of the restaurant I worked in. The picture it presented—the triumphant incursion of the female principle into a Pharisaical waste land—struck me forcibly; I took the bloody napkin home with me that night in the car, now and again glancing carefully down at it as though it were half alive or only unconscious. I had no immediate plans. The variations in color, and in scent, of the dried blood denoted a variety of sensual experience I felt excluded from; I couldn't decide whether this made me feel happy or sad. I had been trained in all the rituals of the mysterious menses, and malice made me whip up some more of my own devising. Several nights later I parted the warm reddened cheeks of Sean's ass and inserted the mass into his rectum, using the bowl end of a teaspoon for leverage. He gave no sign that this intrusion was anything new in his life, giving off the impression, rather, that he welcomed its renewal. The language he spoke said as much. It hurt, but only a part of his body he was beginning to believe belonged to somebody else entirely. Today I hope what I did to him during those months caused him no long-term health problems. But he was young and strong then—I bet he's still strong today, if no longer young. I pressed him. "You've never never had this before and don't tell me different." Finally he nodded as if ashamed, ashamed of novelty, ashamed of youth and how it loves to lie; even its dreams are lies, as opened to the white blankness of truth that coats the dreams of its elders. Like the buffering that makes swallowing Valium tolerable instead of a sin. I got a kick out of fucking Sean, with whatever came to a mind so inventive and protean it tried out for *College Bowl*. He acted like the man with a hundred prostates, but that's enthusiasm isn't it. When our bodies broke apart with a sucking sound, ripples of dark pink and carmine had impressed themselves across the width of my hipbones like the bloody handprint in *A Study in Scarlet*. Revenge.

These were signals I was trying to throw out into the world. But he saw them rather as further evidences of homosexual life in the universe that he hadn't suspected. I unraveled a few inches of the napkin and tied it to the base of the Tensor lamp, then I left. "Homosexual life?" I couldn't concentrate on what that meant. My own life I viewed, perhaps mistakenly, as serious and coherent. Out in the swimming summer air a clump of forbidding pines stood blocking out the starlight from the roof of the Cruise-mobile. I went down to the "Raspberry" disco at Port Jefferson harbor; it was the time when disco had begun to die, and in its final, decadent, overblown gasps—like the Jacobean drama— produced its most beautiful flowering. I was as far away from Arthur Russell as I ever would be, and yet listening to the music of Donna Summer's "Summer Fever" I felt close to him for a minute. If this was today I would have reached for my cell phone and called him. It was very late, but I knew him to be something of a night owl. But this was before we could reach anybody at any time and in the darkness of the club all I could do was try to find his funny face among the patrons rushing to the dance floor the minute her voice began to purr, beg and moan.

Oversized plate glass windows, like those of a municipal aquarium, reflected the harbor below and its regatta of ghostly sails quivering in the night.

I didn't know where he was, really. I had his phone number but he rarely answered it. And he lived in Manhattan and I was in the suburbs of Suffolk County, in this tourist trap of a summer village. That had always been my tragedy, is how I saw it. That I would never be cool, and that, my friend, is why I was so mean to my fellow suburban outliers like Sean back there with his butthole stuffed with Kotex. The sails continued to shiver slightly, and now and again the sailboats hulls bumped up against each other like Frank O'Hara in bondage. I heard no squawks— the seagulls must be sleeping, heads tucked under one wing, the night coating them like candy.

In New York Arthur Russell and I hadn't much in common, as I was soon to discover. He knew so much about music he made me feel dowdy and square, like all my experience listening to *Hunky Dory* and *Diamond Dogs* counted for nothing, not to mention the Rosemary Clooney and Bing Crosby duets my mom and dad had filled our house with growing up. *He'd* known Terry Riley and Robert Wilson and Yvonne Rainer and all these people I had never actually even heard of, whereas I was from Hicksville—literally, that's the town I was born in. That was all right because I was still better looking than he was—or so I thought then, and maybe that delusion saved me from an utter ignominy. But delusion is what it was.

I can only remember knowing one thing about music that he didn't already know. But we did share some enthusiasms. We both liked ABBA and their weird, jolly English, "Knowing Me, Knowing You," "Dancing Queen," "Waterloo," "Fernando." We would repeat those lyrics as though they were keys to a deeper understanding of some far-off thing—not just Scandinavian studio mastery, but instructions from another world—an Austin Osman Spare world. "The judges will decide/ the likes of me abide." If you could figure out the turns of phrase you might be on to a different mentality, as might one who would know the sex of angels.

In silly moods we would play like we were Frida and Agnetha, proffering hands drawn up as though they were clawed, and paw the air, singing in unison, "I am behind you, I'll always find you—" paw, claw, —"I am the tiger! People who fear me, never go near me—" growl, claw, —"I am the tiger!" I don't know why any of Abba's songs are still popular, all these years later, because they were so juvenile, and yet I suppose, like this tiger number, they not only partook of human suffering but there was maybe something eerie, unheimlich, about them. He and I were just two guys, neither of us gay or so he said, we just liked to hang out together and to parody the way couples felt—gay or straight—the extravagances of emotion one had come to the Lower East Side to avoid or to sample, like going to a Jack Smith performance, experiencing feeling only through the excess of performance or emotion, as parody. Is there something of the sort going on in Arthur's lyrics? As I listen to them now I think I hear it.

They too, some of them, sound written right on the very *edge of English*.

Arthur liked the wall of sound, or perhaps the super producer in general, so not only Phil Spector and Bo Michael Tretow (he of ABBA fame) but Jack Nietzsche, Joe Meek, Eddie Holland and Lamont Dozier, Mickie Most, Shadow Morton—the guys who didn't know when to stop. He was very hip to the un-hip, people like Juan García Esquivel, or the super un-hip Charlie Calello, who had produced the famous Lou Christie falsetto singles "Lightning Strikes" and "Rhapsody in the Rain" but also the Four Seasons, The Toys' "A Lover's Concerto," Neil Diamond: "Sweet Caroline." Laura Nyro's *Eli and the Thirteenth Confession* LP; we both had the original record that had come packaged with mauve lyric sheets, drenched in patchouli oil. Calello again! Extravagant, even kitschy, at a time when kitsch reigned except among the cool. But Arthur's tastes were unpredictable, for much of the time he had that subtly Buddhist tendency towards stripping down, unplugging, making things simpler. But I don't know much about music and I wonder if carrying these two opposing tendencies with you in a life of music is perhaps common? Commoner than in poetry maybe? Though he knew American poetry quite well, a couple different strains of it, as those who know his lyrics will conclude. I remember him as one of the very few admirers of the poet John Wieners who enjoyed equally both the spare, bleak epiphanies of Wieners' early *Hotel Wentley Poems* (1958), and the manic, Ludwig-eccentric wordtangles collected in *Behind the State Capitol or Cincinnati Pike* (1975).

He would turn to me, tragedy brimming over in his lambent eyes, and ask me, "Where are those happy days? They seem so hard to find." I would reply, from a steely defensive crouch, "I tried to reach for you, but you have closed your mind." By then we would be giggling, like schoolgirls. "Whatever happened to our love?" (with that strange beat on the proposition, "to"). "It used to be so nice," he said. I replied, "It used to be so good." I was one to whom he could unveil these maybe queeny desires, to be one with Agnetha and Frida, to paw at the air, in a way that Allen—or, I don't know, David Byrne or Cecil Taylor—would not. But outside of that we weren't real attracted to each other, and we were both pretty broke all the time. Arthur would moan that he had to break this or that studio date (in which he had planned to record something of his own) because he had to eat. And one time I remember I gave him forty dollars to save such a date and it seemed like an inordinate amount of money to spend on a guy one wasn't even fucking . . .

He acted straight, spoke of having girlfriends, and he danced with the few women who showed up on the floor at the Paradise Garage, seemed to prefer them in fact. It was a shame, then, that I was growing fond of him. He played me a record he had made, a single, sung by a woman, called "Kiss Me Again," and it was fairly tantalizing. I asked him, when you wrote it, who were you speaking to, who did you want to kiss you? Was it Allen? He broke into a grin. "No way, man. Maybe Ronnie Spector."

Matt Wolf's documentary *Wild Combination* emphasizes Russell's background—the past he'd known before I met him. He'd grown up in Iowa, in inhospitable country, flat and hot, and music was an escape, mentally, emotionally. In high school he had listened with all his intensity to the radio hits and low ranking LPs of the art-rock ensemble The Left Banke; once in New York he'd spent some time trying to track down the guy who had written the group's best songs back in the mid-'60s. (I can't remember if Arthur actually met him or not, but Michael Brown was one of his idols.) The cello floating up and around such tracks as "Desiree," "Walk Away Renee," "Ivy Ivy" and "Pretty Ballerina" always calls Arthur Russell to my mind, for I have a mental image of him listening to these songs, as a teen, in a plowed pasture—like the *Children of the Corn*. Or *Cold Comfort Farm*, all lamentation. Maybe I'm just projecting but my sense is that he really wanted out of there. When I heard he had passed on, I wrote a poem for him, named after his song "Is It All Over My Face?" In it random snippets of Left Banke lyrics came rushing onto the paper in splash after splash, "Was I surprised? Yeah! Was I surprised? No, not at all." [Pretty Ballerina.] "Everything returns again; both the laughter and the rain." [Desiree.]

Also the image of looking "beyond the sky," finding or at any rate fishing for something beyond the visible.

When you're a 25 year old drunk like me, with nothing much on your mind but getting laid and trying to be hip, it's disconcerting to run up against a guy who has something going for him. He was quiet sometimes—thinking or feeling deeper than I could. Or than I then wanted to. He got lost in himself easily—just slipped away when you were talking to him. I didn't know how much I ran my mouth till I met him. We'd have long conversations in which, I figured later in blushes, I'd talked in great jags of jokey but earnest bullshit, while he nodded or once in a while interjected a "Yeah," or "No kidding." One afternoon we talked about leaving behind everything and taking a holiday in Hawaii, and it grew so intense for me that I was sure he had agreed to our plans: we were to leave on a week from Sunday, and then it turned out later that he had never registered that I was making a plan and that we were talking about going to Hawaii for that Dennis Wilson feeling of love, love, love.

"It's supposed to be tomorrow," I stuttered. "I'm all packed with like my sunscreen and shit."

"I don't know what you're talking about," he said flatly.

"I know that now, but I don't know why. You said you wanted to see Mauna Loa."

"Mauna Loa," he snorted. "What would you know about Mauna Loa, I met you at the Gay Student Union at Stony Brook."

"Oh and that's right, you're not even gay!"

"All I'm saying is that I would never agree to go to Hawaii with—" He stopped himself from saying, "with you." Instead he said, "With anybody, because I hate tourists and I hate Hawaii."

And there was always his face to convince you. In most lights he had the raw look of Artaud in those stills from *The Passion of Joan of Arc*, and half of it was his hair, and the other his bad skin. He looked like he had been scraped by clamshells, that's how messed up his profile looked. That was the shallow thing that held me back, that gave me the delusion that of the two of us, I was the fairer maiden.

And back on Long Island I sometimes went out with Sean when he was sober, but we'd go drinking and soon enough he was a mess and I guess I was, too.

I know I wasn't altogether in my right mind in those final years of grad school. I had a teacher who had a very wise countenance and a soft, ironic voice who taught us Henry James and Virginia Woolf and Jean Rhys and her emphasis was always on the cruelty of modernism, a byproduct of what she called the "discontinuous universe" produced by the industrial revolution in England. Oh, she scared me to death! She showed how many children in British fiction died, and said it was because they wanted to die, they longed for death because life was so awful—like the little boy in "The Rocking Horse Winner," or Paul Dombey, or the boy in *The Fallen Idol*.

In bits and pieces I resumed work on my long, comic novel *Waterloo Sunset*, introducing a character based on an old romance but blending, finally, into a version of Sean.

I made him an auto mechanic instead of a waiter. There were already too many waiters in the story. It was getting confusing trying to distinguish the restaurants.

One good thing about working in a restaurant is how much your food bill goes down. My grocery bill was only twenty dollars a month and this was almost entirely on Tab, cigarettes and beer. It also leaves a lot of room in your refrigerator and kitchen cabinets to store your books. Why not? You don't need pots and pans. Trained chefs do all that bullshit for you . . . Carl's bookshelves were full of books already: leftist theory, Cortazar, Black Mountain, Burning Deck books, his own work. I forgot to say he was a waiter too. And a poet.

In those two ways he was just like me. Now that Carl was in the hospital and I was in his house I thought: the whole world has gone topsy-turvy.

Gail decided to teach Carl French in the hospital room. Sensibly enough she began with the names of flowers—*des fleurs*.

A woman who's been married twice knows what it's like to take the *rough with the smooth*.

I wonder why the lethargy of off-duty waiters hasn't been more widely noticed. It's an economic principle: the deftness and speed of waiters is balanced, in a zero-sum game, by what the customers don't see, when they're not around—a fantastic, deadening amount of laziness, procrastination, dilation, lead. When I came to California I took a course in acupuncture; I enjoyed the needles and for the first time felt that all the metal in me was seeping out from my pulses into the open fertile air. This was like heroin, in reverse perhaps; this was my heroin. Sean was a student at the local community college and I knew one of his teachers socially. Don't let anyone fool you about confidentiality, which does not apply to adjuncts anyhow. As soon as he knew I too was having sex with Sean, Teacher spilled every bean in his bag, and more, about Sean's attitude in class. To avoid failing the course, Sean had given him a sloppy blow-job in the mimeo room. I should have reported my teacher friend to the Modern Language Association perhaps, but my parents didn't raise no snitch.

Sean was unregenerate, he said. The kid was falling asleep in class. In private, Sean's agility drooped, his public facility and bonhomie grew bumptious and dull, like a county squire in a Trollope novel. I didn't need to be told anything about sleep or about failure. I nodded and clicked and clucked and popped the razorblade ring on another can of beer, each sound or action a signifier of sympathy without any sign to make it real. I began to think of him as a prod—

I BEGAN TO THINK OF HIM AS A PROD
but the proof's in the pudding
I began to refer to him as a god
So gingerly he came to me

I began to think of him as a scumbag
then as a salad I had tossed myself.
Something has to give to give way.

Fetching a stick he began to breathe
out through the corner of his wet mouth
and I began to react in maneuvers.

Nothing like color appeared in his skin
but a veiny pulp plastic or hemoglobin
it got to be a joke between us.

I began to think of him as death
Coming at the end of a bed round
A corner as neat as a hospital nurse

And lifting a leg thick as a log
I could throw on the fire
And he would try to fetch it back

It got to be a joke between us
That I couldn't shake him
That he was like a cold in that respect,

his face bulging, filled with sperm,
a seedy looking man with red gold hair
like a collie, a very sick collie.

O STEPHEN KING! you should be living
in Port Jeff at this hour instead of on
that farmsite in Maine, Port Jeff has

need of you.—Not that you're much
sweeter-scented than this compost heap
impaled on my cock but you'd find grist

here,—grist there, for that MILL OF
SATAN you're running a factory.
Pet cemetery: come bury this body.

Under Gail's influence I spent months steeping myself in Canadian literature and recently, lying in bed at home, I came across
this romantic passage from *Variable Winds at Jalna*, by Mazo de
la Roche, published in 1954: "He had always been a handsome
boy but, of late, the clear fairness of his skin, the sheen of his hair,
his heavy-lidded azure eyes, the perfection of his features, all had
been intensified. As he had grown in stature, so he had grown in
beauty. Piers, looking at him now, thought he was, as Pheasant
declared, the image of what he himself had been as a boy, but the
truth was that young Philip much more resembled her great-
grandfather, Captain Philip Whiteoak. The young Whiteoak
males, sons of Renny, Piers, and Finch, appeared to assert, almost
arrogantly or at least proudly, the Northern origin of their race,
the long, narrow-hipped body, the long flat cheek, the fair skin."
    A red weal appeared on the inner, tender part of Sean's thigh.
By this time the next evening it would be turning yellow and
violet, phosphorescent like marsh air, then brown as cattails. A
ribbon of saliva or mucus made his flushed mouth look larger
and his lips swollen; from the base of his nostrils to his chin a
circle of wet red flesh with a hole in it, through which his tongue
and teeth seemed to hang, mute like genitals. His lower face was

a ripe crushed fruit which contrasted oddly with the pink and blue and yellow pastels of his eyes and forehead: an Elizabeth Peyton watercolor splashed by an anarchist's tomato. Still he instilled in me a sense of pleasure queerly troubled by my fear of enclosure in this bitter fierce world.

Sean begged for a beer, coughing, shifting his kneecaps slightly to open the primitive heat of his ass to a larger locus. He had one of those deep, deep ass cracks that no matter how thoroughly, how widely you spread their thighs, you can just barely make out the asshole. Even in deep stupor he was pretty nimble with his fingers, managing most often to spread his own butt with his hands for visitors to examine his most private of openings. I don't really think he knew what he was doing. The asshole shone like a diamond, and diamantine plinks of light flew off of it, unless I was hallucinating. Or was there someone outside the dark window with a penlight, switching it on and off? Was there a fire flickering in the room and lighting up the faint hairs that blossomed around the borders of the anus? Was Sean bleeding, poor boy, was that why he was crying so piteously, near silently? His asshole had that same crushed strawberry look as his mouth did; it seemed to blink, like the wise owl; maybe wiser than either of us for all we were playing a dangerous game. When I had appreciated the view enough I lowered my face into the seething receptacle, felt with my tongue the heat and the sweat and the faint hairs and I drank from the chalice like I was in some twenties John Cowper Powys novel about finding splendor in the absolute, and in this case literal, ass-end of humanity. But what the devil were those sparks? I tugged at my hard-on for hours while Sean wept, and from time to time I raised my head and spat at his butt—could he even feel that, could he hear me make the indistinct sounds one makes when spitting? The night was so long, it seemed never to end, it seems as if I'm still in it in some way, today in 2018.

I don't think he really knew what he was doing. Sometimes watching his body I wished I had a shroud made of blotting paper I could swaddle him up in. Like a huge industrial strength Bounty, the quicker picker upper. Know how tear gas works? It sucks out from the body all its moisture, so that the flesh swells out under protest. Sean seemed so full of juices that for the first time I understood vaguely what I hadn't since kindergarten, when they told us the human body is 99 per cent water. This irritated me more. A vicious circle. All about Sean. Why, I wondered why can't it ever be all about me? I. Me. Kevin Killian.

Because sleep is so like death I could almost feel a sort of tenderness for him when he slept. When his eyes were open they saw little and reflected less. He liked to feel afraid, I think. As he lay on his stomach with his butt pulled apart, I lost interest presently, and jumped to my feet on the mattress. From what seemed a great distance I observed him nude, his ass a shiny red like a neon exit sign. And then he reached down to his knees and pulled his underpants up to his skinny little waist. He said that it was time we might consider getting a little serious: his parents were having a pool party and he was inviting me to be, like, his date. It was going to be in two weeks time and he knew I had a busy schedule but, if I could come, it would be so hot.

"Your parents?" I cried out. "Who are they? Who let you live?"

"They're just my mother and father to me," he said. I learned later they were a couple high placed in the society of our little town. I was from Smithtown, a middle-class town with plenty of working people and plenty of rich people too. My handbook for living in it was a copy of *A Nest of Ninnies* (New York: Dutton, 1968), a novel by John Ashbery and James Schuyler laid in an impossibly stylized and recondite Smithtown, a Firbankian country that hardly corresponded to the dull, sanitary burg I grew up in. "But these people must be somewhere," I used to think. "These witty, arch, playful, hedonistic scamps!" And when

I went to meet Sean's family I caught a glimpse of them, the playful, hedonistic scamps of Smithtown.

I had never been to Studio 54, "Studio," is how Will and my other young boy friends referred to it, but it was then much in the news, and it was another place, like Hawaii, that Arthur didn't want to go to, in this case because you couldn't hear the music at Studio, and there were too many celebrities there, people without talent, just bone structure and good drugs.

Instead of Studio he took me way over to the west side, the gayest part of the Village, to the Paradise Garage. If he wasn't gay how did he even venture onto that block? It was the late '70s, when the art of cruising had finally been perfected, ditto the whole courtly love apparatus of swooning on the street when a cute trick passed by, or walked relentless in front of one for blocks on Essex Street, his ass a puzzle screaming to be solved, or a moving game like the Tetris of the future, blocks of buttocks to be negotiated and conquered. I would say, "I could eat him up like an ice cream sundae," and Arthur would pause, say nothing, perhaps tilt his head towards me quizzically, almost as if I had said something unpleasant, or so foreign it was like I was speaking in Bjorn and Benny. What was the matter with him? Next to him I thought I was *too gay*, a concept that otherwise did not exist in 1978.

Late, late, late, we got there around 2 a.m. It felt like a prom in a way, there was confetti on the floor, but darker than my prom had been. Soon enough I had lost him in the shadows of the club. An hour or so later I was hanging around and a little short older man challenged me about how I'd gotten in. (You had to be a member apparently.) I explained, he was confrontational in this Brooklyn way that made me sigh inside, thinking, "This sure isn't Studio 54." Had I been ditched? I should have felt shamed, but I was so drunk I was just mouthing off to this little

Danny De Vito guy. "Is it daylight outside?" I said, holding on to last scraps of dignity. "I'll leave if it's daylight." Presently DDVG lost the energy to 86 my ass, and then Arthur Russell returned, blinking from out of the darkness. Had he been watching this ignominious encounter, I wondered? Mostly we were dancing. It was a mixed club filled with blacks, women, Latin guys, Caribbean girls, a fair amount of disco queens in satin shorts and tiny tops. You could hear the music for real there. There was what seemed to be an hour-long mix of the Jackson 5 version of "Forever Came Today." Now that I think of it, Arthur was the one who explained what a mix is! You can see I wasn't very hip. The club played hundreds of tracks I never knew what they were, but I remember he had a fondness for this one song by Norma Jean (was that her name?) and it was called "Saturday." He liked Nile Rodgers and Giorgio Moroder and again, it was how bombastic and pretentious Moroder could be and we both liked *Four Seasons of Love* and *Once Upon a Time* and wondered what would Moroder do next to top that storied grandeur? At the same time, the music always threatened to turn into just pure sound and maybe that's what Arthur liked—that possibility laid out open and threatening.

I remember the Bee Gees had a song called "More than a Woman," and that this intrigued Arthur with the ambiguity of its reference. What would being "more than a woman" entail? Was it in fact a gay coming out number, the Bee Gees acknowledging their gay fans, and giving us a little something? "More than a woman—more than a woman to me." I think now I was just dumb, and socially challenged, expecting everyone to act like they went to Catholic high school—boy's school—as I had, and that everyone was from Long Island's North Shore, since East Egg the byword for vacuity. I thought I had all social types pegged, but I didn't know anything about people beyond my purlieu.

And to be fair to myself, he wasn't all that easy to reach either. It wasn't that he was alienated from other people, not per se; he seemed to be enormously popular. At a coffee shop we'd be eating and our table would get filled one by one by guys he'd worked with or danced with, and I remember having to introduce myself once because he was too high to remember my name. He looked at me and his mouth moved but if you gave him a hundred dollars he couldn't summon my name. One of the fellows sitting two seats away from me was Lance Loud, my gay idol previous to Allen Ginsberg, —Lance Loud of the Mumps, whom I'd adored in the PBS show *An American Family* when I was 20 or so and frozen, transfixed to public TV. Lance Loud who'd had the balls to leave sunny Santa Barbara, his mom and dad, and pound the bell at the desk at the Chelsea Hotel, checking himself in. Those mean desk clerks at the Chelsea. And while we sat there companionably together, I saw another guy's hand slipped into the back pocket of Arthur Russell's jeans and I wondered who this guy was. Of the two of us I was the more alienated in actuality, awash with envy and aggression, while he, Arthur, was merely alienated from his body, and in an interesting way—that's how I see it now, having lived in California for 35 years where these aperçus thrive like the avocados. Again and again I kept running into the basic problem, that I was based on Long Island and that consequently I was a dud. Maybe he was screwed up in his libido, but he was an adventurer, living a creative life, while I was cooped up in my rented house in Rocky Point studying Tennyson, Browning, George Eliot. And bringing guys home, but I wasn't an artist. Every time I emerged from the Midtown Tunnel into Manhattan I would find that Arthur Russell had played some fantastic gig the night before, though he didn't seem to be famous exactly. He wasn't a good fit for me. He deserved somebody better and I deserved somebody who could peer under my anomie and maybe find out I was sort of cool in an ass-backward way. He was handsome but oh, that complexion . . .

Will said I had the shallow personality of the club kid without the appeal—the drive but no charm.

Sean had offered to come by my apartment and pick me up and we could go to his parents' shindig in his car, instead of my old Cruisemobile. "Would you be ashamed," I asked haughtily, "to have my rusty white heap parked in your ancestral driveway? Is that why you're playing it like this, like I should leave my car at home?"

Not at all, he protested. "I know you'll be nervous meeting my folks and when you're nervous, you order another Scotch and Tab. And this way it won't matter if you drink a dozen of them."

"They know I drink Scotch and Tab?"

"Yes."

Part of me was thinking, *My preference is known internationally, and it's so Kevin Killian! Like at the Mardi Gras.*

"My mother thinks it's charming," Sean added. "Charming— that's her word."

"Shall I bring some Tab?"

"My mother bought some. She's like a lot of crazy, like you. She's curious because I found a man I can worship like a god."

"Okay, we can go in your car. But promise me, Sean—you'll get me out of there if I get antsy."

He laughed. "Want to practice a signal? Like you're my batting coach?"

"Yeah, sure, squirt. Like two fingers will mean, get me the fuck out of here. And so will three fingers. Everything will have the same meaning."

"They are going to love you," Sean swore. "You won't need any of our finely worked out finger signals."

"Did you ever bring any boyfriends home?"

His smile sort of died, withered, like a soufflé gone flat. "Yes . . . " he admitted. "It didn't go well."

Our lives were spent in cars all day long, going places, heading out, going home. One day I calculated that I had been on Route 25A twenty-four times in the last 24 hours. You could get to know some intersections pretty well, but only the activity from inside the car. Without getting out and walking, you lost the feeling for nature. But what use had I for nature, I asked myself bitterly. Nature had let me down the day I had assembled that fuzzy bouquet for Allen Ginsberg and it didn't even get me a smile much less a blow job much less a please master push me, my feet on chairs, till my hole feels the breath of your spit and your thumb stroke. Nature hadn't brought him to his senses—

Smithtown had these extra villages abutting it, almost gated communities that we the ordinary people never saw. They had Indian names, like "Nesconset," colonial names, names that were thought up before the land needed names, like "Head of the Harbor." One such village was called "The Branch." I didn't know anyone who lived there. If they had kids, they must have gone to other schools, like maybe schools in Switzerland. And now we were approaching, through a series of rustic roadways with ranch fencing, at 15 miles per hour if that, a town called Nissequogue. That tree there, Sean said, *under that tree is where I first got fucked.* I looked but it was an oak like any other oak. Around its trunk, in every direction, strong roots fingered the ground; it looked like a terribly harsh setting for a physical passion to play itself out.

I didn't even want to ask, but I did, how old Sean was when this happened, and he said he was either eleven or twelve. I thought I was young—fourteen—when a man first lay hands on me. *But this was a girl*, Sean said. *We were boyfriend and girlfriend.* When he said this I felt anew that I was the only gay guy in the whole world. The car drove up through a pair of gates so vast it was like the recent *Mad Max* movie about Fury Road, and then the driveway kept going.

"I was just joking about you having an ancestral driveway, but you do," I told Sean, who nodded, a little embarrassed, the way all rich people are when they are in love with a specimen of lower social register.

"I don't know the whole family tree," Sean explained, "but ask my dad to show you the deed of land. Somebody way back when actually bought it from the Indians, and the chief signed his name like, with sticks." Our town was a mess like every other town in the US, but few of them can have been so vividly embodied with its public art. Look at the status of Whisper for example. The story was told that the founder of Smithtown, Captain Richard Smith, made a deal with some Indians in 1665, telling them that he could ride on the back of a bull, and when they laughed at him, they made a wager that if he could ride a bull they would cede him all the land he could ride around in a single day. What they didn't know is that he had brought a tame bull, "Whisper," on the boat from England, and he picked the longest day of the summer solstice and the Indians realized that they had been fooled, they chuckled pleasantly as they lost a good hundred square miles of their land to the strange white man. When you approached the town from North Country Road, you came across a giant statue of a bull, mounted on a white plinth, spotlit in pin lights, and that was Whisper. Parents had to explain over and over to curious children what the huge genitals of the bull meant, and I know mine were hornswoggled. Schoolboys loved to celebrate holidays by painting the anvil-sized bull cock red and green before Christmas, orange and black for Halloween, pink and yellow as Easter approached, and then crews would be sent out to paint the stone some unremarkable stone color and peace would be restored. It had become a tradition—a romance of genitalia, and *people wonder why I grew up the way I did?*

The house when we reached it wasn't exactly vast, like *Brideshead Revisited*, but it was imposing. Close up it looked as if it was made of old Georgian stone. It was a hot day, but a breeze sweeping up from the river moved around a bed of bright flowers as though invisible fingers were crushing them to produce a headier perfume—zinnias, impatiens, pansies, stalks of lilies tall as Sean was, delphiniums tall as I, their lower leaves stripped so that the blooms seemed to rise floating above the ground . . . Beds of tulips, ringed with daffodils like sentries. Gardeners must have worked on these effects, and afterwards I learned that a friend of the family in the 20s had been a celebrated landscape architect. Here and there a patch of flowers had been run over, luminous color flattened into traces of tire tread. In this way it was like John Cheever's house, that someone drunk lived in a fabulous country setting, but I suspected that was most likely Sean, who sometimes mistook which way the porticos went, and who sometimes, finally seeing his parents' house after a long drive home from work, panicked realizing how blitzed he was and he shouldn't drive a single second longer . . . When I met them I felt sedate, uptight, judgmental. I suppose the rich always keep that power handy, with which to humiliate their inferiors, the power to make us feel incomplete, inexperienced, private and parochial. "They who have the power to hurt, and do none," I whispered under my breath, in my grad student way. You could tell which ones were drinkers, because they already had drinks in their hands—or close by—

The mother, who thought I was so charming, brought me a glass of scotch and Tab, without ice. "Sean says never any ice," she quoted. "So European of you, though I will say that last time I was in Vienna I never saw so much ice: in the bars of Vienna there's been an ice revolution." As she passed me my glass it felt warm from the sun and the whispering bubbles of a freshly poured half pint of Tab winked and blinked under the viscous coating of whiskey. Really, it was the ideal cocktail for so many reasons, I wish I still drank. For pleasure. As I'm writing this, that summer day comes back to me and I wish I still got drunk.

The dad was in the cabana, prone in swimming trunks on a long bed of bamboo and steel, atop a host of brightly colored pillows—red, yellow and green renderings of cactus and burros, Frida Kahlo colors, definitely something Mexican about the décor. (Later I peeked into the women's cabana and it was very different, very femme, with swags of pink chiffon poking down from the ceiling towards the walls.) Captain Whiteoak, as I'll call him, was sober enough, but it embarrassed Sean that he wouldn't get off the phone. Was it his broker? Something financial?

"Pop," Sean whined, "I have to make a call." He threw himself into a lounge chair festive with peasants and lizards. "It's important, pop."

Finally, the Captain ended his call and stood and shook my hand.

Sean picked up the warm phone and dialed a number while I made small talk. Yes, I was Sean's boyfriend. It felt weird to say so in the '70s but these people were cool with it. What was I drinking? Scotch and Tab. Yes really. Yes, I'm in the English Department at Stony Brook.

"How big is your cock," Sean asked on the phone. "What do you like to do?"

The Captain chuckled. "That's when I found out he was gay," he reminisced. "He was on his phone just like this, and he was twelve or thirteen, and he was talking gay sex talk like he was experienced, and overhearing him I grew concerned." Now he grinned and tossed himself into the chair and lifted Sean up and down so he sat on his lap like he was Santa and Sean a child. "But I had an uncle who was gay, so I knew something about it and I knew there was no changing this boy."

Again the Captain stood, abruptly tossing Sean to one side, and with the verve of a golfer he grabbed the right side of his bathing suit and lowered it about ten inches, showing me his tan line. You couldn't see his dick, or even really much of his butt, but it startled me, and when he asked for my advice—should he try to make the tan line more definite—like George Hamilton— or should he go for the totally natural undifferentiated look. His stomach was so flat it was like part of the wall, though less gaily colored. "I don't know," I mumbled, "but I can see you're kind of stuck in between the two states of tan." "Nude," Sean suggested, still on the phone with the potential trick. "Pop, show him your cock." "I'm not gay," said the Captain, "but between me and Sean we keep few secrets," and he took out his cock, and I whistled, and raised my Scotch and tab to my lips, nodding, like both of them were so cool together. But actually in my gay lit class I was teaching as a TA I was having my students read *Pages from Cold Point*—the Paul Bowles story about a similarly close father and son relationship, and my heart was racing faster.

The Captain's cock wasn't immense, but it was the biggest one in the room. He held it in one hand. It wasn't erect, but it was, uh active. "I'm not gay," he said again, "but it's like all things, it perks up when you pay it attention."

"I love it," I said. "Sean told me you were supportive when he came out, but I had no idea."

Sean hung up with his friend, grabbed his dad's arm, pulled up his dad's trunks—rather touching it was, like he was wrapping a present for him. "Come on, you guys," he said, grinning. We could hear some splashing already, like the pool party had begun without us. "Let's go swimming?"

I guess it was just disconcerting that here was another guy who was also not gay, or so he said, and I already had beat my head against the wall about Arthur Russell and his will he, won't he, games of hesitation and avoidance. Later I asked Sean if he and his dad had ever, er, you know—gone the whole way like the boy and his father in the Paul Bowles—and oh, he was scandalized,

"How can you even ask?" I had the feeling that, even if somehow I managed to live past my twenties, I would still never get human behavior right, still never understand relationships between people. How could I be a novelist without that knack? And yet every time I ventured into something I got it wrong. Tearfully Sean insisted his dad was just like a great, supportive, friend with deep pockets. Once in some sort of sex accident Sean had come driving home with something huge stuck up his butt, but it was so far in he couldn't touch it. "Did your dad take it out?" I said. "No, no, but I could tell him about it, and he called in a special doctor. I was afraid he'd hate me. But instead he brought in this specialist and half an hour later, it was out."

"And what did it turn out to be?" I asked. I was a novelist, I felt I had to know every little detail of everyone's stories.

Sean snickered. "I think I knew the guy who put it there, but I may be wrong. But it hurt like a motherfucker."

"Tell Kevin, was this the bad object that hurt my Sean so?"

"It was a silver, like, what do you call 'em? A silver gravy boat—a small one really."

"Yes," I said, "that was very good of your dad to tend to you like that, without asking any questions, just relieving your distress." And I'm thinking, how did the Captain know just which doctor to call?

"Did you have fun swimming?" Sean asked. "My sisters really liked you. Claire now will drink nothing but Scotch and Tab; it just mortifies her fiancé, but she tells him, that's Kevin Killian's drink."

Once Arthur and I went to the movies and argued about what we should see. Perhaps because he wasn't in it for some reason, Allen had advised against seeing *The Last Waltz*, not worth our time he'd told Arthur. One morning we folded the *Daily News* against a mailbox propped open to the movie listings. We wound up deciding on the original *Grease*, then a new release. I can't remember if it was Loews State 1 or 2—whatever the upstairs one was—near Times Square—and moviegoers on line said the management had slotted what might have seemed like a turkey into a small theater, then when it became an unexpected hit there were lines around the block and it became a real challenge to get a ticket. We tried to see it at noon and couldn't get tickets till nine or ten at night. In the meantime we sort of had nothing to do, kicked around here and there, looked at the lions at the Public Library, and as the hours wore on I got the impression that Arthur was not enjoying our date much. In hindsight it was a wee bit ludicrous, dragging him to this show. Finally to save the situation I did what I'd done many times before, acted all into him and came on bi-curious.

I asked him who that man was feeling up his ass at the restaurant.

Arthur at first didn't remember.

I stuck my own hand into his back pocket to improve his memory.

He blushed but kept flipping the albums in the import bin. Even chain stores like Sam Goody's, he always said, sometimes hid treasures. One time, in Berkeley, he had found a case of the Velvet Underground's first album at a church bazaar sale. This was the record with the Warhol banana pasted on the front, ingeniously pink under its yellow peel, and these babies were mint, still in cellophane wrappers. A case! And they were asking twenty dollars for it. He had to borrow the twenty from a girlfriend but it was worth it, for the proceeds of that find saw him through a whole semester of careful eating and dining—already it was a very rare record at least with the banana unpeeled. In his pocket my thumb and forefinger pinched his butt gently. "Who was the guy?" I repeated.

He said the guy was called Steve and he was a musician.

"So you're not gay, but you let him into your back pocket and you just keep his hand there like it's renting a room."

He shrugged, grinned, a grin that said "bi-curious" right back to me, like looking into a mirror.

I hypnotized him into going back downtown, back to the building where Allen lived, on East 12th Street. Arthur lived in the building too, though not perhaps in this very apartment—(this was murky to me, unsettling, as though I were not wanted in his actual dwelling place, where he lived). This was a Spartan flat with only a few pieces in it, all of them white, cream, sand or putty colored. The floorboards were bare, though an area rug covered the lintel between two rooms. It was hot in that flat, and the window opened only a crack. You could see streaks of pink and yellow across the blue of the sky, and the noise was fierce, it was what excited me about Manhattan, so different from San Francisco where I had spent the previous summer, the summer Elvis died. In San Francisco cars don't honk their horns. Arthur said it was the quality of the street noise that made different composers write as they did, that John Cage wrote very differently when he worked in San Francisco than he did in New York, and differently in Seattle than in the other cities. I thought he was projecting, speaking really of himself and the way that he had ridden this trajectory from the prairies of Willa Cather country (or wherever), which must show up in his music somewhere (vague misconceptions of Ives), then he'd gotten blissed out in San Francisco, and now New York was drilling syncopation into his head as it had Lorca and Stravinsky and Piet Mondrian. Like a boy I was always reaching out manually, and for me the direct approach worked, so I had been pawing him all the way from Broadway and Times Square, one palm flat on his crotch, when no one could see, in what I hoped was a masterful or, at any rate, a *practiced* way. In this way I had befriended Sean, picking him up hitchhiking and then measuring his cock through his pants while telling him how red I was going to roast his rump. Wealthy Sean with the hangdog look in his eyes and the fires of hell burning in his soul. Inside Arthur's building, the bright room had a bed but we didn't lie down on it, in fact we didn't even get close to it, we just skinned down our pants and stood by the window, jerked each other off by the window, my back bumping against the painted wall. I blew him a little, cranked myself up, unsteady. His face was damp, rosy. In my hands his cock seemed large, sturdier than I would have guessed, like a stick. I asked him if he was ready, he nodded. Asked if he had any lube, he shrugged. That made me think, maybe this wasn't his place. But that was cool. The whole scene had something to it of the meeting between Brando and Maria Schneider in Bertolucci's steamy 1972 film *Last Tango in Paris*; it made it more exciting that it was the flat of someone else. (And later in life I could see occasions where a trick pad, if that's what this is, could come in handy.) I reached round and bounced his ass in my hand, sluicing his dick. Or maybe when I'd asked about the lube he'd thought I wanted to fuck him, you could tell he wasn't going there. But he had a great Ryan McGinley style ass that felt luminous and insolent in my hand. At that point I was going to shoot and told him so, aim for the floor he whispered. "You too," I said. I kept thinking this is all I had wanted from Allen, but Allen had turned away from me, too busy for mere me.

38:8 And Judah said unto Onan, Go in unto thy brother's wife, and marry her, and raise up seed to thy brother.

38:9 And Onan knew that the seed should not be his; and it came to pass, when he went in unto his brother's wife, that he spilled [it] on the ground, lest that he should give seed to his brother.

Later an expert on Arthur told me that we were probably in Gregory Corso's room—who knew? It was so neat and spare. And Corso had that messy aura to him, but this place was perfect for this Amish sex we enjoyed. Squirt.

Squirt.

Figure X.

I grew comfortable with Captain Whiteoak and one afternoon on a Sunday, when I was bussing tables at the Smithtown Sizzler—the most déclassé place on the North Shore I'm sure—I saw him enter. I was dazzled and surprised, for I had never seen an actually rich person ever come to this two-hit franchise. The highest we aspired to were middle class people who could give generous tips if you buttered them up the right way, and drunks of course, for the place sold beer and wine in all you can eat quantities. The Muzak was playing some snippets of Frank Loesser musicals from the '50s in perfect sheen, like Andre Kostelanetz conducting the Mystic Moods Orchestra, and there he was, Captain Whiteoak, in a honey colored corduroy sport jacket and a broadcloth shirt and a plaid tie, like a golden retriever in a George Selden book.

I put aside my tub and went to greet him, wishing I didn't look like such a schlub, but as all waiters know, people with money are allowed to see the people without money while they're working—they seem to thrive on it. You have to act grateful to be performing labor in front of them. (Sometimes today I feel this way teaching my students.) "Hi there, welcome to the Smithtown Sizzler. Can I bring you some buffalo wings to start off with? Will your family be joining you?"

"They're in Toronto," he explained, as I showed him to a table.

"Oh really," I said. "Neil Young's from there."

"And Glenn Gould," he replied. "It's a musical town. They're visiting family."

I held a finger in the air to indicate Sizzler's scintillating Muzak orchestra. "Do you know this one? 'Wonderful, wonderful Copenhagen, salty old queen of the sea! Once I sailed away, but I'm home today.'"

"Danny Kaye?" he hazarded. Bingo! Another customer was beckoning at me for something. We were still on first base, me and the Captain, and he puzzled me greatly. "I know you're busy, Kevin, but I'm wondering, what time do you clock out?"

"We say punch out." We were studying regional differences in linguistics class at school. "I'll be out at eight."

"Can you come by the house? I want to ask you something."

Like a conjurer he laid down a twenty dollar bill on top of the unopened menu.

"I think I can find my way," I said. "But I should stop home first and shower."

"You can shower at the house," he said. Oh, the thoughts that were tumbling in my brain!

"Will you excuse me?" I said, and darted over to the table 14, which asked for six orders of our famous tapioca pudding. When I returned to table 10, the Captain had gone, leaving me my tip, and a little note that said, "Hurry."

Did that mean, "Please hurry?" or did it mean, "Sorry I had to run, I'm hurrying." Either way I am 100 percent sure today that twenty dollars was the largest tip I ever got in this god-awful place. My face was burning like someone had stuffed it with rubies. *I simply must go . . . the answer is no . . . but baby, it's cold outside . . .*

I didn't really want to "cheat," if that's what you'd call it, on Sean with his father, and he was such a cipher it baffled me what he really wanted from me, but I got out of the Cruisemobile around nine. I had to go home of course and at least put on some nicer underwear, and I made a mental note, as I slammed the car door, to always keep some in the trunk because the truth is, in the '70s you never knew. The house was dark outside, though fragrant with camellias, and as I walked across the flagstone the front door swung open like a dream.

"You look very fresh," said the Captain, holding out a glass of Scotch and Tab. Winningly he said that he was going to join me. "Do you need to shower?"

"I'm good," I said.

"Let's just sit down in the big room there," he gestured. "I really appreciate you coming by."

"You know what I forgot to ask you," I prompted. "Sean said to ask to see the deed of land where your ancestors—"

"—Stole it from the Indians? That's a myth, come look and see." We moved into a shaded alcove where discreet spotlights picked out an ancient manuscript glassed and framed between two windows. I couldn't read a single word, it was in Old English I believed, a hundred years before the Declaration of Independence. I pulled at the Captain's sleeve. "You're historical," I whispered.

Then the Captain took my hand and held it like we were shaking hands, which confused me. Then he asked me if I needed money.

I went back to my cocktail and sat cross-legged on a seductive sofa, patting the cushion beside me, and told Captain Whiteoak that I had a friend who was a genius in New York and all he needed was five hundred dollars to pay for studio space to finish a masterpiece.

"Our family has always patronized musicians," he told me. "Years ago we had Stravinsky stay here when he composed that circus concerto for what's his name."

"Arthur Russell is like the new Stravinsky," I lied. "And he lives in complete poverty."

"I don't know about five hundred dollars," said the Captain, downing his drink. "But how about I give you one hundred forty bucks, and you go away and don't see Sean again." *Reader, what would you have done?* I did feel underbid, like he didn't even think two hundred dollars of me. Or even $150. This was like, wow, how insulting, do you think you can buy me so cheaply? I couldn't claim that Sean loved me, or any such thing, but still, how rude . . .

"Does that figure," said I icily, "include the twenty dollars you dropped on me at the Sizzler?"

That must have stung him, for he showed some emotion, swallowing a cough, his eyes watering up. "No, this is on *top of that twenty.*"

I gave Arthur half, and he was really delighted. Seventy dollars possibly paid for a month's rent on his apartment, I don't know. I didn't mention my shame. I don't know if he would have been interested. His mind was made up about music was his thing.

The only thing I remember knowing about music that he didn't know already was an anecdote about Cole Porter. Porter had been dissed by some competitor for writing complicated lyrics, and Porter retorted he could make a hit out of something as banal as "I Love You." Stupid anecdote, probably apocryphal, but Arthur Russell (who knew the song from its Coltrane rendition) said it just went to show how lyrics might as well and should be reduced to Basic English. I asked Ginsberg to sign a copy of the radical gay arts magazine *Gay Sunshine* that he had published some poems in. This issue was a souvenir of my trip to San Francisco the summer before—the summer Elvis died—and I had stopped into Small Press Traffic and bought up this copy, and a few older issues, of this gay tabloid/sex journal/arts forum, folded over like the *Rolling Stone* of that era—probably by the same antiquated factory machines. On the back of the issue was Ginsberg's poem, "I Lay Love on my Knee," one of the little pieces he liked to write in the vein of Blake, were Blake an American chicken hawk. I showed him a manuscript, across it he scrawled, "Allen Ginsberg did not write this book, I hope somebody did." On the rose-colored back of the gay paper he scrawled his name, big florid "AH," and nearby it, in the tiniest hand, Arthur Russell wrote his. That's my souvenir. I remember our ropes of semen crossing on the floor of I don't know whose apartment. When I saw him onstage, his cello pressing his knees far apart, I anticipated he'd be an easy lay. I didn't realize, not till later on, that he saw himself as basically straight, straight if weak and prone to stumbling. He hung out with fags, but walked apart, at least in the time I knew him. What he and I had wasn't very much, but it pushed a button in me, and always after that I preferred to avoid thinking about him, as one might dream of undoing a faux pas. I keep insisting to myself the pain of recollection denotes something. He wasn't the one I wanted—but is that so horrible? That had after all been the theme of *Grease*, Olivia Newton John striding in a hot leather strapless cat suit, turning the tables on John Travolta because he was the one she wanted.

We didn't have sex again, but continued to hang out until I really started to bore him and vice versa. I remember that same summer going to Riis Park on Far Rockaway, way on the very west end of Rockaway Beach—it was then the poor man's Coney Island, and part of it at any rate a de facto gay beach—of sorts.

We lay there on the hottest day and Arthur made triangles in the sand, about a foot in each direction, with some cryptic symbols in hem. You couldn't do very fine work in the muddy wet sand of Riis Park. Nearby a giant clock told the time on four sides, and each big round face told a different wrong time. I haven't been back there in years, but I suppose under Giuliani and Bloomberg that giant clock was fixed to tell perfect time today.

I felt a little embarrassed by these triangle drawings, thinking that somehow Arthur was snidely referring to my feeling that I was part of a triangle with him and Allen Ginsberg. When I mentioned this he said, "We're not even really a line, you and me."

"Yeah, that's true." *Then what about me jerking you off?*

"And you have the little rich boy who waits on tables," Arthur said. I had told him about Sean of course, but I don't know—was I trying to make him jealous, surely an impossible task? No, I was innocent of that particular manipulation.

Arthur pointed to one triangle, the largest? And drew a plus sign in it. "Let plus stand for Allen!" Another one had an ampersand in it already. "That can be me. No, that can be you."

It just came over me, this feeling of hopelessness. I jumped down to the sand and drew myself as a triangle, and put a minus sign in it. "No, that can be me!" I said spitefully.

About an hour later we were on the ferry laughing, it was still bright and hot and crowded, I had forgotten about this stupid triangle spat, until I heard Arthur humming a tuneless, repetitive melody. You know, he had a beautifully expressive voice. I think he could have gone on Broadway. He was like Frida and Agnetha combined with the notes he could reach. "What are you singing," I giggled. Then I heard the words—it was like one of the hums in *The House at Pooh Corner*. "Triangles in the sand," he sang. "Plus and ampersand . . . Minus on demand." It had other words too, but mostly it was these repeated often enough that I caught the tune and, in a if you can't beat them gesture, I joined him.

> Triangles in the sand,
> Plus and ampersand,
> Minus on demand.

Another time we got on the subway at Astor Place, intending to hit the Cloisters, a place I had used to haunt, for sex reasons, when I was an undergraduate at Fordham's Lincoln Center. My gay rabbi Alfredo had told me you meet a "nicer class of guys" at the Cloisters than you did at the piers, say. Anyhow it was rather like a date between a divorced dad and his little girl whom he gets to see only on Sunday afternoons. Something educational and cheap. We sat on opposite sides of the car, facing each other, like straight boys might. I was still reading *The Raj Quartet* and was continuing on to the end out of habit, the way I see many of my friends today trying to get to the end of Elena Ferrante so they can say they've read her and she's wonderful, and who is she. At Union Square the car slowed down, the brightness of the day trickling onto the platform like a veil of water, we came to a halt and when the doors opened, there stood Ginsberg. It was a cinematic moment for me—the buzzing sunlight hummed and sat right on the top of his head, as though he were the Messiah. He wore a trench coat I'd seen him in before, khaki green, and carried an expensive leather book bag with many buckles. As he stepped in, he nodded at me, then surveyed the rest of the car for a better place to sit in, and accidentally his glance fell backwards and landed on Arthur Russell.

I didn't want to be reminded of how little I meant to Ginsberg, but it was plain as paint, for he sat down right next to Arthur and leaned into him confidentially, launching into a conversation that looked like it hadn't stopped since the last time they'd seen each other. People walking on the moon could look down and see how little I meant to Allen Ginsberg. I was dying. Were neither of them planning to acknowledge me further? I knew there wasn't much point trying to extend the invitation to the Cloisters to Ginsberg. He would only brush me off. But if he knew Arthur was coming? Presently Arthur spoke. "You remember Kevin Killian? We're on our way to the Cloisters." I hate myself but I eagerly hopped to my feet and scurried over to Ginsberg to shake his hand and to join the conversation.

"Oh uh yeah—is that your bag over there on the seat? Better keep an eye on it. I lost a book that way, leaving it on the seat when I saw a friend." He turned to Arthur. "It was Mishima's *Forbidden Colors*," he told him, and they continued a previous conversation about Mishima. I was dismissed. I went back to my seat and sat next to my bag. I couldn't look at them so I looked up and down and across at the fantastic graffiti coloring our car like the inside of a capillary. A few stops later Arthur came and sat next to me and told me that he was getting off the IRT with Allen at 68th Street. "It's a gig," he explained. "At Hunter." At least he had the grace to look ashamed. "Sorry to ditch you like this, Kev, but you understand. I need the bread: rent's due and I'm busted."

Steely eyed I stared forward at Allen, his head deep in a book—it couldn't have been *Forbidden Colors*, it was something slim and little like a prayer book. The hell with him. Later I found out it was some old edition of George Herbert that one of Allen's scouts had found for a dime at the Strand. Yeah, the hell with him.

"I'll be big about this," I said grandly, "and let you off the hook." The tragic grandeur of the Marschallin flooded through me, when she congratulates Octavian on his marriage to that young, pretty girl in *Der Rosenkavalier*. Afterwards whenever I thought of Allen I had this image always of him disappearing, evading me, the tails of his green trench coat just flicking out of sight as the subway doors closed on him. And he never looked back. Was I surprised? Yeah. Was I surprised? No, not at all.

One song thudded through my head, as I sat there in the subway tumult, deciding should I go to the Cloisters solo? Or just head back home to Long Island? It was the dreariest question ever asked! "Triangles in the sand," I hummed, "plus and ampersand, minus on demand." Why was it on demand? Arthur had explained he was thinking of another of my favorite songs, Lulu's inane, yet magical 1971 lounge masterpiece "Oh Me Oh My (I'm A Fool For You Baby)" in which the bewitched singer plans never to leave the bed where her man is resting. She'll "stage a ballet on the table top," mimes two fingers scurrying across the table, as if dancing, "command performance, finger-size." After the girl and the boy have sex, the smoke of their conjoined cigarettes creates the illusion of a genie who will grant her every wish. She will "tell her smoky friend, now don't forget, you must keep us side by side." She realizes she's gone mad but it's OK; she spends the remainder of the track shouting in exultation how crazy, crazy, crazy she is, how enslaved by love. I think I did wind up at the Cloisters that day, it was dull, but I had a book with me, something I had to read for my orals like *Daniel Deronda* or *Lord Jim.*

You won't remember, but when I was eating out Sean in my squalid half-built apartment and I thought I saw lights flickering at the windows all around me? It might have been the spirits but it was this guy, Lionel, who was the son of my landlord, rather a vacant guy who was often around with some buddies trying to shore up other parts of the house.

Lionel was a surly, dummy sort of Long Island moombah who had this resentment of college going on. The classic town versus gown thing playing itself out on the outskirts of the Stony Brook campus. "I have to be honest with you, friend," he explained, after I let him into my rooms. He pulled a beer away from a six-pack of Bud he'd brought with him, offered it up to me, so yes, I took it from him.

"Yes, what brings you here?"

"Well, I'm always here," Lionel explained. He said that he slept in his car in one of the sand dunes abutting the rangy derelict house. "You and me we see each other all the time and I know you're helping out Carl with the rent and all, but you see, I don't think my dad would like it if he knew a queer was here in his rental."

Oh Jesus. Lionel sat there in this dilapidated pink chenille covered lounge chair and he had no idea how gay he looked! He said he had looked in the window one night and spotted me administering discipline to a passed out guy. "His ass was bright red like a balloon at a county fair," Lionel saw. "And you had your face right down there like a wolf scarfing up dinner. That's disgusting, man. I ain't never seen anything like it." He kept raising the Bud to his mouth and swallowing, but kept his gaze trained on me past his fingers and past the open can, as if to measure my reaction. "It was disturbing to all my senses, and I said to myself, 'I better tell my Pop.'"

"But you didn't."

"Because when I went back to the Malibu I tried to sleep and I couldn't," he said. "Is that what they teach you in grad school, Kevin, how to chow down on ass like you're on fire?"

"And what do they teach you in middle school, Lionel? That you've got me by the balls? You can make a career out of exploiting homosexuals?"

"I watch you whenever you've got that boy over here."

"You're hooked," I summed up.

Lionel's shapeless face comported itself into a thin smile. He brushed one side of his face as though flies were buzzing there. "Yeah, maybe I am, dude, but you could of gotten some curtains and then you'd have stayed out of this jam."

Hate's a lot like hope, and hope like hate. Presently I broke my word to the Captain, called Sean, and explained my predicament. And a week after that I sat before Sean's face, watching his heavy-lidded azure eyes bulge and close while from behind my landlord's son fucked him with real glee in my room. Sean's head rested in my lap like a child's. That stupid Lionel had no technique, but he grunted and groaned as though the top of his head was coming off. He held Sean's waist like the steering wheel of a bumper car he kept ramming into a wall, but Sean was silent. I thought of holding up the pages of *Life* magazine before his eyes to give him something to look at. He could read the front pages and I could read the back pages. Carl's shelves were stuffed with good books. Cortazar, Elizabeth Bishop, Charles Olson, *Invisible Man.*

An insensible sigh escaped his lips at last, as Lionel cuffed the back of his head with a loosely rolled fist. I said, "Hush, hush, hush baby don't cry."

"Is he always like this," Lionel asked. "He always take what guys give him?"

My mind was spinning, for I was torn with thought, and worst of all, I couldn't tell really if Sean was all right. He loved pain to a

certain degree, and he also glowed with warm pride when someone upbraided him verbally, for having a small dick or whatever,
big nipples like a girl's. Lionel's battering ram was pretty big, but
not too big for Sean I didn't think. But at midnight you get tired
no matter who you are, unless, like Lionel, you are ringing your
brain with garlands of amphetamine, and you just see the farthest
corners of the bedroom and no further. But Sean had that flowery
background, the seat at the top of the cliff like Merlin. I never
worked out what he saw in me, except for some class thing that
made him hard, and my long list of things to slide up his ass. And
I was also from Smithtown. He and I were brothers in a way.

"He always takes what guys give him," I agreed. "Tell you
what, though, you've been in him an hour, can't you come?"

"This is what I'm good at," he said. "Wearing a girl down."

"Are you okay, Sean?" I asked. He wasn't talking, he was on a
lot of drugs, just to loosen him up and dull his senses.

No reply.

"Tell you what, I'm gonna get up and come behind you and
tickle your balls and that will make you explode," I promised
Lionel. "Ever have that done to you, chum?"

"Not by a guy!" he swore. "Next thing you know, you'll be
trying to get a finger in my butt."

"I sure will," I said. I moved my legs out from Sean's head and
saw him put his thumb in his mouth, sucking his thumb like a
monkey, or a baby. I patted the side of his hot cheek, as if to say,
this will all be over soon. "You're trying all sorts of new things
tonight," I reminded Lionel. "And you know what?"

"What, motherfucker?"

"There's still no curtains up on these windows. Maybe your
dad is out there watching us."

"Shit, he'd kill me."

"Yeah, wouldn't that be something," I groaned sourly. Lionel
had kept his T-shirt on but his jeans and boxers were pushed

down below his knees. He stood at the end of the bed and Sean's legs dangled beyond his waist on either side. Without my counterweight at Sean's head, Lionel seemed now to be pushing Sean a foot or more across the mattress towards the wall, then dragging him back, it was pretty strenuous. I was dressed myself, also wearing a pair of jeans and a T-shirt (that read "Todd is God" in glitter), but I could reach in the sweaty mess with one hand, and find Lionel's slick, bumpy perineum, and his balls pressed up the roof of it.

"Be careful with them," Lionel advised. "Cup 'em like they were robin's eggs."

"Okay, will do." I could feel him stop, hold himself still, his dick almost out of Sean's hole entirely. I could feel him willing himself to hold his own ass up to me, to separate his butt cheeks. He wanted that one finger up his ass, just like we all do. And then he would come, and then he would leave maybe.

"One, two, three," I counted. "Ready, you son of a bitch?"

It all worked out perfectly and he lay gasping on top of Sean like a coverlet of human flesh and sweat. "How'd you do that?" he asked, panting.

"Cocktails, my dear," I whispered throatily. "My secret is cocktails."

I learned Arthur was dead maybe ten years ago, and it hit me harder than it should have. I read an article in some general interest magazine, like *Esquire*, and it spoke of how of late canny marketing and public fascination with this hard-to-define one of a kind wunderkind had made him a star years after his death. "Arthur Russell," I repeated. I giggled, thinking that I had once gone out with a boy who had the same name. And they'd both lived in New York. Yet something kept me from identifying that the two boys were the same guy, until I got to the part in the recap of Arthur's life when it said he had played the cello for the poet of *Howl*, Allen Ginsberg. I put down the mag, the tidy paragraphs blurring like bouncy marshmallows. "I think it's gotta be him!" I whispered. It said he had died of AIDS in 1992. So he was dead, like so many others of our generation. It said that after 1980 Arthur had gone on to make some of his most delicious and inspired work. It named his disco tracks, released most often under another's name, and I recognized some of the numbers, having danced to them in the clubs of San Francisco early in the '80s. "Is it all over my face? You caught me love dancing. Is it all over my face? I'm in love dancing." I remembered them, but hadn't known he wrote them. They sounded so different than the work I had heard him play; and yet they were reminiscent, in many ways, of the work of Giorgio Moroder and Bjorn & Benny of ABBA and of Michael Brown from The Left Banke. I kept thinking, I should call him. Google had been invented by now— I could just go on it and find his number. Just to say hi.

Why had I been so mean to him? It was embarrassing to admit it was because of his looks but that was a lot of it. If he had no acne he would have been too good-looking for me, out of my league. But that seemed to shallow me the price he paid for being so brilliant, that equitable God had not let him out of heaven before scarring his face like he was one of the tribe of Cain. I thought God was equitable, but all I can think of now is how blind I was—perhaps blessedly blind? I raised my hands and experimented, imagining my fingertips were clamshells scraping my face raw. Prodded my fingers into my skin. Above San Francisco the clouds were bumping up against each other, and I had a flash that, if I could look behind these skies, maybe I could make him out—make out Arthur, his averted glance, his forearms, his dream wave, triangles appearing inch by inch in the damp sand of Riis Park Beach.

IS IT ALL OVER MY FACE?

Spring 1978, clutching old
copy of *Gay Sunshine*, on verso
Allen Ginsberg's poem
I lay love on my knee

"I nurs'd love where he lay
I let love get away
I let love lie low . . ."
in Stony Brook, Long Island where once

Denise Levertov nearly expired of an illicit passion in
wartime

Spring, so difficult to keep Allen Ginsberg's rhythms out
of my head, the numb, dumb beat that he compared to
the stroke of a cock, its pulse when you're holding it up
(or out?) in front of you. His affect was strong, unruly, he
was so used to getting what he wanted, indeed maybe it's
a Buddhist trait, their accent on humility some kind of

bizarre cover-up for the emotional thing
he was away on business
Always the two tails of his beige trench coat disappearing
into subway car doors
Is it all over my face, when I talk with you I feel myself
grow red, your wispy beard and heavy
        smell of cigarette smoke,
With you I feel the obviosity of Ginsberg's doggerel verse
grow into baton-like accent and stricture,
        like it is going to pound me to death.

Is it all over my face?
You've caught me love dancing

Everything returns again, everything comes back, the
return of the repressed, both the laughter and the rain

She is living somewhere far away
and I send her this poem to give her options
ask her in my lonely way,

Today the skies over our little park are grim, pink,
streaked with black and white like a cat

nothing can hold back the rain

I could see through the clouds to this place where
Arthur Russell brings his hand around my cock
cello wet with tears, and how he's gone

I told my friends he was not the boy for me

Was I surprised? Yeah
Was I surprised? No, not at all

Desiree, you know how it hurts me, he caught
me love dancing

Heeding the warnings of Allen Ginsberg, the American Buddhist
poet who predicted that their love would lead to untold suffering,
he and Arthur Russell lived apart from the day they were married.

His death from AIDS in April 1992 inspired some of my own
most beautiful work. My own premature death in June 2004

marked a great loss to contemporary Buddhist art. "Where do I run to? Is it real?"

Fifteen stitches across my face,
one for every man that hurt me.
Fifteen apparitions I have seen—the worst, a coat upon a
    coat hanger.
Players and painted stage took all my love,
and not those things that they were emblems of. Is it
all over? My face feels scarred,
my teeth stretched across Botox and bandages.

In the silhouette he casts
the window of a moving train
moving faces—temporary hook-up
he touched the other side of my face

red maple
pepperbush
cranberry

is it all over the Internet, series of short,
    sharp, abdominal pains, is it
    common lingua franca the
    way my soul seeks to engulf you

is it all over my face, the shame
    of belief, the way the ears of George
    Bush Jr sprout from his head,
    for he fears the angel

is it all over the world, red
  maples of Xanadu, cranberry, the simple
  gift of Long Island, almost the way
          Arthur Russell, Lou Harrison played on it
          Allen Ginsberg all noble
          Arthur Russell, Lou Harrison played on it
          till sunset, spring, 1978, and far
          away fingerprints for Kylie
          on cat-tails
          still finds a way to haunt me
          always and forever

Sources and Acknowledgements

Some of this material has appeared, in an altered form in *Zyzzyva*, *Libido*, *The James White Review*, *The Sentinel*, *Archives Newsletter* (UCSD), and in the catalog of *Against Nature*, an exhibition at LACE curated by Dennis Cooper and Richard Hawkins.

"The Honey Bear," by Eileen Myles, originally from their book *A Fresh Young Voice from the Plains* (Power Mad Press, 1981), also appears in the recent new and selected volume, *I Must Be Living Twice* (Ecco Press, 2016) and is reprinted here with their kind permission.

"Chain of Fools" appeared first in *Wrestling with the Angel: Faith and Religion in the Lives of Gay Men*, ed. Brian Bouldrey, in 1995, and later in *The Soho Press Book of 80s Short Fiction*, ed. Dale Peck, in 2016.

"Hot Lights," first appeared in *Gerbil #4* (Rochester, NY), ed. Tony Leuzzi, Fall 1995, and then in *Best American Gay Fiction* 1996, ed. Brian Bouldrey.

"Man and Boy" appeared in *Pills, Thrills, Chills, and Heartache*, ed. Clint Catalyst and Michelle Tea (Los Angeles: Alyson Books), in 2004.

"Spurt," appeared first in *Flesh and the Word* 4, ed. Michael Lowenthal (New York: Plume), May 1997, and was reprinted in *The Best American Erotica 1999*, ed. Susie Bright (New York: Touchstone/ Simon & Schuster), February 1999.

"*Santa*, after Brad Gooch's *Satan*," was excerpted in *New Langton Arts Catalogue of Programs January–December 1989*, Summer 1990, and the whole thing came out as a chapbook from Leave Books (ed. Juliana Spahr) in 1995.

"Who Is Kevin Killian?" is the transcription of a live talk (with audience interaction) given at San Francisco's Intersection for the Arts in April 1993 and first appeared in print in *Avec #7* (Penngrove, CA), May 1994, edited by Cydney Chadwick.

"Young Goodman Brown Effect" was published in *Life as We Show It: Writing on Film*, edited by Brian Pera and Masha Tupitsyn (San Francisco: City Lights Books), 2009.

Triangles in the Sand began as my answers to Tim Lawrence's questions for his 2009 bio *Hold On to Your Dreams: Arthur Russell and the Downtown Music Scene 1973–1992*; some years later Paul Chan and his editors at Badlands Unlimited helped me grow it into a book of its own. *Triangles* incorporates "Homage to Chrissie Hynde," originally published in the 1989 book *Bedrooms Have Windows* (Amethyst Press).

ABOUT THE AUTHOR

Kevin Killian is a San Francisco-based poet, novelist, playwright, and art writer. Recent books include the poetry collections *Tony Greene Era* and *Tweaky Village*. He is the coauthor of *Poet Be Like God: Jack Spicer and the San Francisco Renaissance*. With Dodie Bellamy, he coedited *Writers Who Love Too Much: New Narrative Writing, 1977–1997*.